THE DARING YOUNG MEN

Portrait of W. J. Stillman as a Study for the Head of Christ, by D. G. Rossetti

The Daring
Young Men

THE STORY OF THE AMERICAN PRE-RAPHAELITES

by David Howard Dickason

BENJAMIN BLOM, INC.

Acknowledgments

To THE Graduate School of Indiana University and to the Huntington Library and Art Gallery of San Marino, California, I express my appreciation for grants in aid of research. I also wish to acknowledge the courteous assistance given me by the officials and staff of the Indiana University Library, the Huntington Library, the Newberry Library, the Concord Free Public Library, the Library of Congress, the Boston Museum of Fine Arts, the Harvard Library, and the Fogg Museum of Art. My special thanks for their help and for permission to use manuscript and art materials are due Mrs. Jessie C. Rockwell, the first Curator of the Samuel and Mary R. Bancroft Pre-Raphaelite Collection in the Delaware Art Center of the Wilmington Society of the Fine Arts, and to her successor, Miss Jane Driver. I should also like to nod gracefully in the direction of my wife—who refused to be my amanuensis.

The following publishers and individuals have generously allowed me to quote from the books indicated: George Allen and Unwin, Ltd.: William Michael Rossetti, *Ruskin: Rossetti: Pre-Raphaelitism, Papers 1854 to 1862*. Appleton-Century-Crofts: Sir Hall Caine, *My Story;* and Homer Saint-Gaudens, *The Reminiscences of Augustus Saint-Gaudens*. Baker and Taylor Co.: Russell Sturgis, *History of Architecture*. G. Bell and Sons, Ltd.: Walter Crane, *Ideals in Art*. Miss Janice Biala: Ford Madox Hueffer [Ford Madox Ford], *Memories and Impressions*. Ernest Benn, Ltd.: George Birkbeck Hill, *The Letters of Dante Gabriel Rossetti to William Allingham, 1854–1870*. Cassell and Co., Ltd.: Sir Wemyss Reid, *The Life, Letters, and Friendships of Richard*

v

Monckton Milnes. The Columbia University Press and the Ralph Waldo Emerson Association: Ralph L. Rusk, ed., *The Letters of Ralph Waldo Emerson.* Miss Margaret Conklin: Sara Teasdale, *Helen of Troy and Other Poems.* The Duke University Press: Clarence Gohdes and Paull F. Baum, eds., *The Letters of William Michael Rossetti.* E. P. Dutton and Co., and J. M. Dent and Sons, Ltd.: *Poems and Translations by Dante Gabriel Rossetti.* The Fogg Museum of Art: *Paintings and Drawings of the Pre-Raphaelites and Their Circle.* Prof. Edward Waldo Forbes: Edward Waldo Emerson, *The Early Years of the Saturday Club, 1855–1870.* The University of Georgia Press: Richard Webb and Edward R. Coulson, *Sidney Lanier, Poet and Prosodist.* Miss Rosamond Gilder: *Letters of Richard Watson Gilder.*

Harcourt, Brace and Co.: Horace Gregory and Marya Zaturenska, *A History of American Poetry, 1900–1940.* Harper and Brothers: Merle Curti, *The Growth of American Thought.* Harvard University Press: Frank Luther Mott, *A History of American Magazines;* and Janet Camp Troxell, *Three Rossettis—Unpublished Letters.* Houghton Mifflin Co.: Henry Adams, *The Education of Henry Adams;* Christina H. Baker, ed., *Diary and Letters of Josephine Preston Peabody;* Royal Cortissoz, *John La Farge, A Memoir and a Study;* Edward Waldo Emerson and Waldo Emerson Forbes, eds., *Journals of Ralph Waldo Emerson;* Ralph Waldo Emerson, *Poems by Ralph Waldo Emerson;* Richard Watson Gilder, *Complete Works;* Nathaniel Hawthorne, *Passages from the French and Italian Notebooks;* Josephine Preston Peabody, *The Piper, A Play in Four Acts;* and W. J. Stillman, *The Old Rome and the New.*

Hurst and Blackett, Ltd.: William Michael Rossetti, *Prae-Raphaelite Diaries and Letters.* The Johns Hopkins Press: *Centennial Edition of the Works of Sidney Lanier.* John Lane The Bodley Head, Ltd.: T. Earle Welby, *The Victorian Romantics, 1850–1870.* Mrs. Vachel Lindsay: Vachel Lindsay, *The Golden Book of Springfield.* Macmillan and Co., Ltd.: H. Allingham and D. Radford, *William Allingham, A Diary;* A. C. Benson, *Rossetti;*

and W. Holman Hunt, *Pre-Raphaelitism and the Pre-Raphaelite Brotherhood.* The Macmillan Co.: G. Burne-Jones, *Memorials of Edward Burne-Jones;* Walter Crane, *An Artist's Reminiscences;* John La Farge, *Considerations in Painting;* Vachel Lindsay, *Adventures While Preaching the Gospel of Beauty;* Charles Herbert Moore, *Character of Renaissance Architecture,* and *Character and Development of Gothic Architecture;* Edwin Arlington Robinson, *Collected Poems;* Sara Teasdale, *Dark of the Moon,* and *Strange Victory;* and Cecilia Waern, *John La Farge, Artist and Writer.*

David McKay Co.: Elizabeth Porter Gould, *Anne Gilchrist and Walt Whitman.* The Modern Language Association and Prof. Randall Stewart: *The English Notebooks by Nathaniel Hawthorne.* Methuen and Co., Ltd.: John Guille Millais, *The Life and Letters of Sir John Everett Millais.* New Directions: Ezra Pound, *Sonnets and Ballate of Guido Cavalcanti.* "Yeux Glauques" is from *Personae* by Ezra Pound, copyright 1926 by Ezra Pound, published by New Directions, and reprinted with the permission of the publisher. The New England Trust Co.: Charles Eliot Norton, *Letters of John Ruskin to Charles Eliot Norton.* W. W. Norton and Co.: Babette Deutsch, *This Modern Poetry.* G. P. Putnam's Sons: Elisabeth Luther Cary, *The Rossettis: Dante Gabriel and Christina;* The Century Association, *Clarence King Memoirs;* and Stuart P. Sherman, ed., *The Poetical Works of Joaquin Miller.*

Reynal and Hitchcock: Alfred Kazin, *On Native Grounds.* The Ronald Press: Ralph Henry Gabriel, *The Course of American Democratic Thought.* Charles Scribner's Sons: Edgar Lee Masters, *Vachel Lindsay, A Poet in America;* W. M. Rossetti, *Family Letters of Christina Georgina Rossetti,* and *Some Reminiscences.* Stanford University Press: Martin S. Peterson, *Joaquin Miller, Literary Frontiersman.* Harr Wagner Publishing Co., and Miss Juanita Miller: *Joaquin Miller's Poems* (Bear Edition).

The editors of the following magazines are also to be thanked for the use of quoted material: *Architectural Record, Atlantic*

Monthly, and *Scribner's.* I have likewise made brief quotations from *Hound and Horn* and the *Independent.* The editor of *Art in America* has kindly agreed to let me incorporate in Chapters VII and VIII of this book some articles which I had previously published in that journal.

Miss Agnes Elpers and Mr. James Thomas Farrell of the English Department of Indiana University have been very helpful in the preparation and indexing of this book.

Contents

Illustrations

THE DARING YOUNG MEN

ONE

The Pre-Raphaelite Movement in America: an Introduction

JUST A century ago a group of young British artists and writers became spontaneously vocal and derogatory. They produced some paintings and poetry of varying merit in defiance of the dominant artistic conventions, made a sharp but temporary impact on their cultural milieu—"fought their way into public disfavor," as William Michael Rossetti put it—and, after a mature apology for their youthful fervor, completely disappeared. Thus, in the popular view, the Pre-Raphaelite Brotherhood.

It may indeed be true that for many individuals the English P.R.B. art and artifacts now seem outmoded. Pre-Raphaelite poems are read chiefly in required college courses; their paintings, typified by the meticulous, photographic rendition of detail and by the seraphically vacuous expression on the face of the constant heroine, have suffered from Ruskin's misinterpretation of art principles and from changes in public taste, and so have sunk into some neglect; and original Morris designs in wallpapers and tapestries and examples of his fine printing are now only collectors' items. For Pre-Raphaelite art, itself originally a revolt against convention, soon became conventionalized—"the high finish," as Madox Brown admitted, became "too obtrusive." Even W. M. Rossetti himself in 1899 looked upon the once-solemn code of rules which the young Brotherhood had drawn up as now "almost comic"; and concerning the early exuberance of his fellow P.R.B.'s he further commented:

It may be freely allowed that, as they were very young, and fired with certain ideas impressive to their own spirits, they unduly ignored some other ideas and theories which have none the less a deal to say for themselves. They contemned some things and some practitioners of art not at all contemptible, and, in speech still more than in thought, they at times wilfully heaped up the scorn. You cannot have a youthful rebel with a faculty who is also a model head-boy in a school.[1]

Nevertheless, the ultimate significance of the British Pre-Raphaelite movement* should not be minimized. Insular and transient though it may have been in some of its aspects, it actually marked a very definite though limited artistic revolution. For at its inception the new Pre-Raphaelite view was "an artist's protest . . . a recall to nature, to simplicity and sincerity" in art[2]—a declaration of independence from the long-continued and dogmatic dictates of the Royal Academy in painting and from "genteel" taste in literature.

Furthermore, the Pre-Raphaelite movement was not a solely British phenomenon. Across the Atlantic a ferment was working among certain young American painters, authors, and architects who were directly inspired by the English P.R.B. attack on sterile conservatism. This progressive group in turn denounced what they considered the slavish adherence to mere tradition. They too became less polemic, but through the latter half of the nineteenth century and into our own times they and their followers did

---

* Two extensions of this term are implicit in this study: first, Ruskin, although not a member of the Brotherhood, was so closely associated with them in the minds of the American Pre-Raphaelites that frequent reference must be made to him; and, secondly, although the actual P.R.B. organization existed for little more than five years, investigation of the continuing careers of its members and of such later associates as William Morris is of course essential.

succeed in exerting an influence on the artistic expression and even on phases of the economic life of the United States that cannot be ignored.

Three noteworthy periodicals in this country stemmed directly from the tenets of Ruskin and the British Brotherhood. The first journal clearly Pre-Raphaelite in its origin and sympathies was the *Crayon,* edited by William James Stillman, a painting-companion of Ruskin and a close associate of the whole Rossetti family. This review appeared in the 1850's and conveyed to American readers the heart of the P.R.B. theories. Another little magazine, the *New Path,* was the organ of a superbly self-confident American Brotherhood known as the "Society for the Advancement of Truth in Art," which centered in New York City in the Civil War years. Charter members of this group included several young men of a liberal cast of mind, who were to gain some public recognition: Clarence King, later the good friend of Henry Adams, author of *Mountaineering in the Sierra Nevada,* and first Director of the U. S. Geological Survey; Charles Herbert Moore, subsequently a respected art historian in the Norton tradition and the first administrator of Harvard's Fogg Museum; Clarence Cook, who became editor of the old *Studio;* and two men who made names as architects and critics, Peter B. Wight, a proponent of the Gothic Revival in America, and Russell Sturgis, art editor for *Scribner's* and designer of four Gothic buildings for Yale University. A third American magazine deriving from British sources, in this case from William Morris and his Arts and Crafts movement, was the *Craftsman,* which achieved the impressive circulation of 60,000 before ceasing publication during the First World War. Its pages gave a comprehensive account of the American handicrafts revival that flourished for over two decades and was inspired chiefly by Morris's

"Red House" and the London Arts and Crafts Exhibition.
In a socio-economic direction not only the Arts and
Crafts movement may be largely credited to P.R.B. origins,
but, in its wider ramifications, the founding in this country
of an experimental Utopian community, the ill-fated "Ruskin Commonwealth," which flowered for a few years in
Tennessee and Georgia.

In the more specific field of the visual arts the spirit of
Rossetti and Morris is definitely recognizable in the painting and stained-glass work of John La Farge and in the
varied products of Louis Tiffany, "the William Morris of
his generation in America." Richard Watson Gilder of the
Century, who acknowledged Rossetti as his literary godfather, likewise was linked directly with the liberal art movement through the activities of his artist wife and their "little
salon" in their New York home, "The Studio." Several other
less known painters, such as Thomas Charles Farrer, a student of Ruskin, and J. Henry Hill, were of the American
Pre-Raphaelite school. The exceptional collections of manuscripts, sketches, and paintings made by the late Samuel
Bancroft, Jr., of Wilmington, Delaware, and by Grenville
L. Winthrop, who bequeathed his extensive holdings to the
Fogg Museum of Art, are further evidence of a continuing
American interest in original Pre-Raphaelite materials.

Literary contacts, too, were frequent. Personal associations, some fugitive but others of lasting significance, were
established between the British P.R.B.'s and their American
sympathizers. Thomas Buchanan Read, for example, was
Dante Gabriel Rossetti's first friend among writers from
this country. Joaquin Miller worked his eccentric way to the
dinner-table of "The Master," as he labeled Rossetti. W. J.
Stillman, already recognized as the editor of the *Crayon*,
later displayed talent as an autobiographer and critic, and

added intimate details to the Rossetti canon; and both Still-man and his beautiful Greek wife, Marie Spartali, were themselves artists of some ability and served as models for Dante Gabriel. Hawthorne, Emerson, Whitman, Longfellow, Moncure Conway, and others knew the Pre-Raphaelites in-dividually, and were concerned with their ideas. Some later American writers also owe something to the concepts of Ruskin and the young Brotherhood. The verse of Christina Rossetti, on the periphery of the group, was among the models for Sara Teasdale's poetry. D. G. Rossetti and Morris had a considerable effect on such diverse figures as Richard Hovey, Josephine Preston Peabody, and Ezra Pound; while Vachel Lindsay in his "Gospel of Beauty" expounded much of the Ruskinian aspiration for the better life.

These Britishers and Americans were, in the main, expo-nents of the second of the two chief aesthetic attitudes of the latter half of the nineteenth century. Put simply, one view held that the effective creation of artistic beauty, in whatever form, was an adequate and justifiable end in itself —art for the sake of art was enough. But to many sensitive persons this interpretation seemed too precious, too other-worldly, too esoteric. Beauty is not a supreme and absolute value. Art cannot be abstracted from the conditions of art, but must take its inspiration from its time and place, and must, in full circle, bear a constructive relationship to its surroundings.

Although pioneering chronologically, Poe's dreamworld, "out of space, out of time," demonstrated little visible con-nection with the American environment; and through its sensuous vividness and easy intelligibility, it led a reader smoothly into the convolutions of Walter Pater and Oscar Wilde. The purity and aloofness of art might be even better illustrated by the French, with whom the "art for art's sake" movement largely began: Flaubert, Gautier, Baudelaire, and the brothers de Goncourt.

But other writers and artists, sometimes labeled as mere sociological thinkers, looked about them at the masses of humanity struggling for a better life or even for mere existence, and believed that an artist had a moral as well as an aesthetic duty. To lead the masses the artist must serve the masses. The majority of mankind laboring under inescapable pressures must still be awakened to the power of beauty. And the materialistic proprietors of the new machine-made wealth must likewise be made to see the artistic and humanitarian light. Victor Hugo and Zola in France; Carlyle, Ruskin, and Morris in England; Whitman, Emerson, and many of the later, lesser writers in America saw what they considered the logical and inevitable link between art and literature and common, everyday life.

The core of the Pre-Raphaelite attitude, however, was a more inclusive desire than merely to apply art to society to bring about visible improvements. The touchstone, if one well-worn phrase must be selected, was "truth to nature," to Nature capitalized. Empty and trite interpretations, deliberate manipulations of subject matter to gain meretricious effects—in a word, artistic insincerity, illogicality and dishonesty in all their guises and applications—these were the foes of the Pre-Raphaelites on both sides of the Atlantic. And against them they rode manfully—and loudly—to battle.

This attitude of the Americans, which is our chief concern here, is of particular significance when viewed against the backdrop of its historical period. The low estimate of human nature and its potential which was inherent in the theological determinism of the Puritans had yielded to the optimistic faith in man and his perfectibility through reason which the

Enlightenment had offered. This "rational" attitude had found magnificent political expression in "life, liberty, and the pursuit of happiness," and had found brief philosophical application in Deism, and thereafter in the more organized concepts of Unitarianism. In the Transcendental mode man achieved an even nobler level, sharing a spark of the Divine fire, himself but little lower than the angels. And on a practical level the rich new continent seemed to stretch out endlessly, with equal opportunity and success and satisfaction for all comers.

But some acid facts of American life, both national and individual, began by the middle of the century to corrode the foundations of this high faith and hope. The cynicism evidenced in the acquisition of the great Southwest from Mexico; the self-interested regional economic struggles (as well as the genuine humanitarian concerns) of the Civil War; the corruption and self-seeking of Grant's administration and the era of the carpetbaggers; the incredible "robber barons" and their shameless pride in exploiting the nation's wealth; the thin tinsel and superficiality and "conspicuous waste" of the Gilded Age; the shock of Darwinism, biological determinism, pragmatism, and literary naturalism; the disconcerting ideas of Karl Marx and his exponents; the mushroom growth of grimy industrial centers and workers' slums; the acquisitive overseas activities and imperialism in the Philippines, the Caribbean, and Panama—these and other crises and problems seemed to leave little energy or opportunity for a serious consideration of art and the role of aesthetics in nineteenth century America.

So, whatever the ultimate residue from their efforts, these American figures about to be discussed were at least a lively, corporate antidote to the materialism and artistic stagnation of "American Victorianism." As Russell Sturgis, one of the most outspoken of the New York group in the 1860's, later viewed the Pre-Raphaelite movement in both England and the United States:

We may gravely doubt whether it occupies an exceptionally high rank among the fine arts of the nineteenth century, and yet it is necessary to admit its intensity, its narrow and simply acting force, its vigorous attempt to make painting into a vehicle for religious, literary and patriotic sentiment, and its profound interest to the student of intellectual experiments.[3]

T W O

The British Brotherhood

IN 1848, a year in which autocratic political power was challenged on the Continent, a casual artistic fraternity was formed in England that in its own more limited scope was to become a liberating force in the arts, not only in that country but in the United States as well. Because the Americans reflected the influence of their British confreres so directly—with almost no appreciable "cultural lag"—it seems pertinent before investigating the Pre-Raphaelite activities in the United States to recall a few salient facts concerning the English group.

The original Pre-Raphaelite Brotherhood was not, of course, a closely knit organization of artists consistently defending the same novel and iconoclastic ideas in art. Ruskin was not its founder, nor was Dante Gabriel Rossetti its prime mover; and the term Pre-Raphaelitism had no fixed definition but from 1848 onward went through a widely varying cycle of meaning. For no sooner had the component elements of the fraternity united on a few specific matters of principle and method than each began to follow his own distinct and often quite disparate path. A brief analysis will make this clear.

When the Brotherhood first evolved, John Everett Millais, a cherubic child prodigy who had won Academy prizes at ten, was nineteen years old; Dante Gabriel Rossetti, "the

11

gifted, erratic . . . volatile young poet and painter whose last name was Italian and whose first two seemed to place him under the high patronage of the greatest of poets and an archangel," [1] was twenty; William Holman Hunt, already a deeply religious figure, was twenty-one; and Thomas Woolner, an aspiring but untalented sculptor, was two years older. These young men were soon drawn together at the Royal Academy school by a shared discontent with the formulas of contemporary popular painting.

It was in the beginning of the year 1848 [said Holman Hunt years later to Millais's son and biographer] that your father and I determined to adopt a style of absolute independence as to art-dogma and convention: this *we* called "Pre-Raphaelitism." D. G. Rossetti was already my pupil [after having worked discontentedly with Ford Madox Brown] and it seemed certain that he also, *in time,* would work on the same principles. He had declared his intentions of doing so, and there was beginning to be some talk of other artists joining us. . . .[2]

Rossetti had acquired Madox Brown's habit of applying the term "Early Christian" to the experiments of Millais and Hunt, but the latter convinced him that "Pre-Raphaelite" was a more apt label. Rossetti thereupon, "with a pet scheme of an extended co-operation in mind, amended my previous suggestion by adding to our title . . . the word 'Brotherhood.'" [3]

All four young men were interested in literature as well as in art. Rossetti had already written excellent poetry; Woolner, the stone-carver, was about to compose "My Beautiful Lady"; Millais was writing amateur verse; and Hunt was reading Keats with gusto. And as to painting, William Michael Rossetti noted in his concurrent journal:

They entertained a hearty contempt for much of the Art—flimsy, frivolous, and conventional—which they saw in practice around them; and they wanted to shew forth what was in them in the way of solid and fresh thought or invention, personal observation, and the intimate study of, and strict adherence to Nature.[4]

The quartet soon expanded. Dante Gabriel Rossetti, having admired a painting by a mediocre young artist named James Collinson, invited him into the fellowship. Hunt suggested the inclusion of Frederick George Stephens, who was to become a better critic than painter. And William Michael Rossetti, whose talent was literary rather than pictorial, became the unofficial but prolific recorder and historian of the Brotherhood.

The bond of union among them was unassuming and direct—in William Michael's own phraseology:

1, To have genuine ideas to express; 2, to study Nature attentively, so as to know how to express them; 3, to sympathize with what is direct and serious and heartfelt in previous art, to the exclusion of what is conventional and self-parading and learned by rote; and, 4, and most indispensable of all, to produce thoroughly good pictures and statues.[5]

These seven young men, with Hunt and Millais as the dominant figures, formed the nucleus of the early group. Many others from time to time appeared in the Pre-Raphaelite circle. Arthur Hughes, Frederic Sandys, Charles Collins, and Walter Deverell sympathized with P.R.B. aims and worked on comparable lines. William Bell Scott, John Brett, W. S. Burton, Thomas Seddon, Henry Wallis, and others had tenuous connections. Coventry Patmore, poet and later Librarian of the British Museum, was in frequent contact, but was ineligible for membership because he was not a working artist. The Irish poet, William Allingham, was likewise an associate. And Madox Brown, as Rossetti's first teacher and himself a proponent of minute finish in painting, had a continuing influence on the Brotherhood.

The omission of Ruskin's name in these early years is significant, for the misconception is still prevalent that Ruskin "discovered" the P.R.B. and was their first champion. This of course was not the case. The American journalist and Pre-Raphaelite painter, William J. Stillman, who was well acquainted with both Ruskin and the British Pre-Raphaelites remarked: "I have heard Rossetti say none of the Brotherhood had ever read ten pages of his writing before Ruskin had constituted himself their advocate." [6] And Holman Hunt apparently was the only Brother who ever troubled to read even the first volume of *Modern Painters*. Ruskin's first knowledge of the Brotherhood came through Coventry Patmore, an old friend of Rossetti, who urged him to write in defense of the P.R.B. Ruskin's first letter on that subject to the *Times* was not written until 1851—three years after the inception of the movement—in which he declared he had "no acquaintance with these artists and very imperfect sympathy with them." His friendship with Rossetti did not begin until 1854 when the P.R.B. had in effect already dissolved, and that artist had already painted and sold his "Girlhood of Mary Virgin" and the "Annunciation." From that year until 1866, however, Ruskin was a generous patron and strong defender and ally. Throughout his writings he perhaps gratuitously attributed to the Brotherhood some of his own concepts, and read into their works some of his own principles. Nevertheless, his *Modern Painters* had strong influence on Hunt in particular; and Ruskin's exegesis of the original Pre-Raphaelite platform is largely reliable.[7] In America his name has been linked almost indissolubly with those of the P.R.B.

The more or less formal Brotherhood had disintegrated before 1854 out of sheer divergence of its members' tastes and interests; only "a solemn mockery" of the original fraternity, as Holman Hunt wistfully recalled, it "died of itself."[8] So many hangers-on and pseudo-Pre-Raphaelites had grafted themselves onto the basic organization that Lady Trevelyan wrote in 1860 to William Bell Scott:

I am glad the Academy have ill-used the Preraffs, it will perhaps lop off some rotten branches in the shape of weak brethren, who paint boneless imitations of the school and bring discredit on it. If these are convinced it is unpopular and does not pay they will give up, which will be an unmixed good. . . .[9]

During the following years the term Pre-Raphaelite continued in popular—and unpopular—usage, but inevitably took on various shades of meaning. Holman Hunt alone continued to uphold and apply the early Pre-Raphaelite principles (making an extended tour of the Near East in 1854 to supply authentic backgrounds for his religious pictures), as his highly literal canvases ("The Scape-Goat," for example) indicate; and at the end of a long career—holding the same art principles as he did at the age of twenty—he could view the rising school of Impressionism only as "the threat to modern art, menacing nothing less than its extinction."[10] Millais, who in the early years, according to his son, "sought to paint exactly what he himself saw in Nature, omitting no detail," declared his own "emancipation from the excessive detail of Pre-Raphaelite expression" by a major canvas produced in 1858, the "Vale of Rest." Here, and in such later works of the 1860's as "Rosalind and Celia" and "Jephtha," he could still give careful attention to the minutiae, but allegedly "showed a further development . . . in the style and character of his work, marked . . . now by a greater breadth of treatment."[11] The American Pre-Raphaelite Russell Sturgis regarded this evolution in style somewhat less charitably. "Millais," he declared at the turn of the century, "followed sincerely the principles of the school for ten years, then dropped them absolutely and followed as sincerely a path of more popular, more easy, more fruitful, more speedy execution which led to his immense social and pecuniary success." [12] Millais's continuance in a kind of artistic orthodoxy was indicated, however, by his unanimous election in 1896 to the presidency of the Royal Academy. "Beginning as a *préraphaélite enragé*," says a contemporary critic, "he promises to end a true successor to Gainsborough and Reynolds." [13]

The widest divergence from the original P.R.B. platform is to be seen in the work of D. G. Rossetti himself. As Sturgis asserted, "Rossetti never obeyed, even for a day, the Pre-Raphaelite principles, but painted . . . his brilliant dreams as unconcernedly as if he had never vowed allegiance to serve fixed principles of graphic art." [14] Millais emphatically denied that "the mysterious and un-English Rossetti" had ever influenced his own work: "My pictures would have been the same if I had never seen or heard of Rossetti." [15] And after labeling him "a queer fellow, and impossible as a boon companion—so dogmatic and irritable when opposed"—Millais continued:

His aims and ideals in art were also widely different from ours, and it was not long before he drifted away from us to follow his own peculiar fancies. What they were may be seen from his subsequent works. They were highly imaginative and original, and not without elements of beauty, but they were not Nature.

Then, with some feeling, Millais asserted:

At last, when he presented for our admiration the young women which have since become the type of Rossettianism, the public opened their eyes in amazement. "And this," they said, "is Pre-Raphaelitism!" It was nothing of the sort. The Pre-Raphaelites had but one idea—to present on canvas what they saw in Nature; and such productions as these were absolutely foreign to the spirit of their work.[16]

The subject of all this discussion himself made a pertinent comment, indicative of his attitude in the 1870's. To a lady inquiring whether he were "the Pre-Raphaelite Rossetti," the artist sharply replied, "Madam, I am not an 'ite' of any kind; I am only a painter." His brother, William Michael, accepted the veracity of this statement, but added: "It is not the less true that in 1848 and for some years afterward he meant a good deal by calling himself Pre-Raphaelite, and meant it very heartily." [17]

Be that as it may, friendly relations between Rossetti and Millais lasted only until 1852; they saw each other occasionally during the next few years; after 1856 they did not meet. Hence, with the loosening of his bonds with the Brotherhood, Rossetti—essentially a highly social creature—was heartened both personally and in his artistic principles by the advent in the 1860's of two young men from Oxford, Edward Burne-Jones and William Morris, both of whom had decided to renounce a clerical for an artistic career. To these three, Rossetti, Burne-Jones, and Morris, the new life of the movement was due which, as the later Pre-Raphaelitism (sometimes labeled "Rossettianism" in Millais's phrase), obviously abandoned the original tenets of simplicity, earnestness, and fidelity to nature, and took on an other-worldly, half-ascetic, half-voluptuous tone in the "quaint sexless beauty" of Burne-Jones's work, and a new freedom of subject, interpretation, and treatment in the widely ranging imagination of Rossetti.

Because, in 1848, most of the young Englishmen of the Brotherhood were destined to be of considerable influence in America, it is well to inquire why, as artists, they chose their particular name-label as a means of denouncing the popular standards of early Victorian art. Raffaello Sanzio, who died in 1520, was rejected not because he failed as a technician or as an interpreter of life, but rather because he had become, as an erudite British critic phrased it for the Royal Society, the "300-year-old godfather of a dead school of painting—so dead that it had begun to stink. Raphael, that great creator of form, had been reduced to a recipe. . . . 'Style' and 'the grand manner' were things fixed in mediocrity, and a mannerism too grandmotherly for words. And, therefore, Pre-Raphaelitism." [18] The fresh vision of the Renaissance had indeed degenerated into a formula, which Ruskin sardonically summarized:

We begin, in all probability, by telling the youth of fifteen or sixteen, that Nature is full of faults, and that he is to improve her; but that Raphael is perfection, and that the more he copies Raphael the better; that after much copying of Raphael, he is to try what he can do himself in a Raphaelesque, but yet original, manner: that is to say . . . this clever something is to be properly subjected to Raphaelesque rules.

It may be a shock to find how carefully prescribed the treatment was to be. This clever something must "have a principal light occupying one-seventh of its space, and a principal shadow occupying one-third of the same." No two people's heads might be turned at the same angle; and "all the personages represented are to possess ideal beauty of the highest order, which ideal beauty consists partly in a Greek outline of nose, partly in proportions expressible in decimal fractions between the lips and chin." And this, says Ruskin, "is the kind of teaching we give our young men. And we wonder we have no painters!" [19]

The contemporary British exhibitions thus were filled with the anecdotal works of such insipid figures as Stanfield, Cooke, Creswick, Mulready, Gaudy, Cooper, and President Eastlake of the Royal Academy, which Ruskin categorized as an endless and weary succession of "cattle pieces, sea pieces, fruit pieces, family pieces." [20] With the exception of the romantic Turner no artist had arisen to replace the popular but stylized eighteenth-century masters, Gainsborough, Romney, and Reynolds. In 1821 even Constable cried: "In thirty years English art will cease to exist" [21]—and without the impetus supplied by the Pre-Raphaelites his prophecy might well have been realized.

To the eyes of the young Brotherhood the contemporary art scene was completely bound by custom. Thus they felt impelled to break out of the confining integuments of the "old masters," to assert the validity of their own new, direct apprehension. They chose their label, then, because in the art of the fourteenth and fifteenth centuries they thought they had discovered "a sincerity of purpose, together with a sensitiveness to natural form and colour and to decorative effectiveness, which was quite beyond the powers of any of their contemporaries," [22] who were hampered by the fixed anatomical and perspective standards and the technical methods then current in the academies. Thus the young Pre-Raphaelites deliberately became neo-medieval and anti-authoritarian.

Obviously there had been brilliant artists before Raphael. The historical pre-Raphaelite epoch might be said to begin with Cimabue (born 1240) and extend through Perugino (born 1446), the teacher of Raphael; the intervening period embraced such important figures as Giotto, Fra Angelico, Masaccio, Mantegna, and Botticelli; and in the Flemish School, Memling and Jan van Eyck. But the nineteenth-century Pre-Raphaelites' acquaintance with them was comparatively slight.[23] They were symbols of freedom, not literal patterns to copy, and the later British figures did not trouble to be specific about their artistic forebears. What they saw in the old Italians was the twofold ability to choose elevated and original subjects, and then to embody them in forms demonstrating the utmost fidelity to nature—a nobility of conception and an exactness in transcription which had for them a high appeal. As the American Pre-Raphaelite journal, the *Craftsman,* put it:

They turned for aid and inspiration to medievalism, as to the rightful and common inheritance of modern nations. They rejected the facility fatal to ideas, the artistic subterfuges and conventions of the followers of "the grand style"; seeking their guides and models in artists who lived in a time when human thought teemed, although it struggled with an imperfect medium of expression. . . . Thus in the old Italians and old Flemings they found their masters, whom they did not servilely imitate, but to whom they were attracted as to the founders of a national and popular art.[24]

Since the usual stress is on the Florentine group it is interesting to note that Dante Gabriel Rossetti himself accented his admiration for the Flemish School, following his visit to Bruges:

By far the best of all are the miraculous works of Memling and Van Eyck. . . . I assure you that the perfection of character, and even drawing, the astounding finish, the glory of colour, and above all the pure religious sentiment and ecstatic poetry of these works, is not to be conceived or described.[25]

In spite of their early efforts at literal rendition of the model and the employment of vivid, living color, the work of the British Pre-Raphaelites was not, in any sense, pure "realism," for basically it was their own highly individual expression which was a subjective, a "romantic" thing. W. M. Rossetti phrased it: "The English revivalists recur to one primary school—nature, *as interpreted by their own eyes and feelings.*" [26] And his brother Dante Gabriel at one time remarked, in reply to the argument that a realistic picture "was both vulgar and dishonouring to Art"—"I fear we shall not agree on that point; we should all be both realists and idealists." [27] Pre-Raphaelitism was, indeed, an "endeavour to express romance in terms of nature, with great intensity of individual feeling, and with a strong sense of character." [28] Hence it was completely logical for the P.R.B.'s to seek their subjects, both pictorial and literary, in the conventionally romantic characters of the Middle Ages. But in the hands of Morris in particular these figures were metamorphosed into living individuals true to the tenor of their own part chivalrous, part barbaric times, and not, as in the works of Tennyson, transformed into figurines who were actually refined and conscientious members of British Victorian society.[29]

The British Brotherhood assumed in several fields an originality not completely theirs. It is a defensible conjecture that their neo-medieval tendencies, if not shaped by the Oxford religious movement, at least had an intimate alliance with the aims and methods of that group. Without the effect on the public mind of Newman, Keble, Pusey, and the *Lyra Apostolica* and the whole trend toward the recovery of Gothic design and medieval sentiment, it is quite possible that the Pre-Raphaelites would have cast their seed on stony ground.

So too in literature. Wordsworth, Coleridge, and Keats, and before them Crabbe and Cowper, Blake and Burns, had each in his own way attempted to avoid the old formulas of rhetorical gesture, and to present a new type of intense, sincere, human literature. A sharp focus on small objects, attention centered on the significance of the phenomena of nature, originality in the employment of stark figures and vivid similes, a specific inventiveness in the visual symbol—

all these suggest the essence of Pre-Raphaelite poetry long before it was analyzed and so labeled by the P.R.B.'s.

In the techniques of painting the Dutch genre artists and their Flemish fellows had long since thoroughly explored the possibilities of representational art. In England, Hogarth in literalness, Blake in grandeur of subject matter and revolt from materialism, and Turner in color and subjective interpretation were certainly to be recognized as exemplars of their craft. And in France, Degas, Monet, Renoir, and Cézanne were already painting their early brilliant canvases —in their own effort to escape from stultifying conventionalism, an effort destined to catch the popular favor to a much greater extent than did the works of their contemporary experimentalists in England. For although their directions and methods were radically different, the rising French Impressionists and the British Pre-Raphaelites were both searching for some new and better art forms and expressions than those they found ready-made and transmitted to them by the academies and accepted masters of their day. It is, indeed, an irony in the history of art that the Pre-Raphaelites, who began their crusade with courage, originality and intelligence, failed—with the notable exception of Dante Gabriel Rossetti—to produce any ultimately great art, whereas the romantic individualists of the new French school succeeded in producing works now almost universally revered and enjoyed.

Why this should be so is a subject rich for speculation. Two factors might suggest a partial answer. The Pre-Raphaelites by deliberately cutting themselves off from traditional studio practices perhaps also cut themselves off from the necessary training in manual techniques. They were literally amateurs, and (with the exception of Millais) had to paint and scrape out and repaint to get their effects, largely by trial and error, while the Frenchmen were masters of their materials and were fluent in the media of art. A second suggestion is implicit in a remark by D. G. Rossetti already quoted. On both sides of the Channel the painters rejected the contemporary academic standards in art, and went back to earlier, more spontaneous expression. But as Rossetti said, English artists saw "above all the pure religious sentiment and ecstatic poetry of these works"—that is, they were attracted primarily by the literary and emotional content. The French Impressionists, by contrast, were not concerned so much with subject as with treatment. Largely ignoring content as such, they were free to experiment in non-academic methods and techniques suggested by the older painters, and devoted themselves to working out new concepts of plastic form which did succeed in establishing the direction that modern art was to take.

The question inevitably arises, also, why Ruskin and Morris—with all their courage and brilliance, their penetrating analysis of the society of their time, and their practical moves toward its betterment—should seem vulnerable in the eyes of modern art criticism. Perhaps the basic flaw in their critical armor was their simple refusal to recognize the inevitability of the machine. Faced with the drudgery and degradation of nineteenth-century industrialism, they could think of escape in one direction only—backward into the medieval age of individual self-sufficiency and spontaneous joy in the manual crafts, and of inspired, communal architectural expression in the Gothic cathedrals. A modern social thinker, Lewis Mumford, has pointed out that our capacity to go beyond the machine rests upon our power to assimilate the machine. This fundamental fact Morris and Ruskin failed to appreciate; and there is inevitably some falseness in the objectives which they set up. Nevertheless, although Morris never became reconciled to the industrial age, he did realize, near the end of his career, that irksome labor could be eliminated by planned employment of mechanical aids. In the visual arts he failed, perhaps, to concern himself with the central problems of form and structure, and dealt rather with applied ornament and decoration. But he was talented in handling flat surfaces; and his two-dimensional designs in fabrics, wallpapers, and especially in typography and fine printing have continuing effectiveness and charm. And his crafts idea has certainly affected modern industrial design, which attempts to produce logically and beautifully designed objects—but by mechanical rather than manual processes. Ruskin, likewise, may have failed to penetrate to the core of some problems of art. W. J. Stillman pointed out this weakness as concisely as any other critic. Ruskin did not comprehend that "art does not lie in *representing* nature, but in the *manner* of representing her. . . . No art can be gauged by its fidelity to nature . . . its adherence to physical facts. . . . In my opinion Ruskin cares nothing for the plastic qualities of art, or for the human figure, otherwise than as it embodies human and moral dignity." [30] But within the limitations of his mind, Ruskin was unquestionably one of the liberating forces of the nineteenth century and a major social prophet and critic.[31]

In broad outline, then, it is valid to consider the Pre-Raphaelite movement, in its various manifestations, as a belated evidence of the nineteenth century's "romantic" reaction against the rational, "classical" temper of the eighteenth. In poetry the revolution in subject, form, and treatment seemed already mature in the *Lyrical Ballads;* the religious reaction at Oxford was initiated in 1830; but the artistic recoil is scarcely visible before 1850, except in the isolated figures of Blake and Turner.

In plotting the course of the Pre-Raphaelite movement in America we must, therefore, draw as clear a line as is feasible between the general impulse of romantic individualism, on the one hand, which flooded west from British and Continental sources, and on the other, the effect on American artists, writers, and life in general which is directly attributable to the members of the British Pre-Raphaelite Brotherhood and their literary and artistic expressions.

The story of the Pre-Raphaelites in England has been well and frequently told.[32] But their cis-Atlantic impact has not previously been dealt with. American poets, painters, and architects—and even the proponents of the Arts and Crafts movement and various economic schemes—reacted strongly and specifically to the new perspectives and the fresh assertiveness of the British group.

THREE

Buchanan Read and the Rossettis

THOMAS Buchanan Read, Dante Gabriel Rossetti's first friend among American artists and writers, might well have made a more memorable place for himself in the history of the American arts had he not too completely divided his energies between painting and poetry. He was a protégé of Washington Allston,* and during his career as an artist produced some sixty major canvases in studios in this country and in London, Liverpool, Manchester, Düsseldorf, Florence, and Rome. Of these, "Sheridan's Ride"—his largest painting, some ten by thirteen feet—is probably his most popular work because of his famous poem commemorating the same event. During his own day, however, he was recognized as a successful portrait painter and among his sitters he numbered Lincoln, Longfellow, General William Henry Harrison, Tennyson, the Brownings, and the ex-Queen of Naples. Aside from these portraits the majority of his pictures leaned heavily on literary inspiration, as suggested by "Abou Ben Adhem and the Angel," "Excelsior," "The Culprit Fay," "The Flight of the Arrow," "Titania," "Cleopatra in Her Barge," "The Star of Bethlehem," "Three Marys at the Sepulchre," and others.[1]

* Allston (1779–1834) had been a pupil of Benjamin West, with whom he shared the belief that art should tell a story appealing to the spectator's sentiments. Well known in England, Allston was a friend of Coleridge, Wordsworth, and Southey. Samuel F. B. Morse was another of his students.

Although Read tried his hand at prose and at longer poems such as "The House by the Sea," "The Wagoner of the Alleghenies," and "The New Pastoral"—which he considered his own best work *—what little literary fame remains to him comes exclusively from his shorter verse. In addition to "Sheridan's Ride" with its obvious patriotic appeal, "The Oath," which was read in Congress, received the praise of Lincoln. His best lyric perhaps is "Drifting," a description of the Bay of Naples. And in general his small gift as a poet manifested itself primarily in the ability to visualize natural scenes—to present evocative detail with the vividness of a practitioner of the graphic arts.

With this double interest in poetry and painting, and his concern with poetry as picture, it is not surprising that Read should have made contact with his slightly younger contemporaries, the British Pre-Raphaelites.

A cosmopolitan English couple, William and Mary Howitt, in the 1850's varied their task of translating old Norse ballads and writing a history of Scandinavian literature by keeping open house for literary visitors to London. Throughout her lifetime, in fact, Mary Howitt was something of a collector of Americans, including among her friends not only Read, but Harriet Beecher Stowe, Louisa Alcott, Moncure Conway, Emerson, Joaquin Miller (whom she met in Rome), Bayard Taylor, and Lucretia Mott. Several editions of her own poetry also appeared in the United States, and she was a fellow contributor with William Michael Rossetti to W. J. Stillman's Pre-Raphaelite journal, the *Crayon*.

The cultural interests of the Howitts also embraced the fine arts. During the first half of the century, wrote Mary

---

* With an Introduction, Prelude, and 36 Books, this recounted the extensive adventures and vicissitudes of a group of pioneers from Pennsylvania on their western migration.

Howitt, "the general public was wholly uneducated in art." Among the forces alleviating the ignorance and lethargy of the British masses a "famous band of art-innovators" fortunately had arisen, and these Pre-Raphaelite Brothers were now "startling the world by the novelty and oddity of their composition and coloring, combined with a marvelous fidelity in detail," which fact brought down the edict from Sir Charles Eastlake, President of the Royal Academy, that his Hanging Committee "would admit this outrageous new school of painting" to their walls no longer. That Mary Howitt had the personal confidence of the young P.R.B.'s is indicated by the fact that, lacking a banker, one of them asked her to cash a check for £14 received for a small canvas in Manchester.[2]

In July 1850, Buchanan Read, then in his late twenties, visited London on his way to study art on the Continent, and spent an evening with the Howitts. He had made previous contact with them by a gift of his first volume of poems, and he brought in hand the second. His hostess at first sight thought him "a timid nonentity" and had to make a special effort to prevent his suffering from neglect. But the young Irish poet, William Allingham, who was among the guests, was apparently impressed and a few days later reported the affair to Holman Hunt and Dante Rossetti.

As far as the records show, Read was the first American artist-writer whom Dante Gabriel Rossetti knew intimately. His initial meeting with Americans had occurred, however, some four years earlier when he was a youth of eighteen, studying in Cary's Drawing Academy in Bloomsbury after leaving King's College School. Among the boys at Cary's was the son of a self-taught American landscape painter of the Hudson River School who had taken his family to London where some of his landscapes had been well received. This lad, Thomas Doughty, Jr., was for a year or two, according to W. M. Rossetti, "my brother's chief intimate." After school the two Rossettis frequently drank tea at the Doughtys' semivilla residence in Regent's Park. The elder Doughty was convivial and outspoken, his wife "a pleasant bright-mannered little lady" who suffered more than her share of domestic difficulty; and the Rossettis became so attached to the family that when they returned to America early in 1848 William Michael and his brother saw them off at their ship.[3]

Doughty, a brash youth two years older than Dante Gabriel, had also introduced the Rossettis to a friend, another "quick-witted lively young American, Charley Ware, leading a harum-scarum kind of life in lodgings off Leicester Square." Ware, among other literary likings, was much concerned with Edgar Allan Poe, which gave him an immediate bond of sympathy with Dante Gabriel. He also was an amateur painter, untrained but with some sharpness of natural faculty. As a memento of one social occasion, William Michael recalled, Ware painted a small oil sketch of Doughty, Dante Gabriel, Ware himself, and the Devil, all four engaged in playing whist in Ware's rooms. But Ware too returned to America; and neither of these early friends achieved enough public success to come again to the Rossettis' notice.[4]

Thus Rossetti, on the advent of Read, was not completely unacquainted with examples of the American character. When, as previously indicated, Allingham returned to the studio to report the affair at the Howitts' and the encounter with Read, Rossetti failed to recognize the name. But he replied with the indiscriminating enthusiasm of his years:

By the bye, some of those Americans write glorious things. I have come across some lyrics in the *Philadelphia Courier*, signed "A Miner" and written from Hazeldell, on the Schuylkill, as fine as any I know. I first met with one specimen, and was so delighted

with it that I sent to Philadelphia for all the papers containing the
poems from Hazeldell, cut them out and pasted them in a book
with other gems of poetry.

Immediately Rossetti brought out a big scrapbook, read a
number of lyrics, and commented on them effusively. With
the desire to do a little literary sleuthing Allingham suggested that perhaps Read as an American might be able to
identify "the poet of Hazeldell" for them. The errand accomplished, Read's face, as Mary Howitt reported the occasion,
"became crimson, and his entire frame agitated. 'I am the
writer of these poems,' he replied, with tears in his eyes." [5]
Allingham forthwith dragged his prize back to the studio,
but at that moment Rossetti was absorbed in work with a
model. He only looked up, "gave a sharp little nod, and went
on painting." But Allingham, walking up to him, interrupted,
"I have brought you the poet of Hazeldell bodily!" Where-
upon Rossetti dropped his brush, and "with a face glowing
with excitement, cried, 'You don't say so!' He quite overwhelmed the bashful stranger with his joyous acclamations,
adding, 'How delighted Woolner will be, for he prizes your
poems as I do!'"

Read was received at once as an intimate of the group, and
was in constant contact with his host, Dante Gabriel, and
with Hunt, Woolner, and William Rossetti. Allingham jotted
an entry in his diary for July 19, 1850:

With Woolner, two Rossettis, and Buchanan Reid [sic] in omnibus
to Chelsea, to Holman Hunt's lodging, large first floor room looking on river, near the old church. Deverell—much talk on pictures,
etc.; we have coffee and fruit; some lie on the floor smoking.[6]

Read accepted Rossetti's invitation to paint in his studio; and
on a dinner call to the Howitts, Mary Howitt, who meanwhile had availed herself of the opportunity to read his two
volumes of verse, now found him to be "a very generous,

grateful young man, possessing much original power and fine discrimination of art."

Despite the artistic fellowship which he was enjoying, Read eventually found it necessary to continue his interrupted journey to Düsseldorf. A farewell dinner, a great gathering of all the P.R.B.'s took place, to celebrate their last evening together. He was, of course, the center of attention, and the Brothers read his poetry aloud, made much of him, and prolonged the festivities until early morning. Since he failed to appear at the proper hour at his lodgings in the Strand, "it was reported that the Pre-Raphaelites had carried off Read in a chariot of fire." [7]

Certain other, perhaps tenuous, relations were established with the Pre-Raphaelites following Read's first visit to London in 1850. Coventry Patmore, then Librarian of the British Museum, in 1855 wrote to the poet concerning his *magnum opus,* "The New Pastoral"—but before reading it:

It gives me great pleasure to hear that you are bringing out a work for which you seem excellently fitted. My feeling is that you are the only real poet America has had [!], and it is very well, therefore, in my mind, that you should have hit upon the only American subject [i.e., the expansion of the frontier and westward migration].[8]

After the appearance of the work in America, Patmore's enthusiasm was such that he volunteered to sponsor a London edition. In a letter to his friend, Henry C. Townsend, Read wrote on August 25, 1857, from Italy:

By the way, that fellow Patmore, who took upon himself to oversee the bringing out of the new English edition, has had the impudence to alter several stanzas and leave out some of the matter. He has especially marred the "Closing Scene" by tinkering at the closing line, but I flatter myself that it will bear it. . . .[9]

And in a later communication to the same correspondent Read added:

This edition has annoyed me, and cheered me a good deal— annoyed on account of the mutilations practiced upon it by [Pat- more], who had charge of it (curious how brother poets work these things, eh?) and cheered on account of the reception in spite of those mutilations. [Patmore] left out passages and changed lines, whenever it seemed to him that he could mar anything. Well, no matter; it succeeds, notwithstanding all this! [10]

That the first flush of Read's pleasure in his contacts with the Pre-Raphaelite group soon faded is further indicated by some ironic comments made in 1856, while he was painting in Liverpool and Manchester, en route to Italy:

Through the influence of Ruskin, to my mind a brilliant charlatan, Pre-Raphaelitism is rapidly overrunning the island, and it prom- ises to be as complete a conquest as that of the Normans. . . . [Hunt's] pictures are quite in the popular style. . . . But no one in England buys a picture on his own judgment. It must have passed the ordeal of some great exhibition and have been praised by some journal of note. In this respect the English are far behind the Americans. . . .[11]

The Howitts met Read again, in Italy in 1870. There, blessed by a wealthy wife, he was "dispensing hospitality with a most lavish hand," particularly at an extravagant reception for his hero, General Sheridan. The "task upon his vital powers in his character of poet, painter, and most sociable host," added Mrs. Howitt charitably, "led to the con- stant use of strong stimulants, which ruined his health." This regimen was too wearing on his five-foot physique, and two years later the state of his health forced him to return to America, where he died of pneumonia on the day after his arrival.

FOUR

William J. Stillman:
"The American Pre-Raphaelite"

W
ILLIAM James Stillman (1828–1901) was the American of his generation who was most closely associated with the British Pre-Raphaelites. He was for a time a confidant of the brothers Rossetti and an ardent admirer of Ruskin before becoming one of his sharpest critics. As editor of *The Crayon: A Journal Devoted to the Graphic Arts, and the Literature Related to Them,*[1] he was also the most vocal among his countrymen in his exegesis of Pre-Raphaelite principles.

Stillman's career was one of variety and adventure—"of multifarious occupation and random life," as he surveyed it.[2] His first formal art training, following his graduation from Union College in Schenectady in 1848, was with the popular American landscape painter, Frederick Edwin Church. During his one winter in Church's New York studio he was deeply impressed by the personality of Edgar Allan Poe, who dropped in for a chat one evening shortly before his death, "a slender, nervous, vivacious, and extremely refined personage," as Stillman saw him. But perhaps the most memorable event of the year was the young artist's discovery of *Modern Painters.* "Like many others, wiser or otherwise," he wrote fifty years later, "I received from it a stimulus to nature worship, to which I was already too much inclined, which made ineffaceable the confusion in my mind between nature and art."[3]

His teacher, Church (soon to be known for his "Niagara," "Heart of the Andes," and other spectacular landscapes), by temperament and technique was essentially Ruskinian in his attitude toward detail in the physical world. He was, recalled Stillman, in many respects

the most remarkable painter of the phenomena of nature I have ever known. . . . But he had little imagination, and his technical training had not emancipated him from an exaggerated insistence on detail, which so completely controlled his treatment of his subject that breadth and repose were entirely lost sight of. A graceful composition, and most happy command of all the actual effects of the landscape which he had seen, were his highest qualities.[4]

Although Stillman was later to believe that this literal rendering of the object, without benefit of emotional coloring or individual perception, lacked the higher and broader qualities of art, he spent the following summer sketching in the Mohawk Valley with a fellow-student, and made as he described them his "first direct and thorough studies from nature." One sketch which resulted was bought by the New York Art Union for $30; so, with this pragmatic proof of his artistic success, "I decided," he said, "to go to Europe and see what the English painters were doing."

Stillman carried with him to London a letter to S. C. Hall, editor of the *Art Journal,* who in turn introduced him to the British painters Leslie, Harding, and Creswick; "these artists," he later wrote, all "found me attentive to the lessons they gave me on their own excellences and led me no farther." But he was particularly eager to meet Turner. To that end Stillman made the early acquaintance of Griffiths, that artist's dealer and special agent; and it was at Griffiths' gallery that Stillman ultimately encountered his idol. Here, however, he was first to meet Ruskin, an event which profoundly affected his later career.

I was looking at some little early drawings of Turner, when a gentleman entered the gallery, and, after a conversation between them, Griffiths came to me and asked if I should not like to be presented to the author of *Modern Painters*, to which I naturally replied in the affirmative. I could hardly believe my eyes, expecting to find in him something of the fire, enthusiasm, and dogmatism of his book, and seeing only a gentleman of the most gentle type, blond, refined, and with as little self-assertion or dogmatic tone as was possible consistently with the holding of his own opinions. . . . A delightful and to me instructive conversation ended in an invitation to visit his father's collection of drawings and pictures at Denmark Hill, and later to spend the evening at his own house in Grosvenor Street.

There he met G. F. Watts and others in Ruskin's circle, and came away believing that Mrs. Ruskin was the most beautiful woman he had seen in England. Not until years afterward was Stillman to realize that the "teaching of *Modern Painters*, and of Ruskin himself later, was in the end fatal to the career to which I was then devoted." [5]

Shortly after this encounter the art dealer suggested to Stillman that Turner himself was coming in on business, and if the young man would happen in, a meeting could be effected.

At the appointed hour Turner came and found me in an earnest study of the pictures in the farther end of the gallery. . . . Griffiths . . . introduced me as a young American artist who had a great admiration for his work. . . . It was difficult to reconcile my conception of the great artist with the little, and, to casual observation, insignificant old man with a nose like an eagle's beak, though a second sight showed that his eye, too, was like an eagle's. . . . Half awed and half surprised, I held out my hand. He put his behind him, regarding me with a humorous, malicious look, saying nothing.

Confused and mortified, the young man turned away and attempted to hide his embarrassment in a minute scrutiny of some canvases. But having made this whimsical test, Turner advanced, shook hands, and talked engagingly until Griffiths took him away to transact the business in hand. This greeting was, according to the dealer, unusually cordial on the part of Turner, for he "had never seen him receive a stranger with such friendliness." Turner gruffly invited Stillman to call on him when he came back to England, but on the American's next visit Turner was dead.

On this first trip Stillman did not encounter any of the Pre-Raphaelites in person, but he did see one of Rossetti's paintings, "The Childhood of Mary Virgin," at the old National Society; and one by Millais, "Christ in the Carpenter Shop." This last canvas impressed him particularly, with its "straight thrust for the truth," and, in fact, he declared: "It determined me in the manner in which I should follow art on my return home." To a friend he emphasized his opinion "that if ever English figure painting rose out of mediocrity it would be through the work of the P.R.B." [7] When he crossed the Atlantic (on the same ship as Jenny Lind) he took home with him "a fermentation of art ideas" stemming chiefly from Ruskin, Turner, and the work of the Pre-Raphaelites.

For the next two years Stillman worked hard and monotonously painting directly from nature, but without guidance or any correct appreciation of what he was doing. His larger studies were exhibited, attracted attention, and won for him an "Associateship of Design," and, as he put it, "the appellation of 'the American Pre-Raphaelite'—all of which for a man so lately embarked in the profession was considered a high honor, as it really was." [8] His canvases, with their extreme fidelity to subject matter and completeness of detail, startled some of the observers, "gave a jog to the landscape painting of the day," and admitted him to what he then considered one of the highest places among his contemporaries.

But in his long critical view this initial success seemed paradoxically a disaster, for it merely confirmed him in the Ruskinian doctrines and carried him farther away from an apprehension of the "elements of true art."

There followed then a decade of varied and colorful adventure as international agent for Kossuth; art student in Paris—where he knew Theodore Rousseau and J. F. Millet; recluse in the Adirondacks and in the Florida wilderness; New York painter and art critic for the *Evening Post* under Bryant; brash confounder of Bronson Alcott in public debate;[9] and originator and co-editor of the *Crayon*. To recoup from the rigors of the last position he retreated to the shelter of Cambridge, to continue his painting and his friendship with the Cantabrigians. Here, he recalls, "to insure Pre-Raphaelite fidelity" in an outdoor portrait he was guilty of "the martyrdom of Longfellow" in making that venerable model perch hour after hour on unyielding granite boulders. The associations in the newly-formed Adirondack Club were fondly recalled in his memoirs, his friendship with Emerson, Lowell, and Agassiz in particular.

Just before Christmas in 1859 Stillman's "uneasy and thriftless spirit" drove him again to England, in a move that was to end the American period of his life. Settling in Charles Street, London, he delivered letters from Charles Eliot Norton introducing him to Arthur Hugh Clough; from Lowell to Thomas Hughes; and from Agassiz to Professor Owen. Hughes took him to the Cosmopolitan Club, where he also met Millais and the poet, Monckton Milnes, Lord Houghton. Millais soon called at his studio, as did Dante Rossetti who knew of him through his brother William's correspondence with the editor of the *Crayon*.

With him to England Stillman had taken his major work up to that time, a study of a deer and hunter painted during three months at Saranac Lake, entitled "Bed of Ferns." Rossetti, who was in Stillman's eyes "very honest and blunt in his criticisms, and not at all inclined to flattery," praised it loudly. But Ruskin, viewing it shortly thereafter, pointed in disgust to the dead deer and exclaimed: "What do you put that stuff in for? Take it out; it stinks!" [10] So in his reverence for his mentor's critical opinions he promptly painted out the central motif of the picture, only to be greeted by Rossetti's subsequent disgust: "You have spoiled your picture!" Nevertheless he submitted the retouched work to the Academy, and on its refusal tried to remove the covering pigments. But the varnish was refractory, and after unsuccessful efforts he finally cut up the picture in a fit of anger and burned it. But even this sad passage did not yet serve to dampen his enthusiasm for Ruskin.

During this period Stillman happily developed his associations with William Michael Rossetti, which had been begun by correspondence; the "relations were constant and cordial, and he was for many years my most valued English friend. Through his extreme honesty and liberality, and his extensive knowledge of and wide feeling for art, there was a great community of appreciation between us, and our friendship lasted long beyond the direct interest I had in English art matters." [11]

Dante Gabriel was at this time living by himself; and although Stillman later was to share a house with him for some weeks, at this juncture they saw comparatively little of each other. As a close friend of the family, however, Stillman enjoyed their informal and cordial hospitality, and admired Christina for her "noble serenity and dignity . . . the spiritual exaltation that . . . dominated her and made her, before all other women of whom I know anything, the poetess of the divine life." She attracted him very strongly, but he would have "as soon thought of falling in love with the Madonna del Gran Duca as with her." [12]

In the summer of 1860 after Stillman had exhibited a large painting at the British Society, Ruskin suggested that the American go to Switzerland with him to assist in making some Alpine studies. "Unfortunately for both of us I could not draw well in traces, and he did not quite well know how to drive, and the summer ended in disappointment, and finally in disaster." [13] Admitting his own lack of discipline in working only when he felt like it, Stillman also added that Ruskin wanted things which were of no intrinsic interest to him; and these facts, coupled with the disparity of mood of the two men, made a satisfactory tour impossible. With Geneva as a center they went by carriage and foot to various points of artistic vantage—the Perte du Rhone, Chamounix, Freiburg, Neuchâtel, Montanvert, Lausanne—with almost daily mountain climbing as part of the program. Some of his companion's sketches Ruskin praised. But one painting in particular, of Alpine roses against a huge granite boulder, incurred such harsh comment from the elder man that Stillman, greatly piqued, destroyed it.

In the evenings they varied their art discussions with chess problems and arguments over sabbatarianism. But in point of view and in method they were by now sharply divergent. Ruskin insisted on the technique of laying on in one stroke the finished color, bit by bit, as in a mosaic; while Stillman's practice was to sketch the whole in lightly, then bring the entire canvas to completion by gradual reworking and building up—the better to keep proper relationship among the parts. "But Ruskin said that was incorrect. . . . Another discouragement!" [14] And although the younger man appreciated the "princely hospitality" and kindly companionship of his critic, they agreed neither in temperament nor in method; and since the Alpine scenery awed but did not inspire him, Stillman felt the whole experience to be nothing short of a catastrophe. He was further depressed by an extreme case of eyestrain at Neuchâtel which deterred him for two years from further serious art work. "Our ideas clashed continually, and what he wanted was impossible,—to make me see with his eyes; and so we came to great disappointment in the end. . . . I lost my faith in myself, and in him as a guide to art." [15]

Ruskin's own reaction to the summer was not so sharply negative, although he obviously felt the tension. From Neuchâtel he wrote on July 12 to their mutual friend, Charles Eliot Norton:

I have had great pleasure, and great advantage also, in Stillman's society this last two months. We are, indeed, neither of us in a particularly cheerful humor, and very often, I think, succeed in making each other reciprocally miserable to an amazing extent; but we do each other more good than harm—at least he does me, for he knows much just of the part of the world of which I know nothing. He is a very noble fellow—if only he could see a crow without wanting to shoot it to pieces. We made a great mistake in staying half our time at Chamouni, which is not a place for sulky people by any means. . . .[16]

After Ruskin returned to Denmark Hill, he recapitulated to the same correspondent:

I enjoyed my Swiss sojourning with Stillman exceedingly—I don't know what I should have done without him, indeed, for I couldn't work, and yet moped when I did nothing. Even as it was we moped a little, both of us being considerably out of heart; but we did better than either of us would have done by himself.[17]

Following this unsettling experience, Stillman went alone from Switzerland to Paris. Then "a radical republican" (in his own phrase) in his political sympathies, and unable to paint, he was on the point of joining the Italian patriot, Garibaldi, on his Marsala expedition, when he was called back to America by an urgent letter from his fiancée's father, saying that the young lady, Miss Mack of Cambridge, was in "great distress of mind" over their projected marriage. Stillman took the next steamer home, married her two days after landing, and brought her back to Paris a few days later. Among the young couple's neighbors and close friends that winter were the Brownings, the father and sister of the poet. A treasured gift from the elder Browning was a life of Raphael, purchased in a bookstall along the quay. The terms of intimacy were such that the Stillmans were invited to join their friends, together with Robert Browning and his wife, at Fontainebleau for the summer, but the death of Mrs. Browning kept their plans from fruition.

The spring of 1861 further complicated the lives of the young Americans when, on the outbreak of the Civil War, a Massachusetts friend, Colonel W. B. Greene, offered Stillman a commission on his staff. He immediately hurried to Washington, only to be turned down by the medical examiners; and as a poor substitute he decided to accept an appointment as American consul at Rome. "I went to Cambridge," he says, "to get information and advice, and, at Lowell's met Howells for the first time. We could, each of us, offer condolence for the other's disappointment; for Howells had asked for Dresden and was appointed to Venice, while I had asked for Venice, intending to write the history of Venetian art. But Rome had always been given to an artist; and, although there was no salary, but fees only, it seemed to have been a much-sought-for position, and I accepted." [18] Most of his official duties and contacts in his Roman consulate were unhappy, and as an occasional escape he took long walks into the Roman Campagna where he resumed his sketching. If this revived interest in painting "was not the rapture of art," he commented, "it was the passion of poetic nature." [19]

A transfer of post took Stillman to Crete—in time to witness the anarchy of the insurrection against the Turks, and to incur the sharp enmity of the Sultan's officials. Privations and extreme personal danger were horribly climaxed by the insanity and suicide of his wife, and an injury to his child of such a serious nature that return to America was imperative. In passing through London he found the Rossettis, Christina in particular, most sympathetic and thoughtful.

Back in New England he turned again to his art for consolation as well as for financial support, and from a generous and not too critical friend, J. M. Forbes of Boston, he received a commission for some work in the White Mountains. But his long abstention from painting had apparently destroyed his manual facility—"the hand had always been too far behind the theory" under any circumstances—and at the end of the summer he made the major decision to abandon any further efforts at painting in favor of a career as a journalist. His first move in that direction was to find a position with *Scribner's Monthly,* and soon thereafter to return to London. [20]

Stillman, who was born the same year as Dante Gabriel Rossetti, was at this time to become more intimately—if not more happily—acquainted with him. In America in 1856 or 1857, while he was working on the *Crayon,* Stillman had met an English landscape painter, Barbara Leigh-Smith, who was to become better known as Mme. Bodichon following her marriage to a French physician. Herself an artist of some note, [21] she had become interested in his painting, and now, after the lapse of some years, he renewed the friendship. As spring came on, Mme. Bodichon offered Stillman the use of her charming rustic cottage at Robertsbridge; and with her consent he asked Rossetti to share it with him.

At this time Rossetti was beginning to suffer the morbid attacks which later destroyed his health completely. Stillman reports that he was sleepless, excitable, and obsessed by the monomania of persecution. Rossetti's family wished him to leave the city in hope of a betterment of his condition; thus Stillman succeeded in getting him away from London to stay for a long visit at Robertsbridge. Here the relaxation and quiet and long daily walks in the woodland, the simple life and freedom from all causes of excitement rapidly brought him back to his natural condition, and he resumed work, doing some of his best drawings there, and completing his poems for publication.[22]

Here by necessity intimacy flourished for a time:

Rossetti was one of the men most dependent on companionship I have ever known. When not at work he needed some one to talk with, and in our long walks he unfolded his life to me as he probably never did to any other man, for he had a frank egotism which made him see everything and everybody purely in their relation to him. And in these circumstances he and I were, after a manner, the only people in our world. As he himself said, "In this Sussex desert one tells all his secrets," and I doubt if even in his own family he ever threw off reserve so completely as with me in the solitude of Robertsbridge, where he was very happy and very well.[23]

Rossetti's view of this companionship in its initial stages is indicated in a note to William Allingham, in early March: "You will be surprised at my address, which is Barbara's Cottage, not far from Hastings. . . . I have been here a few days in company with Stillman, W^m's American friend. . . . Stillman and I have this house to ourselves, and he is an utterly unobstructive man. . . ."[24]

As a gregarious creature, however, Rossetti apparently tired of the limited social contact, and without consulting his host or the owner invited Madox Brown and William Morris and their respective wives to visit the cottage. Since they were all excellent friends of the American he could not gracefully object. But since Rossetti and Stillman were to split all expenses on an even basis this extension of the domestic circle evidently stretched Stillman's purse-strings and patience to the snapping point; and, irked by Rossetti's "sublime and child-like egotism which simply ignored obligations," with Mme. Bodichon's consent he withdrew from the menage and left Rossetti in full possession.

Against Stillman's version of the events here narrated, it is interesting to balance William Michael Rossetti's, recorded twenty-four years after the occurrence:

My brother's health continued to be not good, and his eyesight bad; and in the spring of 1870 he went down to an estate belonging to his kind friend of long standing, Mrs. Bodichon, who placed it quite at his disposal for a while—Scalands, near Robertsbridge, Sussex. Here, after a period of much depression, he at last revived considerably; and, when he came back to town in May, I found him . . . much better.

At Scalands, [continues William Michael] Rossetti was joined by an American acquaintance of his, a friend more especially of my own—Mr. William J. Stillman . . . originally a landscape painter, then a literary man and journalist. . . . Few men could have been better adapted than Mr. Stillman—none could have been more willing—to solace Rossetti in his harasses [sic] from insomnia and other troubles; but it is a fact that a remedy worse than the disease was the result of his friendly ministrations. Chloral, as a soporific, was then a novelty . . . [Stillman] introduced the drug to Rossetti's attention. . . .[25]

To Stillman thus belongs the doubtful distinction of starting his friend in the use of the potent narcotic which later had such a terrible effect on Rossetti's temperament and constitution.[26] Himself a victim of insomnia, Stillman had used chloral by prescription with excellent results, and always carried some with him. In London, before the relaxation at Robertsbridge, he had offered some twenty grains to Rossetti with instructions to take it in three doses; but having instead taken it all at once Rossetti said it only made him sleep stupidly for a few hours and awaken worse than ever. Stillman maintained that at that time Rossetti refused to experiment further with it; and only later on the recommendation of his own physicians, Drs. Marshall and Hake, did the poet resume its use, ultimately to his own grave hurt.[27]

W. M. Rossetti is not so generous in interpreting Stillman's part in the incipient tragedy: "My brother," he declares, "was one of the men least fitted to try any such experiment with impunity. With him it was a case of any expedient and any risk to escape a present evil." So, by implication, as soon as Stillman had pointed out the efficacy of the drug, "he began, I understand, with nightly doses of chloral of 10 grains. In course of time it got to 180 grains"—though W. M. Rossetti hoped that that was the watered-down rather than the true content. But William Michael, in extenuation of this practice, suggests that insanity or even suicide might have resulted without it; and that at least as much harm may have been done by Dante Gabriel's custom of drowning the nauseous taste of the chloral by wine-glass chasers of whisky neat.[28]

In fairness to Stillman, however, the evidence of Dr. Hake should be added; in his *Memoirs* the doctor makes it clear that he had only the finest impression and most pleasant memory of his contact with the American and makes no reference to the drug question:

Mr. Stillman [was] to my mind almost the only one of Rossetti's set whom . . . I can refer to with unmixed pleasure—Stillman, a gentleman of high culture, and his faultless lady, a Greek by birth! He is now the *Times's* correspondent in Rome. I have met him and lost sight of him often, and when I meet him after an interval of years, he is always the same kind, attentive friend, though we have no interests in common beyond each other.[29]

Not long after his return from his sojourn in Robertsbridge in the spring of 1871, Stillman married Miss Marie Spartali, the daughter of the Greek consul-general in London. He had met her through the P.R.B. connections, since both Marie— "a celebrated beauty, and the most cordial, accomplished, and amiable of ladies, herself a very elegant painter," according to W. M. Rossetti—and her younger sister, Christine, who served as a model for Whistler * and later became the Countess Edmond de Cahen, had studied under Madox Brown; and "Mr. and Mrs. Spartali and their beautiful daughters" were considered among the members of the Rossetti circle.[30] In spite of his numerous journalistic trips to the Continent, the intimacy between the Stillmans and the Rossettis continued; † and Marie Stillman, with her exotic Mediterranean charm, later sat for Dante Gabriel's one important painting of 1878, the "Fiammetta," a study of Boccaccio's mistress. She also appeared as one of the figures in "Dante's Dream." [31]

In his reminiscences, written almost twenty years after Rossetti's death, Stillman looked back on him as "one of the most fascinating characters" he had ever known, "open and expansive," and a delightful talker. He was, indeed, "the spoiled child of his genius and of the larger world of his admirers," but "there was no vanity about him, and no exaggeration of his own abilities." The sensuous quality in his paintings, the harmony and play of color, and the artist's imaginative force and intensity were such that for Stillman Rossetti was "undoubtedly the most gifted of his generation of artists, not only in England . . . but in Europe." [32]

* For his *"La Princesse du Palais de Porcelaine."*
† Further data on the later relationships of the Stillmans and the Rossettis are to be found in Chapter XVIII.

FIVE

The Crayon:
the First American Pre-Raphaelite Journal

PRIORITIES are often difficult to establish. Of the *Crayon*, which appears to be the first American journal devoted exclusively to the critical discussion of art—and which is certainly the first magazine in the United States which may be labeled Pre-Raphaelite in tone and origin—Professor Frank Luther Mott writes:

> The *Crayon* was the best art journal of the period. It was founded and edited by W. J. Stillman and John Durand; Durand was left alone in the work after the second year. Broad in its scope, handsomely printed, it was written with a certain authority. Bryant and Lowell were among its contributors.[1]

Initiated in 1855, the *Crayon* antedates by a year the *Cosmopolitan Art Journal* (which died in 1861 as an effect of the war). But specialized publications had existed earlier, such as the *Bulletin of the American Art Union*. Various general magazines of the period typically carried art news notes and reviews of current shows, particularly *Putnam's*, the *North American Review*, *Vanity Fair*, *Sartain's*, the *Lantern*, etc.[2] But in the broad sense it was doubtless true, as Stillman asserted, that in 1855 there was no popular publication in America exclusively "devoted to the interests of art."[3]

Stillman, at that time aged twenty-seven, was working in his painter's studio in New York. He had previously met Ruskin and Turner in England, and had been impressed by some

47

Pre-Raphaelite work. In Paris he had visited their studios and talked at length with Delacroix, Gérôme, and Theodore Rousseau; and had met Delaroche, Ingres, and J. F. Millet.[4] On returning to this country he had spent three months painting a woodland scene on his uncle's farm in western New York, which was so realistic in its treatment (the suggestion for such treatment coming, he says, from Millais's "The Proscribed Royalist") that on its failure to sell for $250 to the American Art Union, Stillman had it photographed and submitted the print anonymously to the conservative head of the Union; his amusement was considerable when that worthy remarked: "What is the use of Stillman making his pre-Raphaelite studies when we can get such photographs from nature as this!" [5]

In New York, provoked by the general incompetence of the newspaper critics of that day, Stillman felt a strong disposition to enter into all art controversies which arose or which might be surreptitiously stirred up; and to that end he wrote numerous letters-to-editors. Having thus acquired a certain publicity—if an unmerited reputation—he accepted William Cullen Bryant's suggestion that he serve as fine arts editor for the *Evening Post*. This position neither paid well nor necessitated much time away from his studio; the chief result was, he says, his "intellectually profitable relations" with Bryant, whom he admired for his inflexible integrity and firmness of character—which in Stillman's view suffered rather from repression than from coldness or innate lack of sympathies.

It was the custom at that time for various young artists studying in New York to foregather for informal *conversazioni* at the Brooklyn home of H. K. Brown, the first caster of bronze statues in America and author of the huge equestrian "Washington" set up in Union Square, whom Stillman considered "the ablest sculptor of that day." Young Stillman, with his fluency, lack of reticence, and profound belief in the validity of his own opinions, soon became the most prominent member of this "Brooklyn School," as they dubbed themselves. Here one evening appeared Bronson Alcott, who, in spite of Emerson's judgment, seemed to Stillman only "a shallow and illogical thinker" who made grist from other men's grain. During the discussions Alcott was at first irritated, then confused, and finally silenced by the importunate questions and irreverent heckling of the young iconoclasts.[6]

As one significant result of all this talking and writing about art, Stillman's friends suggested that it would be a good and useful thing if he should start an art journal. With an "overweening self-confidence"—as he looked back on the venture—he immediately agreed, borrowed $2,500 from his brother Thomas, and secured a like amount from, and an enthusiastic partner in, his young fellow-student, John Durand, the son of the president of the National Academy of Design.

They had high hopes of making the journal so lucrative that they could paint without any anxiety as to means of livelihood. But in addition to this practical aim the young editors, particularly Stillman, had a message:

I had read with enthusiasm *Modern Painters,* and absorbed the views of Ruskin in large draughts, and enjoyed large intercourse with European masters, and with Americans like William Page, H. K. Brown, S. W. Rowse, and H. P. Gray, all thinkers and artists of distinct eminence. In this school I had acquired certain views of the nature of art which I burned to disseminate.[7]

To illumine the lessons of the master, then, and to enliven the critical approach of the public to the art of the day, young Stillman set about his self-appointed task. "I was an enthusiast," he declares, "fired with the idea of an apostolate of art, largely vicarious and due to Ruskin, who was then my prophet, and whose religion, as mine, was nature." [8]

An early move was a trip to Boston and Cambridge to enlist the aid of some of the famous *literati*. Lowell, in spite of his grief over the recent death of his wife, responded to the high spirits of the young journalist, and in effect became his sponsor. Lowell introduced him to Longfellow, to that poet's brother-in-law, Thomas G. Appleton, and to Charles Eliot Norton, R. H. Dana, Agassiz, Emerson, Whittier, E. P. Whipple, Charles Sumner, and others, and took the New Yorker to one of the monthly dinners of the Saturday Club. When he returned to his studio Stillman bore with him "an abundant response" in contributions, promises of aid, and best wishes, and was particularly touched by the refusal of all of his new acquaintances to accept even the nominal fees offered to contributors. [9]

Starting as a weekly in January 1855, the *Crayon* by the end of the first month had built up a subscription list of over 1,200, and the hopes for the future seemed brilliant. The amateur editors failed to realize, however, the prime necessity of income from advertising, and succumbed to the arguments of "cunning publishers" to take their advertisements for nothing. Too, in spite of promises of contributions from New York and New England friends, the actual number of manuscripts received fell far below expectations, and for the first few numbers Stillman recalls that he wrote "nearly the whole of the original matter, and for some time more than half of it." He thus had to grind out not only editorials, criticisms, and essays, but also poetry, book reviews, and alleged "correspondence." Talking to all comers at the office all day, he was forced to do most of his writing at night; so with the conclusion of Volume III in December 1856 (the journal having become a monthly after its first year), it is not strange that his health failed and he found it necessary to make a complete break from journalism—and to go back to the White Mountains "to paint one more picture before he died." He gave his share of the paper (and its liabilities) to his partner Durand to do with as he pleased, went off to New Hampshire to produce his valedictory canvas, and was rather surprised, in due course, to recover. The *Crayon* continued to carry "J. Durand, Editor and Proprietor" at its masthead through July 1861, when, with Volume VIII half completed, it ceased publication after a final, futile plea to its readers:

Now that the whole feeling of the country is violently swelling with the war fever, now that its two great sections are about to come into deadly conflict, we hope that some small margin is left upon which we may plead the cause of Art and the *Crayon*. . . . War is but temporary, the crash of a volcano, but Art is permanent, and unceasingly working for good. Let us, therefore, hope that our friends will not be unmindful of us, will supply us with the fuel of our machinery, and thereby protect art and the *Crayon* from being lost in the smoke, din and dust of the war tempest.[10]

Any digest of the more than 2,700 pages of double and triple columns of fine print that make up the *Crayon's* files must be stringently selective. Editorial and other comment on the contemporary art scene, in particular its Pre-Raphaelite aspects; contributions from British P.R.B. sources; and a general survey of the journal's literary aspects and interests might best serve to suggest the cultural role of the *Crayon* in its pre-Civil War decade.

In a somewhat Olympian tone Stillman addressed his opening audience on January 3, 1855:

In the midst of a great commercial crisis, while fortunes of years' growth have been falling around us, and the panic-stricken world of business has been gathering in its resources, to save what it may from wreck, an effort has been organized, having for its object the education of our countrymen to the perception and enjoyment of Beauty. And although the time seems unpropitious, we have a faith that to Beauty and its messengers, even times and seasons have a deference. . . . To this glorious work of art-cultivation we have devoted this undertaking, and we hope to prove to all men that it is worthy the highest regard of all earnest minds —that the artist has a place in the heart of mankind. . . .

The modern tendency in America, he points out in his next week's editorial, is to evaluate artists and their work solely on the basis of cleverness or technical ability, or on the prices they receive in the public market. The unfortunate result is a crop of contemporary painters who are superficial rather than sincere, able rather than "worthy," forceful and facile but lacking in truth and earnestness.[11] Hence there is a crying need for a public awakening to the basic significance of art, and to its pleasures and benefits. The *Crayon* will strive toward that end:

To make Art popular, not by making it low, but by opening its principles to the comprehension of all minds in the proportion of their intelligence and moral development; to show that it is a thing which mingles in our daily lives, and in no small degree influences our happiness and our virtue; and to enforce its claims to such influence and demonstrate its power, are a part of the results we hope from the success of our journal.[12]

As the greatest exemplars among artists who have aided in this "true and rational development" of human nature, one must look back to the earlier days of artistic sincerity and directness—for Giotto, Perugino, Bellini, and others of the period before Raphael, "themselves great by the force of that sense of duty," have, alas, no peers among the moderns.[13]

Stillman, to make his approach to art as simple as possible, paraphrases Ruskin's terms. What should one look for in a painting and how should he judge it? The answer is obvious: "On the perfect observance of truth all other qualities of Art are based." [14] This "truth," of course, consists in an artist's "strict following of Nature." [15] And all men are fitted to be critics "not by the time they spend in galleries . . . but by the extent of their knowledge of Nature." [16]

To clarify and expand his terms Stillman ran as the lead-articles in seven months' issues a series of papers on "The Nature and Use of Beauty"—the major opus of his editor-ship. Here, in essence, he asserts that physical man, or the man of execution, may as an artist develop his mechanical skill, his "technique," to become the perfect artisan or "tech-nist." Intellectual man, the man of science, may as an artist note carefully and accurately all the laws of nature in their botanical, anatomical, and geologic forms; he may, if he is also an artisan, become thus a "scientific draughtsman." But it is only "moral man," the man of feeling and sensitivity, who can go beyond the cold mechanics of the accurate rendering of nature to an appreciation of the beauty and nobility inher-ent in the person or scene before him and awaken in the observer these uplifting emotions. Thus a complete art presents a quality of moral beauty not dependent on a strict literalness of representation—rather it is "indefinable, unsci-entific, incommunicable." [17]

Nevertheless, comments can be made concerning the beauty of visible form and color. Beauty may be said to exist for an observer when he experiences a feeling of pleasure, or in its highest form, "a spiritual exaltation." Some elements of beauty may be dependent on the "theory of function"—a conscious or unconscious recognition of the applicability of an object to its use as in the form of the human hand, the graceful lines of a ship's hull, or even the shape of a well-designed kitchen implement. But beyond such a pragmatic approach there is also "a beauty of abstract lines and colors where they indicate nothing," [18] where one is satisfied merely in the intense pleasure derived from observing the external object, without any intellectual analysis of its functions. Beauty may ultimately stem, as Plato put it, from "the ideal Good," for "moral beauty . . . affects the lines, and forms, and motions of our material organization." So it is that man's sensitivity to beauty should be cultivated through a deepening of his moral nature; and the twofold result will be not only his added pleasure in the apprehension of greater beauties in the external world, but also an upsurge of the divine within himself.[19]

In the course of this extended discussion of aesthetics a dissatisfied reader canceled his subscription because the *Crayon* was "not practical enough." The editors replied: "The most nobly practical purpose it can perform is, in our opinion, to make the people think." [20] Although he disclaimed any ambition to explain studio methods or palette mixtures, it is interesting to discover that shortly thereafter Stillman introduced a "Technical" column which offered among other data a lengthy analysis of the qualities of various pigments.[21]

In the first dozen issues Stillman had employed the term "Pre-Raphaelite" on several occasions, and now drew a request from another baffled reader for an explanation. He replied that he himself had been impatiently awaiting a communication from a well-informed English contributor anent that very subject, but meanwhile would essay a working definition:

The name "Pre-Raphaelite Brotherhood" was assumed by a fraternity of young artists, who, being of more than usual earnestness, had become disgusted with the shallow and conventional simulation of Art which seemed to command the public taste and patronage of England, and, feeling that the namby-pamby spirit which actuated the great majority of the artists had nothing in common with the sincerity and intensity in which the great artists of the past had arisen, they determined to go back to first principles, and reject entirely the teachings of artists, working out their own solution of the problem of the representation of Nature. Justly [believing] that conventionalism began with Raphael, they assumed the name Pre-Raphaelite to signify their determination to go behind conventionalism and represent what they saw as justly as possible. Their works were immediately marked by their intensity of thought and elaborateness of finish. . . .[22]

Then with considerable perspicuity Stillman pointed out that, although the ideal of eliciting the union of "perfect truth" and "perfect beauty" in Nature remained quite sound, the British P.R.B. painters in their human limitations fell short of their goal. In their early practice of carrying the elaboration of detail to the limit, one unhappy result of their "exceeding faithfulness" was a constraint and rigidity of form, an element of grotesqueness not agreeable to the observer. Hence it follows that this phase of Pre-Raphaelitism is only "preliminary to the attainment of the ideal of truth and beauty."[23] This "preliminary state of Art-study" nevertheless offers two essential object lessons: conscientiousness, with its rejection of "the smooth-glosed falsehoods" and tricky effects of popular art; and intensity, the artist's supreme devotion to, and self-forgetfulness in "his loved Nature." These are the qualities which divide the P.R.B.'s from "all other modern schools of Art" and link them to "the glorious elder brethren who wrought in the love and fear of God—as they did in the love and reverence of Nature."[24]

Almost as if in rebuttal to some of his own strictures, Stillman received and printed in the following issue William Michael Rossetti's first contribution from England.[25] As "Art News from London" it is phrased in not too gentle terms. The current British exhibitions are largely marked, asserts Rossetti, by "extreme mental poverty and inanity of subject."

The popular artists do their domestic scenes in either "a prettified sentimental," or a "mindless, literal" way. The genre pieces are often clever, rarely valuable. Portraiture has descended to the level of "vacant vanity." And the landscapes are limited in range and wretchedly repetitious, though, here at least, some fresh and lively color is visible, and some vivid perception and easy rendering of nature. Sculpture, although "tolerably skillful" in performance, is "weak and palsy-stricken" in conception, suffering from the current "corpse-like academicism." [26]

On the whole a dark picture to Rossetti's eyes—but fortunately there are exceptions. "Beneficent Pre-Raphaelitism is gradually working a change in the tenor of our pictorial doings." But "let there be no mistake about what Pre-Raphaelitism means." It deals with neither the technique, defects, nor choice of subjects of the old painters, but rather with "the condition of mind which actuated them to represent whatever was in hand . . . with a resolute adherence to truth of feeling and truth of fact, and a resolute disregard of all mere grace and all mere dexterity which would interfere with the first or affect the second." At its lowest, Rossetti admits, Pre-Raphaelitism might be simply a catalogue-compiler's reverent faith in nature; but at its highest ("and the young men who founded the school understood it at its highest") it embraced a far wider range—a new invention and a new conception "truly natural in idea," but not delimited by the physical aspects of viewed phenomena. From this loving observance of nature, expressed through her medium, would spring fresh and individual beauties from the brush of the artist.[27]

In the current "British Institution" exhibit Rossetti singled out for detailed comment "the thoroughly Pre-Raphaelite work" of Ford Madox Brown, who had painted in that

manner before the label as such was coined; and that of
William Bell Scott, who had "benefited very noticeably
by Pre-Raphaelitism in his art"; and as a comment on the
subsequent Royal Academy exhibit Rossetti declared: "I
have not yet spoken of the Pre-Raphaelite pictures, which
are, to my judgment, the most important of all, as marking
an era not only in British, but in European painting, as well
as for the intrinsic loftiness of their qualities." On display
were three canvases each by Holman Hunt and Millais, including the latter's "Order of Release" which was so famed
in the 1853 show that it "substantially crushed the venomous
abuse of Pre-Raphaelitism." [28]

William Michael Rossetti continued to contribute his
monthly comments, in a similar vein, during the two years
that Stillman stayed with the *Crayon;* thereafter his regular
communications ceased.

Together with his primary interest in the American art
scene Stillman pursued, from time to time, this subject of
the British Pre-Raphaelite movement in his own lead articles
and editorial "Sketchings" (which became rarer as the number of his contributors increased). In "The Hope of Art" he
welcomes the "new reform" in England, of which the "first
fruits are Millais, Holman Hunt, Rossetti and their confreres"; and feels if that movement could spread and find
"an abiding place in the unoccupied artistic feeling of
America, we may hope from the intensity and enthusiasm
of the race, something as yet undreamed of." [29] His most extensive discussion of the Pre-Raphaelites did not appear,
however, until shortly before he severed connections with
the *Crayon.* Entitled "The Two Pre-Raphaelitisms," the chapters were spread through four numbers; their announced
purpose was to explain and to justify both the medieval and
the modern movements, particularly since the artists of the

nineteenth-century brotherhood had been the objects of so much "passionate prejudice." [30]

The predecessors of the modern P.R.B.'s were men who, by "the force, earnestness, and fire of their own minds," produced works which for Stillman were "superior to any of their successors" because they "sought to present sacred truths and human wisdom in a form which all might comprehend without difficulty." Thus they began with "bare, stark-naked, and literal facts, tangible as a blow from a hammer." Giotto, for example, pictured a physical hand of the Lord seen visibly in Heaven, or showed the angel, palm-leaf in hand, entering in a straightforward manner through a window to make his annunciation to Anna, seated in a "perfect transcript of a bed-chamber of the age."

A progression beyond this elementary technique is apparent in an appeal to "a rather higher class of intelligence" which responds to the double challenge of subtle suggestion of character, coupled with "the power of design." In Giotto's own later "Salutation to Mary," as illustration, "nothing could be more expressively tender, more full of affectionate adoration, joy, and hope" than the look which Elizabeth directs toward the future mother of Christ. An unknown early Florentine produced, as another instance, "a magnificent Niello work" in the form of a *Pietà* in which the Virgin appears, not young and beautiful as in later popularized treatments, but old and tired, clutching sadly at the heavy burden on her knee. As for the response to design, an observer must react strongly to the power of the Angel Gabriel in the "Annunciation," standing in the center of "an intense, rayed radiance of the gold of heavenly fire." And for "elegant purity and natural grace" of design Ghirlandajo, Benozzo Gozzoli, Fra Angelico, and Masaccio are "remarkable."

But the highest type of all the art before Raphael was that in which the artist became poet—in which the canvas was so filled with emblem, implication, and further meaning ("the whole presented carefully, subtly, and beautifully") that "we wish for wings to follow the inspirations of the artists." Here Stillman has the grace to admit he is "scarcely competent" to instruct the reader, but suggests that Cosimo Rosselli ("Exposition of the Sacrament"), Ghirlandajo ("Death of St. Francis"), Masaccio ("Martyrdom of St. Peter"), and Fra Bartolomeo ("Saints Peter and Paul"), are all superior in some aspects of their work to the much-praised Raphael.[31]

Having thus presented his case for the first Pre-Raphaelites, the writer asserts that that name cannot fairly be considered "a phrase implying crudity and childishness of design," and that anyone so using it merely betrays his own historic and artistic ignorance. The *post*-Raphaelites indeed succumbed in due course to "exaggerated action, conventionalism, gaudy color, false sentiment, voluptuousness, and poverty of invention." And it was to rescue art from this morass that the new Pre-Raphaelites arose. "We hope to show . . . that the name 'Pre-Raphaelite,' which but a few years ago was taken up as a phrase of mocking scorn by the ignorant critics, may become a pass-word of honor to those who have endeavored to restore Art to its proper position."[32]

The two succeeding articles, his editorial swan song, were devoted to that end. After a summary of the formation and growth of the Brotherhood, Stillman suggests the dominant traits of its three outstanding members: Millais possesses "a singularly brilliant dramatic power, with a wonderful gift of color"; Holman Hunt is marked by a "concentrated, solid, earnest vigor, with a more complete system of execution than either of the others"; while D. G. Rossetti appears as "a genius of extraordinary calibre, delighting chiefly in subtle and spiritual subjects which seem to fit no other hand." [33] After describing their major works, in each of which some youthful faults may be found—for each of these painters was still in his twenties—Stillman concludes:

These have been the chief labors of the English Pre-Raphaelites; with very few exceptions they have been works which exhibited the utmost of devoted labor, the love of the subject carried to the extremest extent, evincing thereby the most sincere intention and . . . the intense purpose which led to the formation of the Brotherhood; a fraternity which, in a few years, has almost revolutionized the style of Art in England. . . .[34] If we have erred in executing our task, it has been through love and admiration, and an honest applause of great efforts.[35]

In view of the general Pre-Raphaelite tone of the *Crayon,* it is not strange that Ruskin's interest was aroused. It was he who had originally recommended W. M. Rossetti as British correspondent; and although he refused Stillman's suggestion of becoming himself a regular contributor he offered to answer, in informal letters, any questions about art which the editor or his subscribers might wish to raise, and added:

I have much to thank America for—heartier appreciation and a better understanding of what I am and mean, than I have ever met in England. Nothing gives me greater pleasure than the thought of being of use to an American; and, if I can, in any way, oblige any of your friends who are interested in Art, I beg that you will call upon me.[36]

Several queries and answers ensued, with an occasional interpolation by Ruskin such as: "I am delighted with all your criticism in the *Crayon.* It is full of sense and justice.—I mean by yours, the editorial. The other matter is also very interesting and good. I think you should be well pleased with your London contributor." [37]

Among Stillman's local contributors who also pleased him was Rembrandt Peale, at seventy-seven the grand old man of American art, whose extended "Reminiscences" of early painters and paintings ran through some eleven numbers of the *Crayon*. Asher B. Durand, the president of the National Academy of Design (and father of Stillman's co-editor), obliged with a series of nine articles cast as "Letters on Landscape Painting." The sculptors Horatio Greenough and Henry K. Brown likewise contributed, as did the critic, Christopher P. Cranch and the British Pre-Raphaelite Brother, Frederick G. Stephens, and Mary Howitt. Numerous extracts, presumably with Ruskin's approval, were reprinted from *Stones of Venice* and *Modern Painters*. And many contemporary painters, critics, and essayists who are now only names, among them Daniel Huntington and James Henry,* discoursed at length on such diverse topics as the "Use of Color," "The Poetry of Architecture," "Pennsylvania Forest Scenery," "Wigs and Their Wearers," "Picture Buying," "Sketches of the Great Masters," "Scenery of South America," "Rosa Bonheur," "On Boats," "Allegory in Art," "Iron Buildings," "Genius," "Egyptian Art," "Medieval Gothic," "Landscape Gardening," and so on. Notes were made of the current shows and exhibitions, and of the doings of the National Academy and such other art and cultural organizations as the Boston Athenaeum, the New York School of Design, the Pennsylvania Academy, the Rhode Island Art Association, the New York Gallery of Fine Arts, and—in a very patronizing tone—the Cosmopolitan Art Association of Sandusky, Ohio. The various British groups were often mentioned, not only the Royal Academy, but such institutions as the Arundel So-

---

* In his memoirs Stillman says that Henry James, Sr., was "a not infrequent contributor." Unless "James Henry" is a simple pseudonym, Stillman's memory played him false.

ciety and the Royal Association of Fine Arts at Edinburgh.

A brief word must also be said concerning the literary as distinct from the art interests of the *Crayon*. The journal opened auspiciously with new poems donated by Lowell and Bryant, which Stillman bore triumphantly to New York after his Cambridge visit. Bryant's contribution was without a title, and, said Stillman, "when I asked him to give it one he replied, 'I give you a poem, give me a name'; and I called it 'A Rain Dream,' which name it bears still in the collected edition of his works." [38] Having to economize his wealth, Stillman held this until his second number, putting in the first his own essay on "The Landscape Element in Bryant's Poetry," [39] and gave to Lowell's fragmentary "My Appledore Gallery," which Stillman considered superior to Bryant's work, the honor of the initial appearance. Later sections of this poem were printed in the fifth number, together with a version of "The First Snow-Fall" which had been especially revised for the *Crayon*;[40] his "Invita Minerva" appeared soon afterward. In appreciation of their relationship with Lowell, the editors of the *Crayon* tendered him a farewell dinner in New York as he sailed for Europe before undertaking his Harvard professorship. The occasion was "a splendid success," especially since it contributed to the reconciliation between Lowell and Bryant, who had felt some injury over certain passages in the "Fable for Critics."[41]

Other original contributions from American poets were Aldrich's "Hafiz Ben Ali" and "The Village Clock"; Bayard Taylor's "The Inaccessible"; and William Gilmore Simms's "The Mountain Prospect";[42] together with reprints from Bryant ("The Tides," "Snow Shower," "An Invitation to the Country," and others), Longfellow ("The Children's Hour"), Emerson ("To the Humble Bee"), and N. P. Willis ("Infant Beauty"). But the most frequent names to be found in the poetry columns were those of Lydia H. Sigourney, Christopher Cranch, W. Sylvester, Justin Winsor, and Lucy Larcom, "the truest poetess of that day in America," as Stillman fondly described her.[43]

From British sources are Clough's "Say Not the Struggle Nought Availeth," and William Allingham's "Aeolian Harp." Mrs. Browning's "A Dead Rose" is reprinted, with more than a half dozen poems by William Bell Scott, the poet-painter and friend of D. G. Rossetti and other Pre-Raphaelites. In 1858, some time after Stillman had left, Durand reprinted Rossetti's "The Burden of Nineveh," "The Blessed Damozel," and "The Staff and Scrip" under the note:

The following poems appeared some months ago in an English Magazine, which was published for a year, never reaching a large circulation, and which is now extinct. It contained the writings of some of those younger men who will win fame for themselves, if they live, and who, if they die before fame comes to them, will have had what is better than fame. These poems show such power of expression, such depth of sentiment, such force of imagination, as are rarely found in modern verse. They were written by one of the leaders of the Pre-Raphaelite School in painting, and they are an interesting illustration of the imaginative tendencies, and of the tone, the thought and feeling which pervade that school.[44]

As long as Stillman shaped the editorial expression of the *Crayon* we may assume that the poetry he printed or selected illustrated his critical principles in literature, for there was in his aesthetic a close connection between poetry and painting, e.g.:

We shall make our position clearer, perhaps, by showing the analogy between Art (in our sense) and Poetry, the former being devoted to forms and appearances, the latter to ideas, the Artist and Poet being different manifestations of the same spirit of Beauty. . . .[45]

Thus the "technist" in the plastic arts who relies on clever manipulation approximates the "versifier" who stresses the external literary form. But both the true artist and the true poet must go beneath the superficial, to a fundamental love and presentation of the beautiful, which springs from and is dependent on the development of "their moral nature."

Although Stillman's primary interest in literature was in poetical forms, he and Durand ran extensive review columns variously called "Sketchings" and "Studies among the Leaves," together with longer criticisms in which succinct and pertinent comment was made on American, British and Continental literature. The majority of the reviews, however, were quite properly devoted to works dealing with the fine arts.

From the perspective of a long career Stillman looked back on the *Crayon* as a comparatively successful venture although, "from a large journalistic point of view, it was, no doubt, somewhat crude and puerile. It had a considerable public, sympathetic with its sentimental vein, readers of Ruskin and lovers of pure nature,—the circle larger, perhaps, for the incomplete state of art education in our community."[46] As Stillman asserted, the *Crayon* did have "a real vitality," which is still apparent after the passage of a hundred years. And although its omniscient and cathedral tone may have betrayed, as Stillman suggests, "a relative juvenility," nevertheless the *Crayon* as a lively sheet devoted to art criticism and to poetry served a real purpose in making mid-nineteenth-century Americans more aware of their current art world.[47]

British Pre-Raphaelite Art in America:
1857 Exhibition

EARLY IN 1857, shortly after Stillman had withdrawn from the *Crayon*, a young, retired British army officer, Captain Augustus A. Ruxton, arranged the first formal loan-exhibition of English art in the United States. He had, as W. M. Rossetti recalled, "no particular technical knowledge of art matters," but he was an energetic amateur and had in this case also the hope of profiting from his endeavors. He immediately wrote to William Michael Rossetti as an outstanding art authority, and engaged him as secretary for the whole venture. Together they began in London the collection of a considerable loan-exhibit, and in the process necessarily had contact with a number of art dealers. Among such professional connoisseurs Gambart was one of the best known and most enterprising; and he, by coincidence, had been preparing a parallel exhibit of his own for showing in the United States. Thus they decided to join forces, and Gambart became co-partner with Captain Ruxton in the whole project.

Rossetti meanwhile had written to Ruskin asking for assistance and a little publicity, but was rebuffed. "You must have thought me very hard," replied Ruskin (sidestepping the main question), "not to help you with the American Exhibition; but I have no knowledge of America, and do not choose to write one word about things which I know nothing of."[1]

With W. M. Rossetti acting largely as a one-man jury to select pictures for the transatlantic public, there naturally was evident, as he admitted, "a certain bias towards Pre-Raphaelitism" with an almost total exclusion of eighteenth-century canvases. Since they wished to make an impressive showing—six galleries were ultimately filled, each room "well covered, the pictures all being closely jammed together," the captain later reported—a number of non-Pre-Raphaelite works were necessarily included.

Rossetti had introduced Captain Ruxton to Madox Brown. The suggestion was made that Brown should also go to America as "art-superintendent of the Exhibition"; and although Brown was on the point of acquiescing, he finally refused. Hence Ruxton alone shepherded the show to New York, where he was gratified by what appeared to be official recognition of the cultural value of his project. "I am happy to say," he wrote back to Rossetti on September 29, "I have not miscalculated the feeling towards the English Exhibition. The Commissioner of the Customs has not only given authority to pass the frames as well as the pictures free of duty, but allows them to be handed over to my agent from the ship without examination."[2]

They had concocted the elaborate scheme of splitting the exhibit into two sections to show concurrently in Philadelphia and New York, and then in due course, of shifting the materials. But the hard times of 1857 were at hand—"the sudden panic in the money market," as Ruxton ruefully explained to his English correspondent. "We could not have undertaken our enterprise at a more unfortunate, I may say, disastrous time. . . . The wisest heads are affrighted at the state of commercial affairs in the country. Every day brings some startling crash, and literally, money is not to be had. It may appear absurd, but I could not get a sovereign changed yesterday." So instead of the four sources of return which the original plan of the double showings would have provided, the sponsors had to be content with a single New York exhibit. Chances of sales were also reduced by Ruxton's inability to obtain conveniently located exhibition rooms.

The captain's spirits were lightened somewhat, however, by the interest and encouragement of President Durand of the American Academy of Design, and the assistance of Stillman, now ex-editor of the *Crayon*. Durand, Jr., as sole editor of that journal, was disappointed in an informal preview that none of Dante Gabriel Rossetti's drawings were included, and urged Ruxton to ask that some be sent immediately. "Your brother will not be displeased to hear that great interest is felt here in his works," wrote Ruxton to William Michael.[3] Something by Millais, too, was urgently requested.

The untrained reactions of Ruxton's employees also boded well. "P.R.B.ism," he reported before the show opened, "takes with the working men—they look, and they look, and they look, and then say something that the author of the pictures would be delighted to hear." Arthur Hughes's "The Sailor Boy," "Innocence," and "April Love," Madox Brown's "King Lear," and Hunt's "The Light of the World," [4] Ruxton added, "are immensely popular among my *hangers*." The last work in particular had a wide and obvious appeal. "Please report to [Hunt] that a man said, 'Never mind the gas, that picture will light us up.' " [5]

Affairs seemed to progress well in spite of the hard times, and on October 20 Captain Ruxton drafted his report to Rossetti:

I have to announce a most successful opening of the Exhibition at the private view last night. All the leading people of the city were present—indeed the rooms were crammed, and the most cordial and kindly feeling was manifested. . . . "The Light of the World" creates a great sensation; but Madox Brown's "King Lear" seems to be the most popular picture of the Exhibition.[6]

Stillman three weeks thereafter sent a note of encouragement—and criticism—to his old *Crayon* contributor, W. M. Rossetti. In spite of "the straitness of the time, the Exhibition holds its own and grows into wider favor every day." Not a little of this success, Stillman suggests, lies in the captivating charm of the worthy British captain, "whose management has been most admirable, and whose excellent address and personal influence have won him friends and favor with all classes and parties. . . . The artists unite with him, and the Club welcomes him, and the ladies especially become workers for the success of the gallery. . . ."[7]

But, added Stillman, who no longer enjoyed the editorial columns of the *Crayon* as a vehicle for his critiques, it would not do to talk down to the American public. The show, in effect, was badly padded with poor stuff, and the sponsors should be made to realize this. "The Committee seem to have thought that things which were second-rate at home were fit to represent English art here, while our *amateurs* are in the main as well acquainted with English art as the English public itself. . . . There are many pictures which the public feel were sent here in presumption of ignorance or bad taste on our part, and we are a sensitive people on such points."

Even the P.R.B. contributions "should have been culled more carefully." In view of the fact that certain "eccentricities" of the school were new to the American public, Stillman singled out Hughes's "Fair Rosamond" and Miss Siddal's "Clerk Saunders" as items that should have been omitted. Further, too much general attention was given to pictures of historic incident and episode of comparatively little interest, whereas there was a dearth of good landscape which the public would have enjoyed more. Nevertheless, "the Pre-Raphaelite pictures have saved the Exhibition so far as oil pictures are concerned." Because of "something vital and earnest" in them "the P.R.B. pictures have . . . attracted more admirers than all the others . . . and at the same time have been more fully appreciated than they are *at this day* in England." [8]

By implication, however, sales were not too encouraging, for Stillman pointed out, perhaps to cushion Rossetti's disappointment, that American picture-buyers rarely purchased from exhibitions, but preferred to buy pictures not previously shown. He hoped, however, that specific commissions would be forthcoming.

The exhibit continued in place for some months. In July 1858, almost a full year later, Charles Eliot Norton received a letter from Dante Gabriel Rossetti in answer to such a commission given him by the American. With apologies for his tardiness in filling it, Rossetti described his drawing called "Before the Battle"—these "chivalric Froissartian themes are quite a passion of mine," he explained. In this he pictured a "castle-full of ladies who have been embroidering banners which are now being fastened to the spears by the Lady of the castle"; and uncertain as to its acceptability, Rossetti asked Norton to corroborate his selection. "Worst of all, to be thoroughly sordid," might he also beg "by return post if possible, the amount of the commission (50 guineas if I am not mistaken)"? This importunate "*hook* for the money" he apologizes for by the fact that his "Oxford labours of love" have left him "a little aground." After further news on the progress of the Oxford Union murals, his own work on the Llandaff triptych, and his *Early Italian Poets* then in press, he concludes:

My brother has been largely occupied with duties in your neighbourhood, and I suppose the English Exhibition may be considered *un fait accompli.* . . . I am afraid, from your not telling me,
that no one much liked "Clerk Saunders." All I can say is, if they
don't, they're wrong.[9]

In this 1857 Exhibition, then, the American public had
their first major opportunity to view and evaluate contemporary British art; and in the main, they found the Pre-
Raphaelite paintings good.[10]

SEVEN

The American Brotherhood:
"The Society for the Advancement of Truth in Art"

LESS THAN eighteen months after the demise of the *Crayon*, further action of a Pre-Raphaelite nature ensued. On the evening of January 27, 1863, at 32 Waverly Place in New York City a group of "daring" young men met to diagnose the condition of the arts in mid-century America. Believing in the "overwhelming power of Truth, especially in Art, they had for some time seen the necessity of a united effort to revive true art in America, and had assembled at this time . . . to organize an Association for the better promotion of the end just stated." [1] Several other meetings were held, with sharp altercation over platform principles; but finally, on February 18, the Articles of Organization were reported complete, unanimously adopted, and signed by all the persons present. In such an American manner, a decade after the climax of the Pre-Raphaelite Brotherhood's activity in England, was born the little-known counterpart of that group in this country.*

The lineage of this society may be traced to two definite sources, one British, one American. In 1860 a young Englishman, Thomas Charles Farrer, who had studied art under Ruskin and had become his ardent supporter, moved to New

* See Chapter VIII for details concerning the charter members: T. C. Farrer, Clarence Cook, Clarence King, Peter B. Wight, Russell Sturgis, Charles Herbert Moore, and Eugene Schuyler.

York. Finding, to his surprise, a few sympathizers with his views among some young artists and architects, he soon was instrumental in drawing them together into an organization. But the ground had been prepared; for before the *Crayon* expired in the first year of the Civil War its Pre-Raphaelite seed was ripening, and the journal of the new association soon editorialized: "Less than ten years ago there was but one man in America, W. J. Stillman, who practically understood and believed in the new art. Today it counts its believers [honestly but anticlimactically] by tens instead of units." But, continued the spokesman, "when we think of what has been accomplished in England since the first protest against the old conventionalisms was made . . . we cannot despair of the cause in America." [2]

"The Society for the Advancement of Truth in Art" was their formal appellation, but they soon were popularly referred to as the American Pre-Raphaelites. "We hold," they clarioned, "that the revival of Art in our time, of which the principal manifestations have been in England, is full of promise for the future and consolation for the present. That the Pre-Raphaelite school is founded on the principles of eternal truth. . . ." [3] As the *Germ* (in only four issues) had spoken for the P.R.B.'s in England, so the *New Path* was to be the vehicle for publicizing the credo of the Americans. This small but self-assertive sheet indeed merits attention, for in spite of the exigencies of the war years it saw the publication of twenty-four issues (intermittently, it is true) from May 1863, through December 1865, and in a highly independent manner discussed problems of the arts in America.[4]

There was, in 1863, nothing reticent or self-effacing about the contributors to the *New Path*.

We exist [they declared] for the purpose of stirring up strife; of breeding discontent; of pulling down unsound reputations; of making the public dissatisfied with the work of most of the artists, and, better still, of making the artists dissatisfied with themselves. . . . We refuse our respect to popular verdicts. . . . And we utterly deny the value of the greater number of Academic laws, believing that they and the Academies which made them and uphold them have done harm, and only harm, to the sacred cause of true Art.[5]

Additional entries in their Articles indicate that, akin to Ruskin's aims, the more practical objects of the Association were "to secure encouragement and mutual instruction, to assist meritorious artists who may need help, to develop latent artistic ability, especially among the class of mechanics, and to educate the public to a better understanding of the representative Arts." To such ends meetings should be held for the reading of papers and for discussions and criticisms; approved works of art bought and commissions given to deserving aspirants; prize contests conducted; public exhibitions of "naturalistic Art" sponsored, together with pertinent lectures; and, finally, their magazine, the New Path, issued as a convenient medium for critical notices, essays, and "such appeals to the public as it may be expedient to make." [6]

Such an energetic program again attracted the eye of Ruskin in England, whose letter of approbation the editor of the New Path proudly printed:[7]

Denmark Hill, 5th April, 1864

Sir:

I have been occupied lately with painful business, and have too long delayed the expression of my sympathy with you, both in the labor you have set yourself, and in the feelings with which you undertake it:—no less than of my thanks for the help you are giving me in carrying forward and illustrating the views which I have hitherto endeavoured to maintain almost singlehanded. . . .

I have only time today to ask your pardon for my apparent neglect of your efforts, and to express my thankfulness for courteous references to my own work. . . .

Very respectfully yours,

J. RUSKIN

These "courteous references" to Ruskin and his younger contemporaries are even more frequent in the pages of the *New Path* than they had been in the *Crayon,* and make incontestable the debt of this American group to the English Pre-Raphaelites. A typical entry:

Pre-Raphaelitism has saved the art of England, and made it the first art of the modern world, and Pre-Raphaelitism will save our art, yet, if we can but have the modesty and patience to obey its teachings. . . .[8]

Or:

If ever a body of men stood on a foundation of granite, it is the Pre-Raphaelites, and if ever a cause was absolutely sure, it is their cause. . . .[9]

Among the variegated essays, art criticisms, editorials, letters, and general harangues in the *New Path* a reader may discern three main types: critical and often caustic reviews of current art shows; discussions of the principles of the fine arts and to a smaller degree of literature; and, finally, concrete analyses of and practical suggestions for the improvement of American art, architecture, and interior decoration. Of these categories the last two are of some continuing interest.

The American Pre-Raphaelites' much-argued "Articles of Organization" (in many details similar to the promulgations of Stillman in the *Crayon*) contained the following confession of artistic faith, applicable to literature as well as to the plastic or visual arts:

We hold that the primary object of Art is to observe and record truth, whether of the visible universe or of emotion. . . . The greatest Art includes the widest range, recording, with equal fidelity, the aspirations of the human soul, and the humblest facts of physical Nature.

That the imagination can do its work, and free invention is possible only when the knowledge of external Nature is extended and accurate. . . .

That beauty . . . can only be appreciated and seized by those who are trained to observe and record all truths, with equal exactness. . . . The art which seeks beauty alone, disobeying Nature's law of contrast and narrowing the Artist's mind, loses beauty and truth together.

Therefore, that the right course for *young* Artists is faithful and loving representations of Nature, "selecting nothing and rejecting nothing," seeking only to express the greatest possible amount of fact.[10]

For the Americans the great touchstone in art is thus the variable and now too-familiar term, "truth to nature." "All works of Art, whether pictures, statues, poems, or novels, must eventually stand or fall according to the truth in them. . . . As Mr. Ruskin says, '. . . Truth forgives no insult, and endures no stain.'"[11] In the quest for this minute realism the creative artist must go to nature direct; but even then "we do not believe that mere faithful transcript from nature can ever be the greatest art: but we believe and positively affirm, that there can never be any degree of greatness without this as a basis. . . . Naturalism is not all we believe in, but we know it must come first."[12] Naturalism, not in the philosophical connotation of the individual inescapably affected by his environment and heredity, but rather in its suggestion of "nature-ism"—the substitution of observable, actual phenomena for the inherited classical conventions of the academies—was the goal of the new aesthetic expression.

And since the Americans agreed "to let the term Pre-Raphael-itism pass as a synonym for naturalism," they thereby tightened their bonds with the British group.

Modern Painters was of course the quarry from which most of these ideas had been extracted. Twenty years earlier Ruskin had offered this advice to the young painters of England: "They . . . should go to nature in all singleness of heart, and walk with her laboriously and trustingly, having no other thoughts but how best to penetrate her meaning, and remember her instruction, rejecting nothing, selecting nothing, and scorning nothing. . . . Then, when their memories are stored, and their imaginations fed, and their hands firm, let them . . . give the reins to their fancy, and show us what their heads are made of. We will follow them wherever they choose to lead." [13] This mature development was stressed, too, by William Michael Rossetti, who objected to Ruskin's apparent inclusiveness of subject-matter: "Strict non-selection cannot, in the nature of things, be taken as the rule in a picture of character or incident." [14]

The contributors to the *New Path* at once offered defense and interpretation of their new creed. A comment first on their British friends:

The reform movement of the modern Pre-Raphaelites has been mistaken for an attempted revival of medieval art. . . . Modern Pre-Raphaelite art is as far from being an imitation of early Italian art as light is from darkness. . . . The young men of England who started this movement called themselves "Pre-Raphaelite" because they saw that the painters of that period were actuated by worthiness of aim and put their whole strength into their work. It was the *spirit* of the early workmen that they resolved should actuate them, (i.e. the spirit of truth). . . . The new movement is directed against conventional shallowness and imbecile affectation,—it is a stern appeal to truth.[15]

This appeal to truth is by two media: not only through the "faithful and loving representations" of visible nature already recommended for young artists, but also through the recording of the realities of imagination and emotion. But still the goal is verity, for "that art which is the work of the imagination is the noblest, not because it gives less, but infinitely more pure fact than is possible to mere topography of external nature." [16] There are, fortunately, a few who do possess "creative imagination of extraordinary power, with great ability to express it." This, then, is artistic or poetic genius; and "their mission is to put into marble or music or verse or painted form whatever they see imaged on the retina of their mental vision." The world should indeed "accept with modest gratitude" whatever such artists choose to produce.[17]

These terms may be extended to literature as an art form, since "the Poet and the Artist have the same errand in the world." [18] Lessons in the accurate observation and faithful reporting of nature might well be taken from Thoreau, whose *Excursions* was singled out for extended quotation. Emerson too can see nature in a way which a painter should try to imitate; [19] and Emerson's comments on Ruskin and on the American sculptor, Greenough, are reprinted from his *English Traits*.[20] Others among the American "great or worthy" are Bryant, Lowell, Whittier, Holmes, and Longfellow; and in England Tennyson in his use of evocative, concrete detail in such works as "The Eagle" might well be compared in technique with Millais.[21] Wordsworth and Keats also combined the painter's eye for the definite detail in nature with the expanding imagination and rich emotional experience of the creative poet. Not alone with these men, the *New Path* editorialized, but with all poets and artists—with all literature and art—the public should above all else train itself to be critical in its appreciation.

Briefly now the actual situation of the arts in mid-nineteenth-century America may be reviewed through the eyes of the wayfarers along the New Path. In their "unrelenting vigilance in the pursuit of all interlopers in the domain of Art," these critics were accused by the New York *Tribune* of resembling "rough riders" who ran down pitilessly everything they regarded as legitimate game. In need of less dogmatism and greater tolerance, and guilty even of "ungracious conceit," the magazine nevertheless was redeemed by "its refreshing frankness and honesty, its appreciation of the nobler function of the artists, and even its cool assumption of infallibility" which gave a "zest and vitality" to its pages and made it "a power, though small in size, of not a little weight and significance in our periodical literature." [22]

In painting, in public and domestic architecture, and in interior decoration America, declared the sponsors of the *New Path,* was woefully wanting. With surprising vigor and modernity of approach they declaimed:

American painters have produced no work for forty years that is worth keeping, unless it may be for historical purposes. There has never been one of them sufficiently master of his technics to make his mere painting valuable without reference to the subject treated. . . . Art in America has been pursued on wrong principles. Its aims have been misunderstood; the Artist's work has not been comprehended. And beside that Art has suffered from the provincial character of all our culture, the moral atmosphere at home has been deadly to all high aspiration or achievement.[23]

Popular painters are swept off the board in a broad backhand gesture. The American masters—so-called—Copley, Stuart, Huntington, Leutze ("Washington Crossing the Delaware"),

Bierstadt ("The Rocky Mountains"), are so considered only because of lack of adequate competition; and with "traditional reputations" current among the masses they continue to enjoy unwarranted fame. The younger artists prefer to turn their backs "deliberately and without ceremony on the rubbish of the past"; and with a new way of looking at nature and at their work intend to paint "far better pictures than have ever yet been painted in America." [24] For the modern "school of realists, though numerically small, is yet beginning to be felt formidable by the adherents to tradition and conventionality." [25]

Public architecture likewise suffers from poor taste and lack of artistic sensitivity. The classic revival is the particular target of the Gothic-minded American Pre-Raphaelites. "In that hot-bed of the false and ridiculous in Art, Washington City, the ancient faith in the Greek colonnade still holds sway. . . . But all this is a part of the tradition." City structures elsewhere too often present only a "cold squared front of brick" or a "frozen façade of pseudo-classic columns and pilasters," and make the metropolitan centers only "homes of ugliness." Influenced by Ruskin and contemporary Continental trends, the reformers offer an enthusiastic alternative. Instead of neo-Greek or eclectic designs: "We say . . . build Gothic buildings, because the Gothic framework is beyond all comparison the most noble of all, the most varied and easily adapted to all purposes, the strongest, the most easily suited by all materials, and by far the most susceptible of decoration." [26]

This insistence on the inherent excellence of the Gothic was, in fact, so basic to their creed that their original Articles of Organization contained an extended statement:

We hold that it is necessary, in times when true Art is little practiced or understood, to look back to other periods for instruction and inspiration. That, in seeking for a system of Architecture suitable for such study, we shall find it only in that of the Middle Ages, of which the most perfect development is known as Gothic Architecture. . . . That the efforts for the restoration of the so-called Gothic Art have been, in the main, well directed. That the hope for true Art in the future is in the complete and permanent success of this great reformation. . . .

Again the influence of Ruskin is directly observable, for in his "The Nature of Gothic" he had asserted: "In one point of view Gothic is not only the best, but the *only rational* architecture, as being that which can fit itself most easily to all services." Or again, in the *Stones of Venice*, "It is the best and strongest building, as it is the most beautiful. . . . I plead for the introduction of the Gothic form into our domestic architecture, not merely because it is lovely, but because it is the only form of faithful, strong, enduring, and honourable building, in such materials as come daily to our hands." [27]

In application of this latter statement, the American Pre-Raphaelites asserted that not only the public architecture but also the private homes of the period were subject to stricture. Hollow brick or wooden cylinders called Doric columns, timber lintels and brick arches boxed in with wood panel work, the simplest farmhouses covered over with pilasters and cornices with a wooden pediment over every window, those greatest of "architectural monstrosities"— cast-iron fronts and indiscriminate use of stucco, brick, or wood—such a tasteless constructional hodge-podge made the new artists recoil in aesthetic horror. The honesty and functionalism of the Dutch colonial structures appealed rather than the garishness of so-called Italian villas, the Greek temples, and "embattled sham fortresses" of the rural population. Architectural sincerity or confessed functionalism is the goal: "We would reject all false construction, or that which seems to be what it is not, and would not attempt purposely to conceal anything that pertains to the construction." [28]

And, finally, the furnishings which go within the American homes must be made more sensible, comfortable, and decorative—as the English interiors were being beautified under the inspiration and ability of William Morris and his helpers.

Years ago Edgar Poe published an essay entitled "Philosophy of Furniture," in which he asserted and undertook to show that the Americans did not understand furnishing their houses. He began by assuming that the English are supreme in the matter of interior decoration. . . . He then goes on to treat of the *rationale* of furniture and decoration, details and general effect, harmony and "keeping," carpets and curtains. . . . The essay is good reading. It was Poe's error and his misfortune that he undertook the discussion of many subjects of which he knew too little to think rightly.[29]

His error lay, not in denouncing American interior decoration, but in assuming that the conventional British was any better. For at that time both countries suffered from a plethora of "bandy-legged seats," "wretched little knobs and scrolls as ornaments," "wood sawed into patterns without regard to its grain," glued moldings along the tops of chair-backs "disagreeable to the sitter and quite out of place," "monstrous bed-heads," table-tops of Florentine mosaic—all of which united in an effect of "inevitable ugliness" in a style of furnishing consistent only in a design seeking the avoidance of all straight lines.[30] Scorning all this, purchasers should search for careful workmanship, simple lines, functional construction, comfort, and durability—and be willing to pay the necessary price. Often, however, excellent furniture may be of humble origin—simple kitchen or work tables, the "Kentucky" and the "Mayflower" chairs, woven cane pieces, the common "camp-chairs," colonial cabinet styles, and other household articles.

Thus in general the *New Path's* contributors interpreted and applied a specific Pre-Raphaelite principle, as phrased by William Michael Rossetti: "The absolute rejection of all meretricious embellishment—of all which might be introduced to heighten effect or catch the eye to the disregard or overlaying of actual or presumable fact." [31]

EIGHT

The P.R.B. in the U.S.A.: Charter Members

THE INTELLECTUAL level of the original members of the "Society for the Advancement of Truth in Art" was consistently high. And although the impact of mature experience quite properly mellowed the highly authoritative tone of their early pronouncements, all the participants in the New York group in the Civil War years maintained an interest in the arts throughout their careers; and without exception they made definite contributions to the fields of fine and applied arts, art history and criticism, or creative writing.* While it is true that most of them transcended the limitations of their early Pre-Raphaelitism, its inspiration and initial impetus were highly significant.

* Of the original group of seven, Eugene Schuyler, who became one of the most successful of nineteenth century diplomatic figures, was perhaps outside the immediate artistic orbit. But his interest in languages led to his Ph.D. in that field at Yale in 1861, and after the interlude of a law degree from Columbia and a brief period of legal practice, to application for a position in the U. S. Consular Service. Appointment to Moscow, then as Secretary of the Legation at St. Petersburg and Constantinople, gave him intimate acquaintance with the Slavic languages, augmented by later posts in the Balkans. In 1868 his interest in the culture of Finland led to his edition of *Selections from the Kalevala;* and he made a notable contribution to the initial Western appreciation of Russian novels by his own translations of Turgenev's *Fathers and Sons* (1867), and Tolstoy's *The Cossacks* (1878). The remainder of his considerable literary work fell into the categories of history and international relations. The best known was probably his two-volume *Peter the Great, Emperor of Russia* (1884), which appeared serially in *Scribner's Monthly.*

Thomas Charles Farrer: LINK BETWEEN THE BROTHER-
HOODS

Thomas Charles Farrer, born in 1838, was for a few telling years an adoptive American, and his younger artist brother Henry settled permanently in New York where he became known for his work as an etcher of metropolitan scenes.* T. C. Farrer was originally a Londoner who had learned to draw in Ruskin's classes at the Workingmen's College in Red Lion Square and later in Great Ormond Street, to which Ruskin contributed his services from 1854 to 1858. Heartily in favor of this co-operative educational institution, Ruskin enlisted D. G. Rossetti's services as well, and wrote encouragingly: "There is no fear about teaching; all that the men want is to *see* a few touches done, and to be told where and why they are wrong in their work, in the simplest possible way." Rossetti was persuaded to take the figure-class, while Ruskin divided the elementary and land-scape work with Lowes Dickinson, one of the original founders of the College.[1] Under their tuition Farrer developed some skill as a technician, and accepted as gospel Ruskin's dogmatic principles of art.

In 1860 Farrer came to New York, with considerable missionary fervor for the improvement of the intellectual and artistic scene. His concern with the ethics of slavery led him to volunteer in the Union Army for some two years, but by 1863 he appears to have been living again in New York.[2] Finding there some congenial souls, he became the central figure of that little coterie of adventurous young artists, architects, and critics who, largely by his activating energy, formalized themselves into the "Society for the Ad-

* Henry Farrer was born in London in 1843, came to America when he was nineteen, and died in Brooklyn in 1903. His early work showed definite Pre-Raphaelite influence.

vancement of Truth in Art," which organization was, as a friend of the founders declared, "the child of the P.R.B.'s." [3]

In his own technique and interests as an artist, Farrer paralleled the early members of the British Brotherhood. As subjects for his brush he was chiefly concerned with limited and relatively simple scenes, which he elaborated with the minute accuracy of a photographic lens. This devotion to meticulous rendition was coupled, however, with a certain poetic or even sentimental sensitivity to the implication of the simple phenomenon. "A dead bluebird on the snow, a swallow's flight across the pale purple evening, a single hill-crown against a sunset of flaming yellow," wrote an early critic, "glow with an intimation of truth beyond fact." [4] Thus a patch of weeds or tiny wildflowers could present to his eye a revelation of complex and delicate beauty which was its own excuse for graphic representation.

In the pages of the *New Path* Farrer himself summarized his creed: "Those works that give to the world no facts at all will sink into deserved oblivion. . . . It is the absolute facts of everything that we are fighting for, and not for smoothness, not for execution, but for truth and reality." Then he amplifies:

Time and future generations will ask of our art and our literature, "Is this the way the people of the nineteenth century worked, dressed, and acted? Are these their passions, principles, and feelings? Is this the Palisades, and the North River, and the Catskills in the year 1863?" If not, they are absolutely valueless to us, however perfectly they may conform to rules of Art in texture, tone, and central light; for Nature is absolutely right. . . . [5]

But this desire to record, to categorize, is not the basic drive. For "in the artist it is the love of beautiful forms and lively colors" which must first send him out into the fields to work. And his pleasure in nature must be of a degree that inevitably will work itself out in graphic expression, the whole process being for the artist "the greatest enjoyment he finds in life." Even though his execution might be coarse and clumsy, and his canvas demonstrate "all the signs of paint and human weakness," such an artist's product will be "infinitely more valuable to the world than inane nothingness, or absolute falsehood, painted with all the marvelous skill and delicacy of touch of a . . . Gerard Douw." [6]

Because the dubious financial situation of the *New Path* forbade the expense of carrying half-tones or cuts, the editors quite properly felt the paradox of an unillustrated art journal. In the spring of 1864 they therefore planned a special supplement (at $6 per copy) to contain a set of ten photographic reproductions of works acceptable to their critical eyes. Farrer was given the honor of furnishing exactly half of these representative and desirable works of the new "Realist School," in the editor's phrase. They presumably were selected by Farrer himself as his own best work: three were simple but highly detailed pencil sketches of unassuming subjects: "Pumpkin Vine," "Spring Weeds," and "May in the Woods"; one sepia drawing presented a "Yellow Water Lily"; and the most elaborate of the group was an oil genre entitled "Gone! Gone!"

About 1870 or 1871, after having exhibited in the National Gallery such works as "Twilight on the Hudson," "Sunset," and "Coming through the Lock," Farrer returned to his native England. His interest in painting continued; and although his later technique loosened and became more impressionistic, he retained the sharp accuracy of observation and facility of rendition that marked his early Pre-Raphaelite work in this country. His advent in America was, perhaps, the essential catalyst in the New York reaction against conventional academic and anecdotal art in the 1860's; and his extended visit served as one of the closest links between England and the United States in the spread of the Pre-Raphaelite movement at that time.

Clarence Cook: PRE-RAPHAELITE JOURNALIST

After the first editor of the *New Path*, Clarence Chatham Cook, died in 1900 at his country estate near Fish-kill-on-the-Hudson, his wife issued a commemorative volume of some twenty-five of his published and unpublished poems. Although these verses appear derivative, prosy, and overly didactic,* the book is of particular interest for another reason. The portrait used as the frontispiece was selected by Mrs. Cook from a wide variety of photographs and sketches; her choice was a pen-and-ink drawing made in 1864 by the artist, "Thomas C. Farrar [*sic*], pupil of John Ruskin." The central bearded figure of the *New Path's* editor is pictured leaning studiously over a desk, quill pen in hand; on the wall over his shoulder may be seen a copy of Holman Hunt's "Light of the World"; and carved in the wood panel-ing in the background are the names "Rossetti–Turner–"

---

* Clarence Cook, *Poems*, "Privately printed at the Gillies Press, New York, for Louisa W. Cook and her friends," 1902. The subject matter ranges from Biblical material, as in "Abram and Zimri," through the classical ("Ulysses and the Sirens") and the English courtly tradition ("A Sonnet in Praise of His Lady's Hands"), to contemporary nature verse with moralistic overtones, and expressions of his own philosophy. "An April Violet" is a fair sample:

> Pale flower that by this stone
> Sweetenest the air alone,
> While round thee falls the snow
> And the rude wind doth blow,
> What thought doth make thee pine,
> Pale Flower, can I divine?
> Canst thou not wait the morrow
> That rids thee of thy sorrow?
> Art thou too desolate
> To smile at any fate?
> Then there is nought for thee
> But Death's delivery. . . .

A native of Dorchester, Massachusetts, Cook had been graduated from Harvard in 1849, then had from time to time been a tutor, student of architecture, lecturer on art, and public reader of Shakespeare's plays. By the mid-1850's he became aware of the spread of Pre-Raphaelite ideas in this country, and in that connection once crossed critical swords with W. J. Stillman, who was exactly his own age.

The occasion was the absence from duty of the editor of the *Crayon* because of the overwork inherent in the publication of an essentially one-man journal. Cook wrote a polite letter to the editor of the *Independent,* which sheathed a few barbs with reference not only to the co-editor, John Durand, but to the policy of the whole project: [1]

Mr. Stillman has . . . been ill, and has produced we understand but one picture, which we shall probably see in the Exhibition. Mr. Stillman's illness has also had an unfavorable influence on the columns of *The Crayon,* which has hardly satisfied of late the expectations of its readers. . . .

It seems to us that *The Crayon* lacks earnestness, and has altogether mistaken the road to be travelled by those who would awaken an interest in the arts among our people. If art is worth talking about at all, it is worth talking about in a vigorous, sensible manner, and in plain terms. Art has too long been a luxury for the exclusive use of the dilettanti and caviare to the general—We submit that the way in which *The Crayon* treats it is hardly calculated to extend its sphere.

CLARENCE COOK

The editorial rejoinder in the *New Path,* which reprinted this communication, was brief and presumably withering: "Poor Cook."

With his interest thus focused on the public discussion of art problems in "a vigorous, sensible manner," Cook's ideas simmered for a few years. Then—as one of the major events listed in the brief post-mortem chronology arranged by his wife—he began in 1863 a series of articles entitled "American Art and Artists," which as staff critic he contributed to the New York *Tribune* and later collected in a book.[2] This column ran until 1869, and because of the critic's unrestrained and often scathing attacks on contemporary painters, was very popular reading. A delegation of his artistic victims even visited Horace Greeley to protest their treatment at Cook's hands. The editor rejoined with the promise that if they would write a letter to the *Tribune* embodying the points of their grievance, he would print it—if it were interesting enough.[3]

Peter B. Wight, one of Cook's fellow-members in the Society for the Advancement of Truth in Art, indicated that Greeley chose Cook as his paper's commentator largely because of Cook's success with his little journal, the *New Path*, in which he had demonstrated his flair for clear analysis and caustic comment. Because of his growing prestige and his seniority in years (Cook was thirty-five, while Sturgis was twenty-seven, Wight twenty-five, and Moore twenty-three) it was logical for Cook to serve as the editor of his Society's organ. His devotion to, and militant defense of the elementary Pre-Raphaelite principles, as interpreted by Ruskin, have been already demonstrated in the review of that magazine.

After some time abroad as the Paris correspondent for the *Tribune*, Cook had a particularly productive year in 1878. His new edition of Lubke's monumental *History of Art* appeared [4]—in a postscript to which Cook lamented the exclusion of such artists as Rossetti, Burne-Jones, and Madox Brown from its pages; likewise his text for a reproduction of Dürer's *Life of the Virgin;* and a collection of his own detailed articles on interior decoration, reprinted from *Scribner's Monthly* and entitled *The House Beautiful.* Here, under the subtitle of "Essays on Beds and Tables, Stools and Candle-sticks," he presented his theories of home furnishing and beautification, profusely illustrated with woodcuts, and directly reflecting the Morris influence in America.

This work was a further step in the right direction—a campaign for simplicity and good taste, which had already been instituted by his earlier contributions to the *New Path*.

"When people are spending money in furnishing their houses," he urges, "they will find it costs no more to get pretty things than ugly things, things that are in good taste than things that are in bad taste." Honesty of design in recognition of function must control the manufacturer and should direct the buyer; and the illogical over-ornamentation, "the rampant lawlessness" in treatment of detail, "the glare and glitter" of ostentatious but superficial embellishment, must be spurned.

The beauty of simplicity in form; the pleasures to be had from lines well thought out; the agreeableness of unbroken surfaces where there is no gain in breaking them; harmony in color . . . these considerations . . . have been utterly ignored.[5]

Not only had Morris and his co-workers done much to revive appreciation of sincere craftsmanship, but the painters of the Pre-Raphaelite group had enriched the decorator's and designer's palette: "The mistletoe-green, the blue-green, the duck's-egg, the rose-amber, the pomegranate-flower," and so on—"colors which we owe to the English poet-artists who are oddly lumped together as the Pre-Raphaelites, and who made the new rainbow to confound the scientific decorators who were sure of what colors would go together and what colors wouldn't. . . ."[6]

But in spite of the validity of Cook's artistic theories, when a modern reader flips the pages of this old handbook he will, unless an antiquarian, inevitably recoil from the sort of thing that in actual practice Cook recommended—Moroccan inlaid mother-of-pearl stools; Moorish gunracks degraded to the supporting of gentlemen's hats; elaborate faïence water-jugs; heavily mantled fireplaces with symmetrically balanced knickknacks in exact position; Jacobean heavily carved armchairs; and French bureaux with weighty brass mounts. Occasionally pertinent exceptions occur: a simple Chinese sofa of bamboo; straight-line "modern" undecorated bookcases; a novel but functional chaise-longue from France; solid oak chairs of pleasing proportions; American colonial chests and highboys, and so on. But in general it would appear that Cook's pronouncements were more advanced than his practices. The combination nevertheless appealed to the reading and house-furnishing public of that day, and in spite of the potential buyer's difficulty in acquiring many of his exotic recommendations, *The House Beautiful* was Cook's most successful work.

As a change from the position of contributor to magazines and writer of books, Cook again wished to try his hand at editorship, and in 1884 took over the old *Studio*. His taste for fine illustrations left that journal insolvent, and it occasionally failed to appear, finally stopping publication in 1892. But meanwhile Cook had pioneered in the new technique of photo-etching, and made his limited public appreciative of new beauty of format and illustration. The columns of his journal he naturally used for further promulgation of his opinions; and when he died at the age of seventy-two, Cook was recognized as a penetrating and outspoken critic in his particular fields.*

* One of the most publicized of his critical attacks was on the authenticity of the famous di Cesnola collection of Cretan antiquities in the Metropolitan Museum. This campaign reflected to his own ultimate discredit when he was unable to offer specific evidence of fraud in a subsequent lawsuit.

Clarence King: SCIENTIST, WRITER, AND PATRON OF THE
ARTS

A famous anecdote concerning Clarence King, author,
geologist, and critic, has all the earmarks of being apocry-
phal, but is vouched for by his good friends John Hay and
John La Farge. At a picture dealer's in London in 1882 King
quite by chance began discussing a canvas with an anonymous customer, and "argued upon a number of subtle points
which to him were evident." Only after a heated exchange of
opinion did King discover that his opponent was John
Ruskin, the idol of his *New Path* days some two decades
earlier. "The famous writer," continues La Farge, "appears
to have been delighted by the value and form of these say-
ings and criticisms, and the ensuing acquaintance was one of
the many gracious episodes in Clarence King's European
experience." Hay here picks up the account: "Ruskin took
him to heart, entertained him at Coniston, and offered
him his choice of his two greatest water-colors by Turner.
'One good Turner,' said King, 'deserves another,' and took
both." [1]

This contact was typical of Clarence King's lifelong interests. He was born in 1842 in Newport, Rhode Island; and,
after being graduated at the age of twenty from the Yale
Sheffield Scientific School, he went to New York where he
immediately acquired friends among artists and men of
letters. Here in the following winter he became one of the
founding members of the Society for the Advancement of
Truth in Art. But his active association with this group was
brief, since by May 1863, he found himself suddenly bound
by horseback across the plains and mountains for California.
Nevertheless, these few months of meeting and discussion

with fellow-enthusiasts sharpened and crystallized his fervor for Ruskinian Pre-Raphaelitism, and definitely influenced his own later critical and creative writing.

Although familiar with the works of Tyndall, Ruskin, and John Muir, Professor William H. Brewer, Yale's noted geologist of the last generation, once chose to call King's *Mountaineering in the Sierra Nevada*, published in 1872, "the most brilliant and fascinating of books on mountain-climbing." [2] The experiences here recorded date from that summer of 1863 which saw King's tremendous initiation to the mountains through an ascent of Lassen with Shasta towering eighty miles away—"What would Ruskin have said, if he had seen *this!*" he exclaimed. Through the good offices of Professor Brewer, King was hired by Josiah Dwight Whitney as a staff member in his California Geological Survey, and thereafter King rambled through most of the Sierras, scientifically mapping the territory as he went.

On one such expedition, he recalls in the *Mountaineering*, he was riding along a lonely foothill trail, where his thoughts had occasion to wander: "Thus I came to Ruskin, wishing I might see the work of his idol, and after that longing for some equal artist who should arise and choose to paint our Sierras as they are, with all their color-glory, power of innumerable pine and countless pinnacle. . . ." And around the next curve in the trail he suddenly came upon, not a Turner, but appropriately enough a red-flannel-shirted native American artist who announced himself as "Hank G. Smith." Although this fictive character had profited from a rapid winter's whirl through the Academy in New York, he retained his Western allegiances as "California-born and mountain-raised," and his views on contemporary American art may be taken as a colloquial statement of King's own:

"There," he said, "is old Eastman Johnson; he's made the riffle on barns, and that everlasting girl with the ears of corn; but it ain't *life*, it ain't got the real git-up.

"If you want to see *the* thing, just look at a Gérôme; his Arab folks and Egyptian dancing-girls, they ain't assuming a pleasant expression and looking at spots while their likenesses is took. . . ."

He avowed his great admiration of Church, which, with a little leaning toward Mr. Gifford, seemed his only hearty approval.

"It's all Bierstadt and Bierstadt and Bierstadt nowadays! What has he done but twist and skew and distort and discolor and belittle and be-pretty this whole doggoned country? Why, his mountains are too high and slim; they'd blow over in one of our fall winds.

"I've herded colts two summers in Yosemite, and honest now, when I stood right up in front of the picture, I didn't know it.

"He hasn't what old Ruskin calls for." *

In spite of his attack on Bierstadt's style and interpretation, King once chose to invite that artist to accompany him on an extended field trip. In September 1872, about eight months after the appearance of his *Mountaineering*, one of the exploratory parties of the extensive Fortieth Parallel Survey,

---

* Eastman Johnson's genre paintings showed some technical dexterity derived from four years of following the Dutch tradition at The Hague; but they did not approach the monumental sweep of the work of Thomas Cole's apprentice, Frederick Edwin Church. After some not-too-vigorous Hudson River scenes Church (in whose studio William J. Stillman studied for a year) had stressed sharp and detailed realism in his later South American landscapes such as "The Mountains of Ecuador" (1855), and "The Heart of the Andes" (1857), and in his popular success of the same year, "Niagara Falls." "The little leaning toward Mr. Gifford" stemmed perhaps from that artist's visit to Washington, Oregon, and California in 1869 and the commemoration of those Western scenes, which preceded his better known works of the Massachusetts coast and of North African deserts and tribesmen. In Bierstadt the weaknesses here suggested have contributed to his failing reputation; and modern art criticism vindicates King's judgment. Although blessed with some "formal dignity," Bierstadt's pictures betray the lack of any deep mentality or strong technique or warmth; and "the present fashion finds his huge canvasses singularly dull and monotonous, wanting in personal charm like stage painting, without dramatic vigor or imagination." See Charles DeKay, "Albert Bierstadt," *DAB*, II: 254.

to the directorship of which King had graduated from the California Survey, was working in the High Sierras. King and Bierstadt joined the field scientists, and crossed the mountains by the head of the King's and San Joaquin Rivers to the California plain. The artist's two most familiar paintings, "The Yosemite," and "The Rocky Mountains," had already appeared in 1865 and 1871; but on this expedition he made sketches of the King's-Kern Divide which were later re-worked into two popular pictures, and spent many hours as well around the evening campfires discussing art with King.[3]

With the successful conclusion of the Fortieth Parallel Survey in 1877, King was instrumental in seeing formed a centralized United States Geological Survey, with himself installed as its first chief in 1879. So for the next several years, before resigning to carry on private geological investigations in the United States and abroad, King had Washington as his headquarters. Here, following up an earlier acquaintance with Henry Adams which had been formed in Estes Park, Colorado, he became an intimate of the erudite household at 1607 H Street; and, with John Hay and his wife, King was one of the innermost circle who facetiously dubbed themselves the "Five of Hearts." In Adams's anonymous novel *Esther*, which appeared in 1884, King obviously served as the original of the fictional character of George Strong, a congenial and proficient geologist whose description is a close portrait of King himself:

He looked like what he was, an intelligent man, with a figure made for action, an eye that hated rest, and a manner naturally sympathetic. His forehead was so bald as to give his face a look of strong character, which a dark beard rather helped to increase. He was a popular fellow, known as George by whole gangs of the roughest miners in Nevada, where he had worked for years as a practical geologist, and it would have been hard to find in America, Europe, or Asia, a city in which some one would not have smiled at the mention of his name, and asked where George was going to turn up next.[4]

A mutual friend of Adams and King was John La Farge. In New York on one occasion these three got together for a colloquy extending over two evenings and the intervening day—of which unfortunately no written record remains— when they ranged all through the subject of art and its relation to science and society. One such Ruskinian application of art to society, however, is embodied in the joint plans which King and La Farge proposed for the tomb of President Grant.[5] Although their suggestion for the then-novel use of structural glass was rejected by the committee, King's interest in the problem led him to publish an article called "Style and the Monument," in which he both analyzed some of the difficulties in selecting the most fitting architectural form, and offered some significant strictures on the paucity of American art production and appreciation in general.

"We are," says King, with a biting brilliance first felt in the pages of the *New Path,* "an unartistic people, with neither an indigenous nor an adopted art language in which to render grand thoughts. We are ignorant of the meaning and use of *Style*—that spontaneous but concurrent mode which races of men have devised and accepted as the fittest expression of their *race* ideals." Then, warming to his subject, he continues:

Not only are we innocent of all style of our own, but we are phenomenally ignorant and obtuse as to the requirements of the styles of other races and ages. We use them only to abuse them; we adopt them only to mutilate and burlesque them. . . . There must be a sensitive consciousness of the significance and relation of leading lines, in short, for composition, and an instinct for the harmony or inharmony of details, before an artist or a people can rightly use style. From Bangor to San Diego we seem never weary of contriving for ourselves belongings which are artistically discordant and customs which are wholly inappropriate.

Although not the most desirable architectural style, the most fitting for contemporary America he judges to be the Romanesque, because of striking parallels in the national and intellectual patterns of Rome and America:

The chief experiences of the Roman people were what ours have been—war, trade, and sudden expansion into national greatness, an expansion so rapid and immense as to over-shadow and mar the serenity and order of social life. Material prosperity and political administration were the leading pursuits. Rome and America have loved luxury and pomp. Each civilization might be called a political success; both must be judged social failures. Rome loved the big; it seemed in harmony with the prodigious growth of the Roman populations and the gigantic spread of the imperial system. Size, brute mass, the big figures of the census are our pride. Like the Romans we adore quantity.

Then, pointedly, he goes on: "The splendid expansion of the Roman Empire gave an impetus to the production of architectural monuments in which bigness was realized at the occasional cost of greatness. In that they showed their inferior art perception to the Greeks, who only asked of their craftsmen greatness, rarely exacting bigness." Thus it seems that the Roman tradition embraces "monuments adequate to express our thoughts," and in such a traditional style should a modern American memorial be most logically constructed.

But the Gothic fervor of the Society for the Advancement of Truth in Art had not died in King's veins in the twenty-year interim since that organization's end. "Of Gothic architecture," he felt constrained to add, "we have done little more than to cobble up some unsuccessful plagiarisms in the way of churches, and to nail a few rather thin boards together into sad little suburban villas, having a certain sanctimony

of English perpendicular windows." But its essential greatness remains, obscured only by his own century's inability
to comprehend its basic truth and beauty:

It seems to the writer that this is neither the age nor people to
meddle with Gothic art. To do Gothic work requires a Gothic heart,
a Gothic head, and a Gothic hand. We are sophisticated, *blasé*,
indifferent to nature, and conventional to the last degree. The men
who awoke from the sleep of the Dark ages and suddenly broke
loose from monastic authority, prerogative, and precedent, and
within fifty years created a style and carried it to the consummate
flower of its whole life, were simple, direct, and religious. They
made a passionate appeal direct to nature to help them in their
new ideas of ornamentation, and she showered her favors upon
them.

Hence, with only the outer mechanical shell, but not the
spontaneous, inner creative spirit, it is inevitable that modern
copyists should fall woefully short of the greatness of the
originals. . . .

Before King's restless, versatile, brilliant career came to a
tragic end in 1901, he had made a lasting reputation as a
practical field scientist, an original theorist and historian in
geology, a capable government administrator, a clever and
entertaining man of letters, and perspicacious commentator
on aesthetic problems in America. And although his initial
contact with the American Pre-Raphaelite group was brief,
their eager interest and genuine concern in the status of the
arts in America had a lasting influence on King's ideas and
expression.

Peter B. Wight: ARCHITECT IN THE PRE-RAPHAELITE
PATTERN

Peter Bonnett Wight, "student of art and life, builder
and designer," as his obituary notice in 1925 described him,[1]
enjoyed a long and productive career as architect and editor

until he retired in Pasadena at the age of eighty. His early enthusiasm for Ruskin and the practices of the Pre-Raphaelites made a permanent impression on his theory of design, as one particularly noteworthy building proves.

As an undergraduate in the "Free Academy" in his native city (later the College of the City of New York), Wight showed such talent in architectural drawing that he designed a stone country-house, as he proudly recalled, "for pay." Before receiving his B.A. at the age of seventeen in 1855 he had discovered Ruskin's writings and absorbed them with uncritical gusto. Some graduate work followed, since he was too young for an architect's degree, and then a year as a hard-working student draughtsman in a mediocre architect's office before he set himself up, not too successfully, in 1858 in Chicago. Back again in New York in the following year, he designed a bank in Middletown and a hospital in Binghamton; and several years later the Brooklyn Mercantile Library and the School of Fine Arts at Yale. On the outbreak of the Civil War he served as architect for the United States Sanitary Commission and built the first government field hospital in Washington. His subsequent disappointment at being refused an army commission was salved by his success in 1862 in his first and most important architectural competition; as a comparatively unknown youth of twenty-four he was selected from a field of five eminent architects to plan and build the new home for the National Academy of Design at Fourth Avenue and 23rd Street. Since this structure was designed "in an essentially Pre-Raphaelite spirit," [2] it not only was the object of considerable sharp discussion, but indicated sympathy on the part of the National Academy for certain of the Pre-Raphaelite principles, and, further, explained why Wight should appear as one of the founders of the Society for the Advancement of Truth in Art, just a few months later.

The complete issue of the *New Path* for June 1864, was devoted to an account of this well-publicized structure and the ideas behind it. Although the extensive article was unsigned, it probably was from Wight's own pen, for the minute details indicate first-hand knowledge of the whole project; or Wight's architectural partner in New York from 1863 to 1869, Russell Sturgis, could well have phrased the actual report on the basis of their numerous discussions.

After an initial flourish: "We are safe in asserting that very few buildings in our day and generation are designed to be either beautiful or instructive, and in concluding thence that there is very little Architecture among us,"—the author becomes specific. The building for the National Academy "has evidently been designed in entire accordance with the views concerning Architecture which have always been set forth in this journal." "Since it is the first building in this country . . . which has been so designed," some commentary must be offered. Two main principles are involved: "*first*, that all buildings should be designed in the medieval spirit, in other words should be 'Gothic' and not revived classic of any school; *second*, that all carved ornament should be designed by the workmen who cut it, under such superintendence and instruction as the artist in charge may find necessary." Since the modern use of Greek and Roman forms seems only "pompous and luxurious trifling with unbelieved mythology and unfelt allegory," it follows that all "the good and natural" in architecture has come to us "from the Middle Ages," directly from the Gothic, or at one remove as in the English half-timbered houses of the sixteenth century or in the Italianate forms employed in this particular structure.

Honesty of design and spontaneity in the creation of the decorative detail are the major controlling factors: "The building is so planned as to perfectly answer its purposes."

Furthermore, this functionalism is directly expressed through the outer form, for "it is possible, as this building shows, to deny nothing, to deceive in nothing, to add nothing for composition's sake which the occupants do not need." Thus, of its three stories, the first, partly below the sidewalk level, is logically devoted to night-school classes conducted by artificial light; the second, with monumental steps leading up to the main entrance on this level, shows by the spacing of windows and chimneys its devotion to offices and smaller rooms; while the top floor, with skylighting but unbroken wall surfaces except for tracery-filled openings for ventilation, clearly indicates the presence of the major galleries. Alternate courses of white and blue-gray Westchester marble create a color pattern, pointed by a red disc over the doorway and four purple Vermont marble pillars flanking the entry. A "great deal of rich and delicate carving" executed in white marble by the individual workmen and representing their own interpretation of "facts of nature"—chiefly leaves—embellishes the whole interior system of supporting columns. In fine, "the edifice is evidently meant as a renewal of the way of building which prevailed in former glorious times of art," for the "Academy of Design is . . . in all respects, a Gothic building. The design of the exterior is not merely realistic and constructive, it is completely medieval, and in the spirit of medieval art."

The daring experiment of allowing—in fact, demanding—original design in the stone-cut detail seemed to Wight to be basically successful. The workmen at first inevitably made mistakes, for their originality had been previously thwarted by the mechanical reproduction of endless egg-and-dart and other formalized and empty designs. And although a few of the finished pieces "had better been rejected . . . there are capitals in the Academy of Design which are exceedingly

good, interesting, and full of truth in themselves, and, more-
over, most valuable architectural ornaments." Great attention
was also lavished on hand-wrought iron railings in a leaf-and-
vine design which Wight proudly declared were "the only
examples of decorative iron-work executed in the medieval
manner that we yet have" in America. As a friend of the architect later remarked, the charm of all these hand-carved imi-
tative decorations "lies chiefly in the unmistakable sincerity
of the method, the hallmark of true Pre-Raphaelitism." [3]

Shortly after the completion of the building in 1865 (its
dedication was postponed because of Lincoln's death), Wight
issued an elaborate folio volume, dedicated to the president
of the National Academy of Design, Daniel Huntington.[4]
With fifteen plates, an introductory essay, and running commentary, he gave a minute account of the planning and construction of the edifice, including the difficulties encountered
in the war years through three wage strikes and an army
draft. "It is my firm conviction," he declared in phrases
inspired by Ruskin and the Pre-Raphaelites, "that no good
can be done unless the workers are imbued with the right
spirit, and have their hearts in the cause. The only hope for
the arts of the future is in the *conscientious fidelity* with
which all who make any branch of art a calling shall measure
their work by the standard of truth." Since the original decorative detail had caused lively argument, he amplified the
point. Although such indigenous and unassuming flora as the
bloodroot, tiger lily, bleeding-heart, jack-in-the-pulpit, azalea,
clover, narcissus, and pitcher-plant had been used as motifs
by the stone-carvers, Wight did not wish to imply that this
revival of a "system of decoration from nature" was the only
pattern for all future work. Paradoxically, "the essential
point wherein *all* the work [in the Academy] falls short . . .
is its too evident naturalism."

Many, doubtless, who have admired this work will be surprised to hear this; but naturalism is not, as I conceive it, the *end* to be sought, but only the means to that end. Between the two faults of *want of truth to nature* and *accurate copying,* I prefer the latter. *Severe conventionalizing* is better than either, and therein is the vital force and beauty of the best Medieval work. Good conventional work is always full of truth to nature, but can only be done by workmen of long experience and thorough knowledge.[5]

But since his laborers suffered from strict limitations of originality, he thus had to be content with the simple reproduction of natural forms, with as great accuracy as was consistent with the material used; and he reported, a little wryly, that his workmen were now happy to be back carving their familiar Corinthian capitals for a Fifth Avenue mansion.

The architect was young, the building was successful, his pleasure in it was great. As the *New Path* commentator declared in sanguine phrase:

This solidly and admirably built, richly decorated building, a noble design well carried out, will remain for ages unless fire destroy it; its lesson ought not to be lost on this generation, and it will not be lost on the next. . . .

But the tempo of the metropolis accelerated; the "ages" telescoped themselves into four decades; and with the turn of the century Wight's early masterpiece was slated for demolition. The New York *Times* thought fit to mark its passing by asking the architect for his reminiscences. Instead of indulging in nostalgic regret he used the opportunity for the double purpose of making penetrating commentary on the progress of the Gothic movement and the Classic Revival in America, and indicating how he himself had grown with the times and left behind his own medievalist bias.

The basic principles of Gothic architecture, he declared, remained sound. He still knew of no better way "to express the purpose of a building devoted to the fine arts than by seeking inspiration in the best Gothic works of Italy." He had deliberately avoided employing any details, no matter how beautiful, "except when they were not inconsistent with, or when they gave emphasis to rational constructive methods." With strict adherence to these principles the Gothic Revival "would undoubtedly have led to the development of style in our buildings." But unfortunately the Gothic was never genuinely understood or appreciated in this country. Instead, "*caricatured by the ignorant* who tried to copy its surface indications, and to put their own originality into it until it became ridiculous, the works of the earnest as well as of the superficial workers have been confounded by an undiscriminating public until both have met the same fate. Therefore they are a thing of the past." The eclipse of his own building, furthermore, clearly points the fact that "in this age Art must always give way to the power of commercialism."

To Wight it was of course regrettable that most of his contemporaries who once "recognized the principles underlying 'the Gothic movement,' [had] through the tyranny of fashion and patronage, abandoned the principles as well as the forms to which they gave expression thirty years ago." But all of the medievalists, including himself, had indulged in the common error of believing that the only medium for the expression of rational ideas in architecture was through the Gothic, once a completely rational style. "But experience has demonstrated that a *rational use of modern materials* and methods of construction does *not* necessarily find its expression in Gothic forms. Neither is it to be found in any other *historical* style, and time is now being wasted in experimenting with *exotic* styles, while we are waiting for the true evolution of the architecture of our own time and country." And although Wight felt that his own contemporaries had deserted the field, fortunately "a new set of younger men have taken up the task of developing the architecture" to fit the new day, "*not* from the historical styles or at the dictation of fashion, but along *rational lines,* and I confess that I am with them."

That this was more than a mere phrase of graceful capitulation was borne out by the facts of Wight's later career. Following the Chicago fire he had returned to that city, become a partner in the firm of Carter, Drake and Wight, and devoted much effort to the development of modern fireproof construction. For the decade following 1881 he gave up a lucrative practice in order to work out and produce a new type of terra-cotta structural tile. With a younger member of the firm, John W. Root, he developed the reinforced concrete floor-slab or "grill foundation" for commercial structures. And to insure a higher quality of general architectural planning, he influenced the passage in 1897 of the first law in America requiring the examination and licensing of architects.

From October 1904 to the end of 1907 Wight edited a copiously illustrated, slick-paper monthly called the *Fireproof Magazine.* This publication he thought unique in journalism, not only in subject matter but in fearless point of view:

For independent criticism it also stands alone. It has criticized bad material and bad work . . . more severely than any other technical journal.[6]

With a combination of articles, photographs, and designs of new, approved buildings, and detailed data on plans and planners of those destroyed by fire or structural collapse, Wight pulled no punches, and made his journal "a plain and outspoken advocate of all that is good in architecture and construction, and a fearless denunciator of every system . . . which has fallen short in the accomplishments claimed for it."

Forever on the trail of "shams and deceits," Wight continued his campaign for honest and rational architecture; and in his final editorial repeated his essential motto of his early Pre-Raphaelite days: "We are only seeking for the truth."

Russell Sturgis: "PRINCIPAL POPULARIZER OF ARCHITECTURAL KNOWLEDGE IN AMERICA"

In 1909 Peter B. Wight was persuaded to publish some informal reminiscences and extracts from the letters of his late friend and former partner, Russell Sturgis.[1] Here Wight recalled that his associations with Sturgis had begun at college in New York City in the 1850's, when they put in extra time together sketching in the drawing master's office and admiring the finely detailed architectural plans of the All Souls Unitarian Church, then being erected at 20th Street and Fourth Avenue. "We were fascinated, and I may say then and there both were impressed for the first time with the desire to become architects." Their friendship was cemented, he continued, when they began to read architecture together.

We read all the books on the subject to be found in the college library, including a set of Ruskin's *Seven Lamps* and *Stones of Venice*, which had just come out, and Sturgis began to buy books, as he had more spare money than I had, and I began to devour them. This habit, very convenient to me, was continued for fifteen years. . . .

In his analysis of his friend's artistic credo, Wight emphasized Sturgis's early speech to his fellow members of the Society for the Advancement of Truth in Art, which had been delivered on March 17, 1863. These remarks and an expanded article in the *New Path* were of major significance, declared Wight, not only as an early statement of Sturgis's theories of art, but in addition—although the so-called Gothic Revival was well advanced in England—"it was the first and only plea for the fine art of architecture that had been made in America up to that time." Furthermore, asserted Wight, that statement marked "the beginning of his literary career, and that creed affected all his critical articles." [2]

Referring to the Society's accepted platform (and by-passing the primitive forms of carving and drawing), Sturgis had declared:

"We hold," says the article in our name, "that in all times of great art there has been a close connection between architecture, sculpture, and painting; that sculpture and painting, having been first called into being for the decoration of buildings, have found their highest perfection when habitually associated with architecture; that architecture derives its greatest glory from such association; therefore, that this union of the arts is necessary for the full development of each."

The American Pre-Raphaelites, as has already been amply demonstrated, selected the Gothic as the style most nearly incorporating their announced principles: "In seeking for a system of architecture suitable for study, we shall find it only in that of the Middle Ages, of which the most perfect development is known as Gothic architecture." But as a vital reservation, Sturgis insisted that slavish imitation was not the end in view:

The exact reproduction of medieval work is only desirable in so far as it may be necessary to regain the lost knowledge of the vital principles that controlled it. Out of the careful study and application of these principles a true and perfect architecture is sure to arise, adapted to all our wants, and affording the most ample field possible for the display of our artistic power.

In 1863, shortly after this declaration, to launch his neo-Gothic architectural career Sturgis settled down with Wight in a fourth-floor office at 98 Broadway, opposite Trinity churchyard. There they remained happily for five years, until Sturgis moved over to 57 Broadway, taking with him his young draughtsman, George Fletcher Babb (later to head the firm of Babb, Cook, and Welch), and a student architect, William R. Mead. Charles F. McKim shortly thereafter studied with Sturgis for a year before going to Paris—and on his return set up the firm that was to be known as McKim, Mead, and White. Sturgis made one more removal, this time to the corner of 17th Street and Fourth Avenue, where he stayed until he took his family abroad in 1880, to live in Europe for four years.

This foreign residence marked the end of his career as a practicing architect, and from that point on his chief interests were in research, editing, and the writing of architectural history. Concerning this shift in emphasis Montgomery Schuyler, an eminent but somewhat younger architect and art critic, commented: "It was a good thing for the rest of us that he was early withdrawn from design to discussion. . . . Criticism and not creation was evidently the real line of action for Russell Sturgis." [3] His competence was admittedly shown in his Gothic designs for four Yale buildings: three dormitories, Farnham Hall (1869), Durfee Hall (1870), and Laurence Hall (1885), and Battell Chapel (1876); and in such other works as the fireproof Gothic Savings Bank in Albany (1876)—this last in association with Babb.[4] But although these structures entitled him to respect, Schuyler thought that they lacked any significant individuality and were essentially the product of a careful and scholarly, rather than a genuinely creative, mind.

One reason for this reservation in judgment was doubtless the fact that Sturgis refused to join in the popular wave of the Classic Revival which overwhelmed the temporary taste

for the Gothic in American architecture.* The public acceptance of this "fatuous designing" Sturgis considered "a most
depressing and saddening symptom" of our nation's aesthetic
shallowness. The Chicago Exposition of 1893 he thought a
major and "accursed" influence in the reviving of neo-classic
forms in this country. And even the popular and successful
firm of McKim, Mead and White (two of whose members he
had once trained) now were working "in the direction of
mere blank, bare, square, unvaried, unmodified boxes with
square holes cut in them except where a Roman colonnade is
introduced":

They seem to choose deliberately the no-style which consists in
following the blankest and least interesting Italian work of the
seventeenth century, merely reducing it to a still blanker and
barer monotony by leaving out the slight vestiges of sculpture
which that late Italian style had preserved.[5]

These "incomprehensible vagaries" of otherwise sensible men
unhappily indicated to Sturgis the mere blind revival of classical forms without inherent beauty or appropriateness to the
contemporary scene.

After giving up his career as practical designer, partly
because of his health, Sturgis devoted the last three decades
of his life chiefly to the history and criticism of architecture.
As a popular lecturer and as art critic for the *Nation* and the
New York *Evening Post,* and editor for ten years of "The
Field of Art" in *Scribner's* he had ample opportunity in more
than five hundred printed articles, reviews and monographs
for the expression of his forthright opinions concerning his

* It is obvious that Gothic design or the employment of superimposed
Gothic detail continued to influence American architecture, as the Woolworth
Building (1912) by Cass Gilbert and the Chicago Tribune Building (1922)
by Raymond Hood indicate. In Gothic church architecture Ralph Adams
Cram was of vital importance in his Cathedral of St. John the Divine (begun
1911).

contemporaries and the general progress in American arts.

In some of these shorter articles Sturgis made succinct comments that well exemplify the direction in which his mature critical ideas developed. In place of his early Pre-Raphaelite demand for literal "truth of natural form" in the representation of fact, he came to realize that an artist's aim must be "truth of expression." He gives a simple example to clarify the point. To a sculptor the human eye is in form merely a spheroid, a flattened ball; but sculptors have found that a deeply incised half-ring with a central drill-point in the marble or clay suggests much more effectively the brilliance and expression of the eye—although this carving of the eyeball is in no way a "representation of Nature."

All of which is another way of saying that in these matters the language of the art is of such momentous importance that the person who chooses it is borne along by it, and disregards statement, narration, and representation alike—ignores truth in general, as well as of detail, considers only his effects producible in that language of art: or in other words, what he thinks of splendor of color, nobility of line composition, grace and harmony of mass, delicate graduation and also bold contrast in light and shade; all these being included in the resources of that one language which he is using as he paints.

True, an artist as a secondary consideration may present an old tree or a house, or may relate an incident either pleasant or discordant, but "that is not the purpose of his work of art." For, in fine (and the most pointed antithesis of his early Pre-Raphaelite dicta), "No work of art that is worthy of the name has for its principal subject Description or Narration, or even Representation." [6]

The death of Ruskin in 1900 again directed Sturgis's thought—with some lack of charity—toward that critic's theories, and in turn toward his own. Ruskin had an unquestionably "sincere love of art in many forms and a hearty desire to sympathize with the artist." Too, his powers of observation were remarkable, and his retention of impression acute. But, in the final judgment, "Ruskin was not a critic at all, either by nature or by gained capacity." [7]

Ruskin should be read, says Sturgis with some acerbity, only by stringent selection. "An immense amount of what seems almost to be wisdom, and is certainly alert intelligence, is to be inferred from any well-made collection of such passages." But the inaccuracy of the general impressions and the illogicality of the conclusions drawn from the given premises so vitiate his total work that its effect is pernicious. For "in Art criticism, there is, of course, no such thing as Authority":

Art criticism is a matter of suggestion, of comparison, of good-natured and sympathetic hints at possible shortcomings, of hearty praise of probable excellences. Art criticism is addressed not to the artist . . . but to the public. . . . Criticism is always false and sure to be mischievous when it assumes the final and dictatorial tone.

The first two volumes of *Modern Painters* were written, according to Ruskin's Preface to Volume III which appeared in 1856, in a hurry and for the express purpose of checking the attacks upon Turner "which prevented the public from honoring his genius at the time when his power was greatest." The ten years spent more deliberately on the preparation of the third volume, to enable the author belatedly "to judge rightly of art," were in Sturgis's view tragically misdirected; for Ruskin's expression there, as well as in the *Seven Lamps* and *Stones of Venice*, was completely dogmatic and authoritarian. "Neither in his youth nor in his age were there any bounds to his certainty that he was right." By his early thirties he had committed himself to definite theories of architectural grandeur, to the relative values of different styles and periods, that should have been the conclusions drawn from a lifetime of serious study. Thus Ruskin misused his "splendid powers" to lead astray "the whole community which they might have led to an intelligent feeling for fine art." For in spite of all his bold intelligence, unstinting liberality, and poetic cast of mind, Ruskin could "give only bold assertion where no assertion was possible, and the declaration as fact of what was never anything but whim." Thus the world "has reason to regret that John Ruskin ever saw or thought of a work of fine art in his life"; for in his misdirection of students of the arts he has done "an irreparable mischief." [8]

The appearance of Holman Hunt's autobiography in 1905, with the title *Pre-Raphaelitism and the Pre-Raphaelite Brotherhood,* served as another invitation for Sturgis to comment on the Pre-Raphaelite movement as a whole. As major influences acting on their line of thought Sturgis cites the Brethren's distaste for the European art of their time—particularly the French; their "worship of fifteenth-century Italy"; the love of the architecture and decorative art of the Middle Ages, with its "vigorous colors and strongly outlined patterns"; "the growing idea that the unequaled logic and rationality of Gothic architecture were in some way virtuous —even religious"; and a deep concern with "ecclesiology," with Biblical materials and scenes from legendary church history, always embellished with religious symbols and emblematic design. . . . But perhaps the most easily identifiable characteristic "evident in all the Pre-Raphaelite work" was their desire for "realistic drawing of the figure, for natural pose, natural gesture—natural action, in short." In pursuit of this reportorial accuracy in drawing, a certain clumsiness resulted in the effort to avoid affectation of pose. But there is indeed a "verity got by imaginative treatment" that is evident in Millais's "directness of insight and readiness of expression" that gives his work some permanent significance; and Hunt's "realism of movement," taken from life both "accurately and imaginatively," likewise places his paintings far above those of his contemporaries. This desire for realistic treatment could have been further gratified had the English Pre-Raphaelites been appreciative of the French painters of their day—Géricault, Delaroche, Couture, and the rest, whom unfortunately they "despised without knowing." Nevertheless, declared Sturgis, leaving the question open, "there are many kinds of truth in art," and the Pre-Raphaelite version with its peculiar atmosphere of quaintness, remoteness, and medieval tradition, was of wide influence and popularity.[9]

The related problem of the similar aims (of escaping from the lifelessness and restrictions of academic art) but differing practices of the P.R.B.'s and the newer French school of the Impressionists had for some time fascinated Sturgis. As early as his series of university lectures on art he had gone out of his way to say:

It is extremely curious that the English Pre-Raphaelites, of all men the most faithful to delineation, and preaching the most rigidly close adherence to the models actually before them as they drew, and the French "Impressionists," the reverse of their English predecessors in all these respects, should have hit upon the same way of offending careless lookers at pictures. The painters of each of these schools express some curious truths about nature's light and color, and use these for very interesting works of art: and in each case they receive plenty of ridicule and very little sympathy.[10]

As vigorous as were many of Sturgis's shorter pieces of comment and criticism, his name will be associated permanently with his major, serious studies which were scholarly, authoritative, and widely inclusive. His friend, Peter B. Wight, saw "no extravagance" in the assertion: "I doubt if any other man ever lived who acquired such an extensive knowledge of all that concerns the history of art in all its branches." [11]

Among the ten volumes which he wrote or edited during the last three decades of his life the most significant are the *Technique and Principles of Visual Art,* issued as a series of "University Lessons on the Fine Arts" by the International Art Association in Chicago (1900); the popular *How to Judge Architecture* (1903), and its companion volume, *The Appreciation of Sculpture* (1904). But his most extensive work was his *History of Architecture,* projected in four volumes, of which only two were finished at the time of his death.

Volume I, dealing with "Antiquity," presents a minutely detailed and beautifully illustrated factual record of the monuments and remains of Ancient Egypt, Western Asia, Greece, and Rome. His own subjective judgments and aesthetic evaluations are minimized; but occasionally, as in his discussion of the massive construction of Imperial Rome as illustrated in the Pantheon, he speaks personally: "There is no interior in the world more impressive than this; and probably one reason for its beauty is the fact that its overwhelming mass reduces the columnar system to mere decoration—to ornament simply." [12]

Volume II continues with the "Romanesque and Oriental." In the latter category especially he pioneers in presenting careful accounts of the architecture of non-Moslem India and Southeast Asia, China, Japan, and Persia. A subsequent section deals with the Mohammedan structures, in particular the mosques, in India, Persia, Egypt, and the Near East, and in Spain and North Africa. In the lengthy division devoted to the Romanesque Sturgis analyzes the effect on art of the decline of the Roman Empire, and records the rise of the basilica-type of early church. Later Romanesque forms are

tional Academy of Design

Portrait of Clarence Cook by T. C. Farrer

then pursued geographically in the various areas of Europe, including the Armenian, Anglo-Saxon, and Scandinavian.

His third volume was planned to continue with the Gothic; and, inferentially, this type of architecture would have received his most enthusiastic treatment. As Wight indicated, however, despite his basic allegiance to the Gothic, Sturgis also broadened his sympathies in his later years. Occasionally, therefore, we find comments on exotic types such as this: "It is the glory of the Persian designer of the Middle Ages that he knew where to stop and where to emphasize, how to combine by contrast and by harmonious gradation, and, in short, how to produce color decoration on a scale and with a faultless good taste which the other nations of the earth have never approached." [13] But his constant concern with the Gothic is evidenced by his proposition that the typical ribbed vaulting in that form originated not in France, as the popular belief had it, but rather in England, specifically in the otherwise "magnificent Romanesque" Durham Cathedral, as early as 1160 A.D.

Second to this extensive *History* in ultimate importance was his three-volume *Dictionary of Architecture*, still valuable as a general reference. This work was "notable not only for encyclopaedic and accurate knowledge and for soundness of views," according to a contemporary reviewer, but also as "indicating Mr. Sturgis's genius for friendship. The work seems unique because of the extraordinary number of signed articles in it. Most eminent architects would hardly give time and attention to the writing of articles for the compiler of a dictionary, but they were glad to do this service for Mr. Sturgis because of their affection for him." Both comprehensive in material and simple in presentation, these various volumes served to clinch Sturgis's reputation as "the principal popularizer" of architectural knowledge in America.[14] Called "not only a connoisseur, but an inspirer of fine work," Sturgis was the obvious choice for president of the Architectural League of New York, and of the Fine Arts Federation.

In a memorial epilogue to Sturgis's "Field of Art" series in *Scribner's*, Montgomery Schuyler reviewed his career:

> With his tendencies and his environment . . . it was quite inevitable that he should succumb to the spell of Ruskin's eloquence. . . . Determining, in his youthful enthusiasm, to devote himself to architecture, it was a foregone conclusion that Mr. Sturgis would devote himself to the revived, or, in its British phase, to the "Victorian" Gothic.

After his association with "an evanescent and evangelical architectural journal entitled, almost necessarily, the *New Path*," he graduated to the *Nation* as "a more stable organ of a wider culture"; and thence to his other more mature expressions, already discussed above. Blessed to a consummate degree with both "sensibility and conscientiousness," in Schuyler's phrase, Sturgis during his prolific career produced much work of lasting "interest, influence, and authority." [15]

Charles Herbert Moore: DISCIPLE OF RUSKIN

In 1946 the William Hayes Fogg Museum of Art at Harvard University arranged a major exhibition of its holdings of British Pre-Raphaelite paintings and drawings.[1] This collection was first assembled by a Harvard graduate of 1886, Grenville Lindall Winthrop, whose appreciation of art was shaped by the teachings of Ruskin's good friend, Charles Eliot Norton. Winthrop's first acquisitions were the products of Pre-Raphaelite artists, and he went on to spend a lifetime gathering significant paintings, sculpture, and other art objects from many periods and many cultures including Egyptian, Oriental and Aztec, with the intention of bequeath-

ing them to the university; on his death in 1943 these treas-
ures were turned over to the Fogg Museum. Although the
P.R.B. materials form only a small fraction of the total Winthrop Collection,* they nevertheless constitute one of the two
major groups of English Pre-Raphaelite art in this country.†

This gift of the work of Rossetti and his fellows to the Fogg
Museum seems particularly appropriate since its first director, Charles Herbert Moore, had been in his earlier days an
active member of the American Pre-Raphaelite "Society for
the Advancement of Truth in Art" in New York, and a friend
and student of Ruskin. The recent exhibition by happy coincidence marked the semicentennial of Moore's appointment
as head of the Museum; and Winthrop's donations amplified
tremendously the few examples of P.R.B. art which had been
acquired by the Museum under Moore's administration.

Charles Herbert Moore's central creed had been announced
early in his career; for in answer to conservative attacks on
his New York Society he had declared in the *New Path* in
1863:

The revival of the Pre-Raphaelite principles is only beginning to
dawn . . . yet, some works of consummate excellence have been
already accomplished. . . . We are called by some "weak mockers
of Ruskin," and it is said that our principles are not born of
original conviction. Be that as it may, the principles are not affected either way. By the mercy of God, Ruskin has been sent
to open our eyes and loose the seals of darkness.[2]

In sharpest contrast to his fellow-member, Russell Sturgis,
who in his later expressions turned bitterly on Ruskin, Moore
remained throughout his life a loyal disciple. In 1900 as a full
professor of art at Harvard he marked Ruskin's death by an

* A brief description of the Winthrop Collection is included in the Appendix.
† The other, the Bancroft Collection in the Delaware Art Center in Wilmington, Del., is discussed in Chapter XVIII.

extended article in the *Atlantic Monthly*. Here the American admits that Ruskin's architectural studies, *The Stones of Venice* in particular, "abound in misconceptions and mistaken affirmations"; and that in his later years the critic's "self-confidence became almost a mania, which greatly impaired his power for good." But in spite of all this, in the realm of painting few artists "had so fine and so thorough a technical training," and as a practitioner "nearly all of the vast numbers of his drawings exhibit rare subtleties of expressive execution. His sense of form was keen and his feeling for color was exquisite." Furthermore, his total critical work is, "in the main, sound and illuminating. It is on the highest plane of thought and feeling; and no criticism can rob it of its enduring value." [3]

In the thirty-seven years between these two public statements, Charles Herbert Moore had created for himself a scholarly and artistic mode of life. He first attended the public schools in his native New York, then studied painting instead of going on to college; and in the 1860's spent several years in the Catskills where he was one of the lesser members of the Hudson River group. In 1871 he accepted the offer to give instruction in freehand drawing and water-color in the Lawrence Scientific School at Harvard. Three years later, on the suggestion of Charles Eliot Norton, newly appointed professor of the History of the Fine Arts, he offered for Harvard undergraduates a general course in the principles of design, painting, architecture, and sculpture. Here he stressed the then-revolutionary concept that actual studio work in the visual and plastic arts was a prerequisite to appreciating their more subtle values.

In a personal application of this dictum, Moore took leave of his academic duties for the year 1876-77. He bore with him to England in early summer a letter from Norton introducing him to Ruskin, which he delivered at Brantwood. On August 2 from Wales Ruskin sent a letter back to his dear friend Norton:

I want to write to you every day, but must, at last, having quite a feeling of next door neighbourhood to you this last month, in sight of Mr. Moore. . . . I was of course delighted with him; and had true pleasure in the time he could spare to me, increased by feeling that I was able to show him things which he felt to be useful.[4]

They made plans to meet again in Venice. On October 5 Ruskin reported to the same correspondent his daily work schedule there: an early hour of sketching on the Canal, then breakfast at nine, a brief session on his *Stones of Venice*, fourth volume, and at half past ten a visit to the Academy "where I find Moore at work; and we sit down to our picture together." Since both men believed in copying the old masters for training in analysis of design and manual technique they had selected Carpaccio's "Saint Ursula" as their model. "I'm painting a small carefully toned general copy of it for Oxford," wrote Ruskin; "Moore is making a study of the head, which promises to be excellent"—and which was ultimately added to the Fogg Museum collection. Moore usually worked until noon, then went off for lunch with his family, leaving Ruskin to have "a couple of hours tête-à-tête with Saint Ursula," before doing some open-air sketching in the late afternoon.

The two men—Moore in his mid-thirties, Ruskin now fifty-six—were eminently congenial and to Norton his British friend added: "I am very much delighted at having Mr. Moore for a companion—we have perfect sympathy in all art matters and are not in dissonance in any others. His voice continually reminds me of yours. And he's not at all so wicked nor so republican as you, and minds all I say!"[5] On this basis their personal association continued through the following months and into the winter. In February Ruskin again assured his friend Norton: "I have been 'happy'—in such sense as I ever can be—with Mr. Moore, he *is* so nice." [6] In contrast to the less happy experiences with his other young American painting companion, W. J. Stillman, some sixteen years before, Ruskin continued to exert a profound influence on Moore; and in the phrase of a present professor in the Department of Fine Arts at Harvard, Moore may be looked on as "the most talented and serious painter among those who may be considered as the pupils of Ruskin." [7]

With his initial fervor for the Gothic, expressed first in the *New Path* and fostered by his associations with Ruskin and his own personal observations on the Continent, it is logical to look to Moore for further scholarly exegesis of this principle in architecture. And although his friend Sturgis latterly expressed doubts about its desirability, Moore published several laudatory volumes on the subject. In his thirteen years as director of the Fogg Museum and full professor of art at Harvard, Moore's most important studies were the *Development and Character of Gothic Architecture* (1890, with a second edition in 1899), and its sequel, the *Character of Renaissance Architecture* (1905).

In the first of these Moore propounded a thesis that was considered extreme by most historians and critics, particularly the British. The final statement in the volume suggests the theme of the whole: "Of the pure French Gothic of the twelfth century it is hardly too much to say that it is the most splendid architectural product that human genius and skill have thus far wrought in this world." [8] Although his praise is thus extreme, his definition of the term is sharply limited, for as he points out in the preface:

In the works of the true Gothic style we have a new structural system carried out with the strictest logic, and with a controlling sense of beauty. They are works of the highest art, in which sound mechanical principles serve as the secure foundation for the exercise of the poetic imagination. It will, doubtless, seem to readers already more or less familiar with the subject an extravagant position that Gothic architecture, as I define it, was never practiced elsewhere than in France.[9]

Applying the term "pointed architecture" to other types hitherto "erroneously classed with Gothic," Moore declares that the true Gothic is to be recognized, not by the simple substitution of pointed for round arches and the use of a particular type of ornament, but rather in a fundamental plan completely at variance with the Roman and Romanesque: "a system of balanced thrusts in contra-distinction to the ancient system of inert stability . . . a logical adjustment of active parts whose opposing forces neutralize each other and produce a perfect equilibrium." [10] Believing, as he did, that the Lombard churches of Northern Italy first employed the ribbed vaulting and functional grouping of supports typical of the transition from Romanesque to early Gothic, Moore deduced from his study of the actual monuments that it was the people of twelfth-century France who first developed the true "Gothic style and gave to its marvellous constructive system equally new and appropriate types of carved and painted adornment." [11] As for the architecture of England, admirable as it was in its own right, the Gothic there evidenced was essentially secondhand, derived from Anglo-Norman sources and frequently constructed by Anglo-Norman builders. Thus, asserted Moore, "I believe the English claim to any share in the original development of Gothic, or to the consideration of the pointed architecture of the Island as properly Gothic at all, must be abandoned." [12]

Whatever the weight of this particular argument, Moore's definitions are lucid and his comments enlightening. In the subordinate arts of decoration mentioned above, for example, he analyzes the dominant influence on the designers and points out the "modern" tendency toward abstraction: "Everywhere in Gothic art do we find expression of organic life," in both the foliate and floral decorations and the human figures, "but this life is invariably governed by the exigencies of architectural fitness. . . . The artist, while keenly appreciative of nature, has a constant regard to the conditions of his art." Thus in the handling of actual physical detail the Gothic artist was free to present his own simplified interpretations or "abstractions" of his natural models.

In addition to sculpture, the art of color design in stained glass is, of course, associated with the Gothic cathedral. Moore suggests that historically this was incidental to the development of the organic framework in the structure itself. After it was discovered that the walls might practically be dispensed with, the interest in stained glass increased rapidly and soon "it became the universal practice to fill the aisles and clerestory with resplendent fields of translucent mosaic." The supporting mullions and tracery enriched the total effect through their own highly elaborate designs.

Such comments as these on the character of the Gothic are perhaps the most interesting but quantitatively are subordinate in Moore's total work to his comprehensive historical survey of its development. With more than two hundred fifty illustrations in the text, many of a technical and analytical nature, based on his own drawings at the site, the author elaborated on the chronological development of the Gothic cathedral architecture in France, then of the "Pointed Construction" in England, Germany, Italy, and Spain. Detailed studies of the sculpture and stained glass in each of those areas follow, which the author fears "may prove tedious to the unprofessional reader." Because of his clarity of style and incisive tone, this does not occur; and at the end of the volume the reader has almost been persuaded, concerning the "true" Gothic architecture:

In France, and in France alone, is the system complete and the development apparent. There only are the successive steps of change spontaneous and connected, and there alone does the inventive spirit of the builders manifest itself as animated by a general movement.[13]

Having expressed himself thus forcefully on the subject of the Gothic, it was inevitable that Moore should speak deprecatingly of the products of the succeeding age, in his meticulous analysis of outstanding buildings, the *Character of Renaissance Architecture*. His attitude evidences a social and moralistic approach definitely akin to Ruskin's—that a noble people produces a noble art:

The Fine Arts are always an expression of the historical antecedents, the intellectual, moral and material conditions, and the religious beliefs of the peoples and epochs to which they belong. They derive their whole character from these antecedents and conditions, and cannot be rightly understood or appreciated without reference to them.[14]

Moore believed that while the Renaissance fostered independent scientific investigation and realization of greater intellectual freedom, at the same time the "humanist learning bred a Neo-pagan spirit which favoured and strengthened a growing indifference to moral principles and religious beliefs." The man of the Renaissance too often abandoned himself to mundane pursuits and gratifications, and in his escape from ecclesiastical and ascetic restraints proclaimed the "sufficiency of intellectual, aesthetic, and sensuous enjoyments to satisfy the whole of man's nature." All of this meant simply that the fine arts of the Renaissance were called into the service of this extravagant, luxurious, and immoral society, and could only suffer, in Moore's view, an inevitable deterioration. The architects were thus called upon to produce "specious" styles of palatial architecture, and sculptors and painters considered the portrayal of physical beauty as a sufficient end of art.

But aside from demonstrating the moral decadence of their patrons, the artists themselves failed in the basic essential of sincerity. In their eclectic and illogical adaptations of details from the classical styles there was no spontaneity, but rather a labored effort to create showy magnificence which resulted in "freakish irrationality," and a mongrel form never "either really classic or structurally truthful." [15] The fanciful designs of an individual architect eager for fame could never, in Moore's mind, produce work of the inherent beauty and quality of the Gothic building: "The noblest architecture of the past has always been the evolution of the people, the joint product of many minds, and the natural expression of many conditions."

The consistency of Moore's artistic beliefs and their relation to Ruskin's, from his first expression in the *New Path* through his mature scholarly works, are thus obvious. His summary judgment of 1905 might just as well have appeared in 1863:

Beauty in architecture may be . . . defined as the artistic coordination of structural parts. As in any natural organic form, a well-designed building has a consistent internal anatomy, and its external expression is a consequence and expression of this. . . . In the light of what we have seen I think it must appear that the claims which have been advanced for the architecture of the Renaissance as the only architecture of correct principles since that of classic antiquity, and as an architecture in comparison with which the Gothic art of the Middle Ages should be considered as the barbarous product of an unenlightened age, are without justification.[16]

NINE

Joaquin Miller and "The Master," D. G. Rossetti

IT WAS, oddly enough, the "Poet of the Sierras," Joaquin Miller, who succeeded such other Americans as Buchanan Read and W. J. Stillman in their role as transatlantic friend and admirer of Dante Gabriel Rossetti. Miller first met him when Rossetti was approaching middle age and Miller himself was a mature man of thirty. After cutting his California strings the American had bought a second-class passage on the *Europa* from New York on August 20, 1870, bound for Glasgow; and following a sentimental tour of the Burns and Scott country and a visit to Byron's tomb, he proceeded to London. Here his literary pilgrimages continued; and perhaps by coincidence he found lodgings in a garret once occupied by the poet Cowley.[1] His own ambitions had led him to compile a thin manuscript of poems, which he peddled unsuccessfully to almost all the publishers in London. Finally, Miller had one hundred copies of *Pacific Poems* printed at the expense of a pawned gold watch—but without benefit of publisher's imprint. These he cast abroad on the critical waters, and was greatly astonished at their sudden success. "Eureka!" he shouts to his journal, "the St. James *Gazette* says 'Arazonian' [*sic*] is by Browning!"[2]

On the strength of his eccentric, flamboyant personality, and the freshness of his subject matter in British eyes, Miller was at once given entrée into the upper social strata of London. Tom Hood, he says, introduced him to "almost every-body"; and he was made an immediate protégé by the society poet, Richard Monckton Milnes, Lord Houghton. In a letter to Gladstone dated August 5, 1873, Lord Houghton wrote: "Joaquin Miller is most interesting as poet and man. I have known and asked nothing as to his private life." Houghton's biographer carefully points out, however:

When Mr. Miller came to England . . . one of the first to welcome him was Lord Houghton. He had heard of him through American friends, and had been greatly struck by the originality of his writing, and made haste to receive him as a brother-poet and man of letters. He had shown the same attention to so many other visitors from abroad in his time that there was nothing specially noticeable about his reception of Joaquin Miller.[3]

Longmans brought out *Songs of the Sierras* in the spring of 1871, and Miller was astonished at his instant popularity. His subsequent adventures in London—meeting the Prince of Wales and the Queen, dinner with Browning, visits with Tennyson and Swinburne, an invitation from Gladstone, breakfast with the Archbishop of Dublin, strewing rose petals before Lily Langtry at Lord Houghton's reception, mixing everywhere with the elite—make up a fabulous tale.[4] But among his many connections, the only ones of immediate pertinence here are his associations with the Pre-Raphael-ites.

On February 18, 1871, Frederick Locker (later Locker-Lampson) brought Cincinnatus Miller—as W. M. Rossetti refers to him in his diary—to Euston Square for introduction to the Rossetti family. W. J. Stillman, long a familiar, accom-panied the other two.[5] No record of the immediate encounter remains, but it is obvious that Miller was greatly impressed by the personalities and sensitivities of both Dante Gabriel and his brother. In the American's fragmentary journal he wrote on May 3:

I find here among the Pre-Raphaelites one prevailing idea, one delight—the love of the beautiful. It is in the air. At least I find it wherever the atmosphere of the Rossettis penetrates, and that seems to be in every work of art—beautiful art. I am to dine with Dante Rossetti! All the set will be there. I shall hear what they say. I shall listen well, for this love of the beautiful is my old love—my old lesson.[6]

The Rossettis found the newcomer interesting and wanted to know him better. William Michael was constitutionally curious about things American; and Dante Gabriel perhaps saw in the brash, brusque Westerner some of his own later mannerisms: slovenliness of dress, capriciousness of mood, a mixing of boisterousness and geniality. Perhaps the Anglo-Italian felt in the Californian an expansiveness, an openness, an escape from polite forms and restrictions, a sense of freedom and space, that suggested what he himself longed for but never found among "the stolid Britons." And Rossetti must have felt under the surface crudeness and braggadocio of Miller something of the "quest for beauty" which the American tried to suggest in his journal—his "old lesson" which he was still trying to con.

On June 15 William Michael Rossetti wrote an extended and highly complimentary review of the *Songs of the Sierras* for the *Academy*, which appeared as the leading article of the issue.[7] At first glance it appears unreasonably fulsome. "This," he declares, "is a truly remarkable book. To glance through its pages is to observe a number of picturesque things picturesquely put, expressed in a vivid, flowing form and melodious words, and indicating strange, outlandish, and romantic experiences. . . . We have emphatically to pronounce him an excellent and fascinating poet, qualified, by these his first works, to take rank among the distinguished poets of the time, and to greet them as peers"—his fellow authors, of course, including Browning, Tennyson, Arnold, and Swinburne! Then realizing that other readers might hesitate to praise him so extravagantly:

... He is not the sort of man to be abashed or hurt by criticism. Let me add that the less attention he pays to objections, even if well-founded, and the more he continues to write out of the fulness of his own natural gifts, the better it will probably be for both himself and his readers. America may be proud of him.

William Michael himself, however, offers several objections—and thereby adds a greater validity to his own critique. A calmer survey of the poems reveals certain crudities of construction and expression, faulty lines and rhymes, "platitudes of phrase," and a "contempt of quiet common sense." The poet exhibits his subjects with "an effect of abortiveness and gloom. . . . Gratuitous misery is poured forth, as from a bucket, with a liberally cruel hand." In some of the narratives the author shows little gift for constructing a story, for the reader is unable to credit the central fact. But perhaps the most serious stricture is the assertion that "Byron is the poet whose spirit most visibly sways and overshadows that of Joaquin Miller"; there is an echo also of Browning in "diction and versification," and a recognizable "ring of Swinburne, especially as regards alliteration, and a vigorous elastic assonance."—But in spite of these weaker elements, the excitement, vitality, and suggestiveness of the *Songs of the Sierras* have enabled the poet "to realize his poetic identity under very exceptional conditions, highly favourable to spirit and originality." [8]

Before Miller was unexpectedly called back to America in the middle of the summer by the serious illness of his brother in Easton, Pennsylvania, he was able to enjoy the dinner with Dante Rossetti which he had been anticipating with such pleasure. On September 28, some time after the event, Miller made one of his longest entries in his journal to commemorate the famous evening:

I cannot forget that dinner with Dante Gabriel Rossetti, just before leaving London, nor can I hope to recall its shining and enduring glory. I am a better, larger man, because of it. And how nearly our feet are set on the same way. . . .

Here is an odd tone of hero-worship in the voice of the blustering Westerner; and a surprising reticence in declaring that he cannot violate "the sacred secrets" of his host's table, cannot divulge the details of the rich, off-the-record intellectual repast. All "the literary brain" of London was there, "and the brain of all the world," he thought, "was in London"—and mellowed with good red wine. Had he been able to remember and transcribe the evening's long conversations, he would have had "the best and the greatest book that was ever written." But in this belated record "the golden grain is gone, and here is but the straw and chaff."

Dante Gabriel, "the master," in Miller's words, sat for the most part silent at the head of the table where he meditatively rolled a bit of bread between thumb and finger. Leaning toward the American, he confided: "I am an Italian who has never yet seen Italy. Belle [sic] Italia!"

Many topics ebbed and flowed during the evening, but poetry was the central theme. The inspiration of poetry was laid in nature; a true, pure life itself might be poetry without embodiment in any literary form. "All great artists," asserted Rossetti paradoxically, are "above the folly of expression." "Then the master," recorded Miller, "bending close, said softly to me, 'Poetry is soul set to music. . . . Now what do you call poetry?'"

Miller's response, and the discussion it provoked, stress and clarify the Pre-Raphaelite concern with the visual values in poetry:

"To me a poem is a picture," I answered. Proud I was when a great poet then said: "And it must be a picture—if a good poem—so simple that you can understand it at a glance—eh? And see it and remember it as you would see and remember a sunset, eh?" "Aye," answered the master, "I also demand that it shall be lofty in sentiment and sublime in expression. The only rule I have for measuring the merits of a written poem, is by the height of it. Why not be able to measure its altitude as you measure one of your sublime peaks of America?"

To this Miller felt encouraged to respond: "Yes, I do not want to remember the words. But I do want it to remain with me—a picture—and become part of my life. . . ."

The talk drifted to Longfellow as a creator of such word pictures—the Arabs, for example, silently stealing away. Then a "transplanted American" at the far end of the table (no doubt W. J. Stillman) offered: "The poem of Evangeline is a succession of pictures. I have never read Evangeline but once." To this, *sotto voce*, Rossetti responded: "It is a waste of time to look twice at a sunset."

These comments led to further thought on the structure of poetry. "I hold that there never was a long poem written continuously," declared Rossetti, and went on:

As a rule, great poems are built like Solomon's temple, section by section, and are put together without the sound of a hammer. This brings us back to the assertion that all poems are pictures, and long poems only a succession of pictures strung together on some sweet story of devotion and love.

But Rossetti's thoughts soon wandered elsewhere; the conversation lightened; the cigars and bottles passed; the evening eventually drew to a belated end. In transatlantic retrospect, "such was the soul, heart, gentleness," inscribed Joaquin Miller, "of this greatest man that I ever saw walking in the fields of art." [9]

A brief footnote to their relationship may be gleaned from the somewhat synthetic memoirs assembled by Miller's daughter, Juanita, in 1941. As Miller supposedly recalled the dinner in a conversation with his friend Prentice Mulford, he asserted that it was D. G. Rossetti who first introduced him to Whitman's works, placing in his hand one evening a copy of W. M. Rossetti's British edition. Miller was so fascinated at the find that he lay in bed and read the volume through—almost the last reading he was able to do because of weakening vision.[10]

During Miller's brief stay in the United States, his brother John and sister Ella both died; and his estranged wife Minnie publicized on the lecture platform and in the press her version of Miller's desertion of her. After an unhappy interim in Oregon he therefore spent some time in San Francisco and then began again his foreign wanderings. There follow the colorful episode of his stay at the court of Dom Pedro, Emperor of Brazil, and the creation of his long narrative poem, "Isles of the Amazons." But by 1873 he was back again in London, the scene of his first great triumph.[11] Although he was still popular with Lord Houghton's set, he received progressively poorer notices from the press for his *Songs of the Sunlands* and *Life Among the Modocs*, faring particularly hard at the hands of the critic, J. A. Symonds. But he became a member of the Savage Club, where Julian Hawthorne was already enrolled, and diverted the group with his customary practical jokes and tall Western tales.

By this time Dante Gabriel Rossetti was coming into the later, clouded years of his career; and there is only brief record of any other contacts between Joaquin Miller and the

Pre-Raphaelites before he left London for Rome in the summer of 1874. W. M. Rossetti's diary for March 19, 1873, contains the following entry, cool in tone but significant in its evidence that Miller was trying to improve his relations with the Rossettis; the reference is to *Songs of the Sunlands,* published later in that year:

Joaquin Miller looked me up at Somerset House and left with me the remaining proofs of his forthcoming volume. He showed me the dedication, "To the Rossettis." I strongly recommended him to write direct to Gabriel as to the matter before anything further is done. I mentioned the dedication to Christina. She feels some hesitation in sanctioning it, not knowing what the book may contain. If she makes up her mind to object, she is to write to Miller.

W. M. Rossetti's own reactions to the new work were mixed:

I looked through the proofs and noted down some remarks on them. They include a series of poems about Christ, named "Olive Leaves," implying a sort of religious, at least personal, enthusiasm, mixed up with a good deal that has more relation to the sense of the picturesque than of the devotional. These poems, though far from worthless from their own point of view, are very defective, and would, I think, be highly obnoxious to many readers and reviewers. I suggested to Miller the expedience of omitting them altogether.—Christina, I find, has already read these particular poems, and to some considerable extent likes them, which is so far in their favour as affecting religious readers.[12]

Perhaps with Christina's aid the poet overrode her brother's objections; and when the *Songs of the Sunlands* came off the press it bore the dedicatory phrase: "To the Rossettis." Among the poems were eight under the heading "Olive Leaves."

Four years after this episode Miller made a final visit to England, which was cursorily noted in the same journal that had printed W. M. Rossetti's first laudatory review: "Mr. Joaquin Miller, the American poet, arrived in London two or three weeks ago. He is not likely to remain long." [13] As a final gesture of propitiation he dedicated his new *Songs of Far-Away Lands* to Lord Houghton; but it is obvious that in eight years the wheel of Miller's reputation in England had turned full circle.

Since Joaquin Miller came under the spell of Rossetti comparatively early in his writing career, it is difficult to know what directions he might have followed had he not felt some Pre-Raphaelite influence.* Certainly his basic love for "picture" in poetry was strengthened by Rossetti's general acquiescence in point of view. "But beyond that," as a critic of Miller has remarked, "the American failed to approximate either the technique or materials of the man he called 'the master.' " [14]

Hundreds of Miller's lines might be quoted as examples of "word-pictures," but too extensive an investigation would not be rewarding. Although his versatility in theme was considerable, the great majority of such scenes impress a modern reader as being either too obvious or too forced. One of the "Olive Leaves"—which incurred W. M. Rossetti's displeasure —renamed "Songs of the Hebrew Children," offers a sample:

> And camels came in with the traces
> Of white desert dust in their hair
> As they kneel'd in the loud market places,
> And Arabs with lances were there.[15]

The volume in which this appeared, *Songs of the Sunlands,* reflects more than any other not only his contacts with the Rossettis, but also his employment of Swinburnian "alliteration and soft sounds." "The Isles of the Amazons," the longest entry in the volume, aptly applies Rossetti's dictum tossed off at the famous dinner that "long poems [are] only a succes-

* His Utopian romance, *The Building of the City Beautiful* (1893), shows obvious relation to the writings of Ruskin and Morris.

sion of pictures strung together on some sweet story. . . ."
The presumed narrator, "a quaint old crone," sits on the rim
of an island alone:

> Her brown, bare feet dip down to the river,
> And dabble and plash to her monotone,
> As she holds in her hands a strange green stone,
> And talks to the boat where the bent reeds quiver.

The fair young Castilian knight of her legend feels pity for
the conquered Indians:

> For crown'd with fire, wreathed and ruddy
> Fell antique temples built up to the sun.
> Below on the plain lay the burning city
> At the conqueror's feet; the red street strown
> With dead, with gold, and with gods overthrown.

Wounded in the jungle by the "beasts that beset him" and
the serpents "red-tongued and terrible," he escapes to the
banks of the great river where

> The nude black boar through abundant grass
> Stole down to the water and buried his nose,
> And crunch'd white teeth till the bubbles rose
> As white and as bright as are globes of glass.

His rescue is at hand: "The Queen on a prow stood splendid
and tall." In the Isles of the Amazons he is sheltered "below
the banana, with leaf like a tent." The Queen is "as bright
and as chaste as a flash of fire," and with these ingredients
the tale sweeps on through a series of lush descriptions and
sentimental moralizings to the suspected conclusion "that
love should come and liberty pass."

> The Queen was at peace. Her terms of surrender
> To love, who knows? and who can defend her?
> She slept at peace, and the sentry's warning

Could scarce awaken the love-conquer'd Queen;
She slept at peace in the opaline
Hush and blush of that tropical morning. . . .

The poetic qualities of these lines scarcely need comment;
but in their defense the novelty of subject matter might be
urged as one reason for their contemporary popularity. "The
Ship in the Desert," in the same volume, likewise profited
from the sketches of the stupendous wastes of Arizona which
were new to many English eyes. But there is often the feeling
that Miller's word-pictures are not presented in the inevitable or perfect phrase, but rather are offered in a self-
conscious and inept manner.

This tendency may be discerned in practically all Miller's
work, but it is present particularly in one other volume of the
1870's, *Songs of Italy*, which shows some watered-down influence of Browning. "The Ideal and the Real" begins with a
bathetic verse:

She was damn'd with the dower of beauty, she
Had gold in shower by shoulder and brow.
Her feet! why her two blessed feet were so small
They could nest in this hand. How queenly, how tall,
How gracious, how grand! She was all to me,—
My present, my past, my eternity!

In pursuing this vision of ideal beauty the poet has occasion
to employ numerous verbal sketches, both brief and
extended. "The wide-wing'd dolorous birds of the sea" drift
over his gondola; and the doves "hurried home in white
clouds" to Saint Mark, "where the brass horses plunge their
high manes in the dark." The Lady is lost in a wilderness "of
leprous white palaces," while the "troubled sea throbb'd as
if rack'd with pain." On the ultimate encounter she feels
unworthy of love because of "sins that your cruel sex heap'd

on my head," so she will "wait, weeping, in sackcloth" right on "the innermost side of death's door."

There is no profit in multiplying illustrations. The significant fact is that Miller relies heavily upon "picture in poetry," and in so doing reflects a Pre-Raphaelite practice. But in spite of the source of his inspiration it seems clear that Miller's phrases "fall far short of Rossetti's in their attempt to blend the actual with the ideal." [16]

Richard Watson Gilder:
Poet and Art Patron in the Gilded Age

RICHARD Watson Gilder, who is remembered chiefly for his success as long-time editor of the *Century Magazine,* was by his own statement directly influenced in his early writings by the British Pre-Raphaelites, in particular D. G. Rossetti. Too, he was an active member of the group of young, liberal painters and critics known as "The Society of American Artists" who devoted themselves to lifting the face of artistic America in the latter part of the nineteenth century.

In 1870 at the age of twenty-six Gilder became the first managing editor of Dr. J. G. Holland's new journalistic venture, *Scribner's Monthly.* The editorial rooms were then at 654 Broadway, and there for a few months Gilder had as a fellow-member on the staff W. J. Stillman, who had just returned to the United States after his tragic experiences in Greece and Crete. Their mutual interest in art and journalism must certainly have led them to discussion of the career and contents of Stillman's *Crayon.* The associations in the office were, at any rate, both profitable and pleasant, for after Stillman had gone again to England he remarked: "The greatest mistake, from the business point of view, I have ever made was in leaving the collaboration with Dr. Holland—the most friendly of chiefs." [1]

Among the many literary and artistic folk with whom his

137

editorial work served to bring him in contact, Gilder numbered Helen Hunt, later Mrs. Jackson. To the office one day she brought along an attractive young art student, Miss Helena DeKay, then studying painting at Cooper Union. Gilder fell promptly in love with her, and after a proper courtship embracing attendance at art exhibitions, lectures, and concerts, and the reading of poetry and study of Dante in the original, married her. His wife's broad knowledge of European art, literature, and music did much to deepen Gilder's cultural interests; and through her grandfather, Joseph Rodman Drake, she had inherited a certain family enthusiasm for poetic expression which she fused with Gilder's own.[2]

Before Helena DeKay and Gilder were married in June 1874, he had written for her and published in *Scribner's* a short cycle of love sonnets that stirred Edmund Clarence Stedman to a paean of praise (which modern readers can regard only as rash overstatement). "At last you are writing flawlessly," he declared, "and have shown the soul of an artist in perfecting yourself and biding your time. Certainly no American ever has written six consecutive love sonnets to compare with these. . . . Neither I nor any other poet can equal them."

From the elder poet and recognized critic these must have seemed to Gilder high words indeed. "Some fortunate coincidence of art, study, youth, being a poet and *being in love* have come together to produce them," Stedman continued. A literary echo perhaps is audible, but not loud enough to confuse the original voice: "They are wholly your own, by that shade of difference—your own personal flavor—which makes them unlike the work of your masters: Petrarch, Mrs. Browning, Rossetti. . . ."[3]

In a later autobiographical fragment Gilder looked back on this happy and productive period. "The shackles of expression were broken by the circumstance of my getting acquainted with Dante's *Vita Nuova* (through Rossetti's translation) at the time I met Helena DeKay," he wrote. "I began by imitating Rossetti's version of Dante's sonnets. . . ." [4] Thus, instead of the *New Life*, he enlarged his sonnet series for separate publication as *The New Day*.[5] Among the original six in *Scribner's* Stedman preferred these two elaborate polemic metaphors, which bear some resemblance, perhaps, both to Rossetti's handling of Dante and to his own *House of Life* sequence:

I

My love for thee doth march like armed men,
Against a queenly city they would take.
Along the army's front its banners shake;
Across the mountain and the sun-smit plain
It steadfast sweeps as sweeps the steadfast rain;
And now the trumpet makes the still air quake,
And now the thundering cannon doth awake
Echo on echo, echoing loud again.

But, lo! the conquest higher than bard e'er sung:
Instead of answering cannon, proud surrender!
Joyful the iron gates are open flung
And, for the conqueror, welcome gay and tender!
O, bright the invader's path with tribute flowers,
While comrade flags flame forth on wall and towers!

II

Thy lover, love, would have some nobler way
To tell his love, his noble love to tell,
Than rhymes set ringing like a silver bell.
O, he would lead an army, great and gay,
From conquering to conquer, day by day!
And when the walls of a proud citadel
At summons of his guns far-echoing fell—
That thunder to his love should murmuring say:

Thee only do I love, dear Love of mine!
And while men cried: Behold how brave a fight!
She should read well, O, well! each new emprize:
This to her lips, this to my lady's eyes!
And tho' the world were conquered, line on line,
Still would his love be speechless, day and night.[6]

Gilder's interest in Rossetti continued throughout his later writings, although he asserts that after Rossetti's first strong impulse was felt, "almost immediately imitation was lost in the necessity of direct utterance." [7] As late as 1906, however, in writing to his friend Charlton M. Lewis at Yale, he said again: "I am mightily beholden to Rossetti for his translations—for his *Dante and His Circle;* this book, cooperating with other causes, helped me to my natural expression." By that time Gilder had come to prefer Wordsworth and Keats as sonneteers; but in spite of the feeling that Rossetti's poetry was too "odorous of the hothouse," Gilder found that it still attracted him, "for it is intense, exquisite, subtle and in some poems rich with a unique beauty and a new lyricism." [8]

Following their marriage the young couple had settled themselves in somewhat Bohemian quarters on East 15th Street, just off Broadway. Originally a stable, the structure was now converted into a "garden studio" appropriate to Mrs. Gilder's art interests, and although it was not quite a *salon* in the European sense their "Studio" became a popular gathering place for the younger artistic group in the city. H. H. Boyesen, the Swedish novelist, later wrote to Gilder: "I never found a nature more thoroughly sympathetic than yours—unless it be your wife's." Joseph Jefferson and Madame Modjeska were familiar guests; La Farge and Saint-Gaudens dropped in frequently; Stanford White added his architectural interests to their discussions; and even the older Whitman paid this tribute:

You must never forget this of the Gilders . . . that at a time when most everybody else in their set threw me down they were nobly and unhesitatingly hospitable. The Gilders were without pride and without shame—they just asked me along in the natural way. You know how at one time the church was an asylum for fugitives —I was such an innocent and the Gilders took me in.[9]

A revolt in the American arts—of limited but significant dimensions—was initiated in the Gilders' "Studio." The British Pre-Raphaelites' rejection of the authority of the Royal Academy was not its direct stimulus, but the similarity in the two movements is striking; and through the person of the art critic, Clarence Cook, the gesture of defiance in New York had kinship with the American Pre-Raphaelite group.

Helena DeKay before her marriage had helped to found the Art Students' League, and through that organization knew many of the contemporary painters. The ultra-conservative Academy of Design [10] continued to be the arbiter of quality, demanding primarily technical excellence in the rendition of literary subjects; and in its exhibition of 1875 almost all of the younger artists failed to find a place. A number of rejectees decided thereupon to stage a show of their own, and at an indignation meeting at the "Studio" La Farge was appointed to head a Committee on Exhibition. Shortly thereafter the Fifth Avenue showrooms of Cottier and Company announced the "works of some of the most noted as well as some of the younger artists of New York and Boston." Local newspapers which had found the Academy selections "commonplace" thought that the maverick show presented "one of the most important art movements of the day. The pictures exhibited are mainly by certain young artists whose work is not congenial to the spirit which controls the Academy and who find no sympathy or encouragement there." [11] La Farge, Helena DeKay, Abbott Thayer, and

William Morris Hunt were among the exhibitors who received specific mention.

This overt thwarting of authority strengthened the morale of the younger liberals; and their discontent with the old regime increased. Finally, in the spring of 1877, they set up an organization of their own in competition with the recognized Academy, called temporarily the "American Art Association," but soon altered to the "Society of American Artists."

In a letter to Saint-Gaudens's son and biographer, Gilder later reported the highlights of this momentous experiment. After his particular interest in art had been heightened by his marriage to Miss DeKay, Gilder had realized that the "old Academicians were carrying things with a pretty high hand." "So," he declared, "I spoke to a few of the younger men of our American renaissance about starting a new organization." Saint-Gaudens, however, believed that the time was not yet ripe. But on June 1, 1877, he called on Gilder in a highly wrathful mood, reporting that they had just thrown out a piece of his sculpture from the Academy exhibit, and that he was ready to go into a new movement. Gilder promptly urged him to come back that evening for further conference, then hurriedly rounded up two other young dissident artists and a critic sympathetic to their views. "The Society of American Artists was that night founded by Walter Shirlaw, Augustus Saint-Gaudens, Wyatt Eaton, and Helena DeKay, your humble servant acting as secretary. . . . Clarence Cook, the critic, was present, but not as a member." [12]

Cook, with his quixotic and mercurial temperament, "soon hauled off because a certain artist was admitted," went on Gilder. But his defection was brief, and after Gilder had assured him that the whole movement could not be vitiated by the possible error in creed of a single artistic acolyte, Cook rallied publicly to a defense of the new society. The *Tribune* of June 27, 1877, carried an extensive letter by him, accusing the old Academy of favoritism and lack of artistic discrimination. "The dispute between the Academy and the party of reform is essentially a dispute about principles. . . ." In general, the Academy's rejection of certain works on the ground that they are not "good likenesses" is unsound, since the decision depends too completely on the whim of an individual judge. Furthermore, since good work in portraiture is not necessarily limited to the exact rendering of the features of the sitter, "if the whole body of academicians had decided that they were bad likenesses, the wrong done to these artists would have been the same." Specifically, Saint-Gaudens's "Sketch in Plaster" had been submitted on invitation and suitable space had been reserved. Hence, to refuse exhibition on the flimsy plea that there was no room for it was a direct insult to its creator as well as proof of the Academy's inability to recognize meritorious work by younger men.[13]

This sketch, of a young girl reclining on a low couch with an infant in her arms, had been composed while Saint-Gaudens was in Rome; and after the crisis was history he admitted that the National Academy's refusal of the work was justified. "It was entirely too unfinished a product to be exhibited, particularly considering the general attitude of artists at that time." Nevertheless, it served its purpose, for its rejection "so angered me," he recalled, "that with four or five others in the same recalcitrant state of mind, I joined the group which founded the Society of American Artists. After years of increasing success," he wrote in 1906, "that Society is merging back into the Academy of Design, enmity to which brought it into existence." The cycle now bears repetition: "The field is open for another society of younger, protesting men."[14]

ELEVEN

John La Farge

JOHN La Farge is probably the best known among the various American artists of the nineteenth century who had direct and extended contacts with the Pre-Raphaelite movement. A close friend of Henry Adams, Clarence King, and Augustus Saint-Gaudens, La Farge was not only an outstanding painter of his period, but with his lively and graceful memoirs of Japan and the South Seas was a man of letters as well. And although in his latter years his art principles and practice diverged widely from his early application of Pre-Raphaelite concepts, he gladly admitted the formative influence of Madox Brown and Rossetti in his painting, and of William Morris in his brilliant work in stained glass.

La Farge first became acquainted with the historical and literary aspects of art at Columbia University. His professor of English was an Oxford man who had been a member of the Oxford Movement with Newman, and who found great interest and challenge in Ruskin's works. Under his direction La Farge read widely in "anything that would bring up the beauty of the medieval ideal"; [1] and before leaving college in 1853 [2] he felt he had been indoctrinated with the belief that eighteenth-century art and, in fact, everything that did not agree with the medieval was all wrong.

Following his graduation he studied briefly with a French artist in New York, who was the possessor of only "a very small scale of capacity." Nevertheless, the older man directed his pupil's attention to French painters and their methods, as did George Inness whom La Farge saw occasionally at work in his studio. But, said La Farge,

I knew few or no American painters. . . . I only touched the merest corners of what was being done. I did not know of our Pre-Raphaelites here, as a body, though I spent some time with Stillman, who was one of their prophets. I knew Boughton, who was to leave us soon, and a few of the Hudson River men. . . .[3]

With the idea of following a recognized profession La Farge had spent some months reading law when, in the spring of 1856, he broke away and decided to see Paris. His cousins, the Saint-Victors, literary and Bohemian, soon made the twenty-one-year-old American at home in their sophisticated circles. His grand-uncle was a noted collector of art, and his cousin Paul de Saint-Victor "a brilliant, fashionable, successful writer upon art of all kinds." The latter took him to see Gérôme, then only an ambitious young artist. But Delacroix, whom La Farge at that time considered the greatest of living Frenchmen, he did not, to his deep regret, succeed in meeting.

On this first trip to Europe the American followed up his book-knowledge of medieval art and architecture by visiting the great French cathedrals, where his prime enthusiasm was for the stained glass; he then traveled through Belgium where he became "steeped in admiration" of the medieval painting displayed there. Following a suggestion of his father —who evidently despaired of seeing La Farge successful as a lawyer—he gladly acquiesced in the plan of making a serious study of art; and in the winter of 1856-57 an American art-student friend, Edward May, directed him to the Paris studio of Couture. Here La Farge carefully explained that he wished to acquire a practical knowledge of painting only as a basis for a better understanding of art, but that he himself had no intention of becoming a painter. Couture set him to sketching old masters in the Louvre, with occasional work in the studio where, he recalls, Puvis de Chavannes one day came in and used La Farge himself as a model for some sketches.[4] This connection lasted for only a few weeks, however, for shortly he was off to Munich, Dresden, and Copenhagen to see more art. Not long afterward, La Farge received word that his father was ill and so decided to return to America; but en route he stopped for a noteworthy visit in England in the fall of 1857.

"I had plenty of time to give to looking at pictures," he recalled, "because almost everyone for whom I had letters was away from London. After a little while I went to Manchester and spent several weeks at the great Exposition," which was the first special public exhibition in England of paintings collected from private and royal galleries. He felt a rare education in thus being able to view side by side Titian and Velasquez and Rubens. But in addition there was a new art experience: "But besides the miles of old masters, there were some of the quite new; the Pre-Raphaelites, whom I knew by reading and by some prints but whom now I could see carefully. They made a very great and important impression upon me, which later influenced me in my first work when I began to paint." [5]

From a collector of unpublished bits of La Farge's autobiography a few other details may be gleaned:

A visit to the Manchester Exhibition and a short stay in England determined for many years certain admirations, and confirmed me in the direction of my ideas of color. The few Pre-Raphaelite paintings that I saw, and the drawings of some of the leaders in that movement, appealed strongly to me. Nor did they seem disconnected from the charm of Sir Joshua and of Gainsborough, or

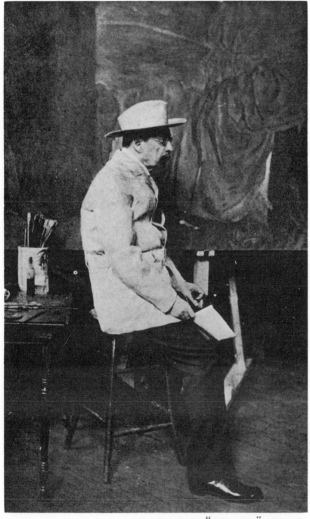

John La Farge

Clarence King

from the genius of Turner, which yet offended me by its contradiction of the urbanity and sincerity of the great masters whom I cared for most. But the Pre-Raphaelites, as seen through my eyes—Millais, and Hunt, and Rossetti, and Ford Madox Brown (Sir Edward Burne-Jones had not yet appeared within my horizon)—seemed to me to be willing to meet many of the great problems of colour, and my youthful energies sympathised with the stress and intensity of their dramatic programme. These likings I retained later when I began to think again of painting, even though Mr. Ruskin's teachings had become stumbling-blocks rather than helps in my likings and judgments. I find the trace of these influences pleasantly lingering in some of the drawings which I made even ten years later.[6]

The "few Pre-Raphaelite paintings" which he scrutinized so carefully at Manchester (as Hawthorne was likewise doing at this time) included Madox Brown's "Christ Washing Peter's Feet," which directly influenced his brush; and one of La Farge's resulting sketches which found its way into the home of a British friend was seen by Rossetti, who with his innate impetuosity immediately wrote La Farge "a handsome message of encouragement. It was the first thing of the sort in his life . . . and it was really helpful to him." [7] Or, as La Farge himself casually recalled the episode: "Some few words of praise accidentally dropped by Millais or Rossetti in favour of some trifle of mine which found its way to England pleased me as establishing a relation to them that my general tendencies of work and study could not imply to many of my friends." [8]

Continuing approval on the part of the Pre-Raphaelites is indicated by a minor episode several years later. In 1868 Horace Scudder, as the editor of Ticknor and Fields' new juvenile *Riverside Magazine,* wrote to William Rossetti that the only artist who gave him "solid satisfaction" was La Farge. As supporting evidence Scudder sent some photographic reproductions of La Farge's designs for the "Pied Piper of Hamelin," which the recipient promptly showed to Dante Gabriel; subsequently William Michael noted in his diary: "He was much pleased with them, and took them off to show Brown."

The shaping of La Farge's artistic expression was gradual and drew from many sources. The "Hudson River men" to whom he had previously referred had been the most prominent group of native artists in the 1850's. With an insistence on the "grand and picturesque," they had painted the Palisades or the Catskills or Lake George in a series of arranged landscapes with conventional sunlight and artfully glassy water—a school which modern taste tends to label synthetic. La Farge felt "the admiration of an earnest beginner for the older craftsmen," but even to the amateur their artificiality and lack of depth was apparent when viewed beside Delacroix, Rousseau, Corot, and Millet, who, said La Farge, then "represented for me the most important of the European development." But his acquired medievalism led him to look favorably, with a Pre-Raphaelite eye, on Giotto and his fellows; for, he declared, "in my first attempts at painting for churches, I certainly had in mind the directness of the earliest masters, at least insofar as to believe that their example represented and contained the main lessons of our art." [9]

In his own immediate art work after returning from his first European jaunt, he put himself in the hands of a friend and teacher, William Hunt, and with him painted for a time in Newport, Rhode Island. In the representation of human figures La Farge was influenced directly by Hunt, but in his interpretation of landscape and still-life details he followed a method of his own, "based on the principles that he had admired in the Pre-Raphaelites." [10]

In 1872-73 La Farge made another trip to England which had a direct effect on his development. Although he carried with him notes of introduction to Ruskin, he deliberately omitted delivering them because "we should certainly have disagreed if there had been any discussion." That he was not alone in this point of view was corroborated by Burne-Jones's remark to La Farge that he himself now refused to read anything whatsoever from Ruskin's pen.[11]

One contact which he did make, however, was of some importance to his growing reputation in England. The French art dealer and connoisseur, Durand-Ruel, had suggested that he look after La Farge's interests together with those of Monet and other French impressionists. So in London Durand-Ruel arranged a show of some distinction, in which one of La Farge's Newport studies, "The Last Valley," was hung between a Rousseau and a Delacroix, where, according to La Farge's artist friend and critic, Royal Cortissoz, "it held its own against that stern test."[12] This canvas, later bought by Professor Agassiz of Cambridge, had been executed under William Hunt's direction, was painted "from nature" on the specific site, and gives, perhaps, the sharpest definition of La Farge's Pre-Raphaelite tendencies.[13] Another similar canvas from the same period was his "Paradise Valley," which La Farge dates as "'66-'67-'68," and describes as his own last "realistic" painting.[14]

But the most important aspect of his second tour was the opportunity to put on a personal basis his admiration for the Pre-Raphaelite group. He was taken into the Rossetti home as an intimate friend, where, as he told his friend Cortissoz, he "immensely liked" Christina, and with her for hours discussed intricacies of the Catholic doctrines in which they both were firm believers. "It was odd," recalled La Farge, "but I could tell her things she didn't know about Romanism, which was blurred for her by . . . the pressure of things English around her." [15] He met the brothers Rossetti, of course, and Madox Brown and Burne-Jones and William Morris; and it was largely through them that the instigation came for his ultimate success as a worker in the craft of stained glass.

When La Farge won a medal first class for his Watson Memorial Window later displayed at the Paris Exposition of 1889, the tribute of the awarding jury may suggest La Farge's contemporary stature in this art:

His work cannot be fully gauged here, where a single window represents a name the most celebrated and widely known in our Sister Republic. He is the great innovator, the inventor of opaline glass. He has created in all its details an art unknown before, an entirely new industry, and in a country without tradition he will begin one followed by thousands of pupils filled with the same respect for him as we have for our own masters. To share in this respect is the highest praise that we can give to this great artist.[16]

Over a period of five or six months La Farge associated closely with the British Pre-Raphaelites. From them, especially Morris, he absorbed enthusiasm for the practical handling of stained glass, the beauty of which had long since impressed him in his visits to the great cathedrals. As La Farge summarized it in a statement prepared for the French Government after the 1889 Exposition:

It was only in 1872, during a trip to Europe, that I thought much again of the question of decoration, that is to say, in so far as returning to its practice. I had naturally taken a great interest, both in early days and up to that date, in the English Pre-Raphaelite school begun by Ford Madox Brown and Rossetti, and at that time (in 1873) distinguished by Mr. Burne-Jones. I saw then something of their work and their methods in stained glass, and the ancient Medieval glass became a subject of interest.[17]

By happy coincidence, on his return to America his friend Van Brunt, an architect in partnership with W. R. Ware,* suggested to La Farge that he design a window for their Memorial Hall at Harvard. La Farge drew the cartoon, and the window was cut and assembled, but the end result was so far below expectations that he would not allow it to be set in place but instead had it destroyed. Since the chief fault lay in the poor quality of the glass, La Farge determined to develop for himself a new type of opalescent glass—suggested, if we are to believe the homely anecdote, by his admiration of a sunbeam transmitted through a cheap colored-glass receptacle holding tooth-powder on his dressing table. He discovered in Brooklyn an old Luxembourg glassmaker, and over several steins of beer succeeded in infecting him with his own new fervor. From the little workshop, in due course, came glass of a new brilliance and iridescence; the Harvard window was re-done; and La Farge went on to execute commissions for McKim, Mead, and White and a

* William Robert Ware (1832–1915), Harvard '52, began his architectural practice in 1860, and three years later formed a partnership with Henry Van Brunt, whom he had met in the New York office-atelier of Richard Morris Hunt. For many years their Boston firm was recognized as one of the best in the East. Among the buildings which they designed were the First Church, Boston; the Episcopal Theological School, Cambridge; two dormitories and Memorial Hall at Harvard; and the Library at the University of Michigan. The eminent critic and historian, Mr. Talbot Hamlin, described this work as "largely under the influence of Ruskin and his English followers, with much use of picturesque detail, horizontal lines, and polychrome masonry." (See DAB, XIX: 452.)

Van Brunt, after the retirement of Ware in 1881, formed a new partnership with Frank M. Howe. With Kansas City as headquarters they designed a number of railroad stations for the Union Pacific, including those at Omaha, Sioux City, Ogden, and Portland. Other projects included the Electricity Building at the Chicago World's Fair, and a residence for the Armours. Van Brunt, too, began his career with "a strong bias for Ruskin-inspired Gothic," but thereafter made adaptations of the popular Romanesque and classical styles. (Ibid., p. 150.)

great many private individuals, producing several thousand windows in the course of his career.

With the craftsman's desire to maintain contact with the complete process of manufacture, La Farge later wrote:

I thought I had noticed in 1873, in the work of the English artists in stained glass, that they seemed to have come to the end of their rope, and that their work in glass had ceased improving; and it seemed to me that . . . this was mainly because the designers had become separated from the men who made the actual windows. . . . It occurred to me that if I made a design for stained glass to be carried out in this country, I should follow the entire manufacture, selecting the colour myself, and watching every detail. . . .[18]

Thus he worked with his assistants at all stages of manufacture, and had the final satisfaction of seeing in material shape the richness of form, line, and color suggested by his original designs.

Although he later turned his interest in the decoration of large surfaces to the production of many murals, it is as a worker in glass that his friend Henry Adams, inspired by their visit to Chartres, gives him the familiar tribute in the *Education*:

With the relative value of La Farge's glass in the history of glass-decoration, Adams was too ignorant to meddle . . . but, whatever it was, it led him back to the twelfth century and to Chartres where La Farge not only felt at home, but felt a sort of ownership. No other American had a right there. . . . Adams himself was an interloper . . . [who] asked no better than to learn, and only La Farge could help him, for he knew enough at least to see that La-Farge alone could use glass like a thirteenth-century artist.[19]

In a survey of La Farge's career the application of the label Pre-Raphaelite to much of his work does not appear to be a willful reading-in of the term. Certainly in the first ten years as a practicing artist he exemplified—as he himself declared—the Pre-Raphaelite reverence for accuracy of statement. He desired to render precisely and literally the phenomena of nature as he saw them; and with the insistence of the early P.R.B.'s made perfectly obvious the structure of the landscape before him and the botanical peculiarities of his immediate settings. He was concerned with the aspects of the atmosphere, of the weather, the season, the direction of the wind, the time of day.

But, as did the best of the Pre-Raphaelites, Rossetti, La-Farge also abandoned the role of literal transcriber and reporter of that fragment of the natural world which he could experience. He came to believe that a given scene could have as many valid interpretations as there were artists using it as a point of departure. He told students at the Metropolitan Museum in 1893:

There can be no absolute view of nature. . . . In these realities with which we are concerned, realism is a very evasive distinction. . . . You need not, therefore, be afraid of the word; you need not be afraid of indulging the illusion that you are rendering the real reality of the things that you look at—that you are copying. . . . If you ever know how to paint somewhat well . . . you will always give to nature, that is to say, what is outside of you, the character of the lens through which you see it—which is yourself.[20]

This attitude and practice, in extension, becomes "expressionism" in its common usage; here according to La Farge there must always be a feeling of movement, in contrast to the photographic staticness of the earlier, more literal renderings. Too, the fondness for representing allegorically various moral and metaphysical notions, so prominent in many P.R.B. canvases, should be outside the realm of art, as inappropriate to the medium.[21] And although his later works, such as his clear and sparkling water colors from Japan (exhibited in Paris in 1895), are quite different from his earlier Pre-Raphaelite studies, there is even here a recognizable concern with the rendering of facts, with form and structure, light and atmosphere.

TWELVE

Whistler: Burne-Jones: Ruskin—
Art on the Legal Scales

THE year 1878 is peculiarly marked in Anglo-American art relations. As is well known, Whistler sued Ruskin for damages as a result of the unflattering comments in *Fors Clavigera* concerning his recent Grosvenor Gallery show—the familiar "pot of paint in the public's face"—and was rewarded with the verdict of one farthing by a solid British jury. In this suit Burne-Jones served as an interested but embarrassed third party; and we are concerned here chiefly with his testimony as it applied Pre-Raphaelite dicta to the judgment of American art.

Whistler had known the Rossettis and their circle for at least fifteen years. An entry in Allingham's diary is suggestive of the atmosphere in 1864:

Got down to Chelsea by half-past eight to D.G.R.'s. Breakfasted in a small lofty room on first floor looking on the garden. Fanny in white. Then we went into the garden and lay on the grass, eating strawberries and looking at the peacock. . . . Then Swinburne came in, and soon began to recite . . . and after him Whistler, who talked about his own pictures. . . .[1]

In 1878 the long-continued association made it very awkward when Ruskin requested Whistler's old friends to testify against him, in particular Burne-Jones who considered Whistler's "technique . . . perfect and his colour always good."[2]

154

Ruskin, however, seemed to be delighted at the publicity that the intended trial would ensure: "It's mere nuts and nectar to me the notion of having to answer for myself in court, and the whole thing will enable me to assert some principles of art economy which I've never got into the public's head by writing, but may get sent over all the world vividly in a newspaper report or two." [3] But unfortunately for this particular desire, his serious physical and mental breakdown occurred before legal action was begun almost a year later, and although he had recovered almost completely he himself was not allowed to testify. Toward the end of 1878 Ruskin therefore wrote to Burne-Jones: "I gave your name to the blessed lawyers as chief of men to whom they might refer for anything which in their wisdom they can't discern unaided concerning me."

Since Burne-Jones had been praised in the same paragraph that vilified Whistler, and since he admired sincerely certain aspects of the work of his American friend, he found himself in a very unpleasant position. To him the only honest and possible attitude was to stress his own conviction that "good workmanship was essential to a good picture." His testimony at the trial is illuminating as it applied his own Pre-Raphaelite values to the paintings in question, and further as it demonstrated the effect that Whistler was making on the British art-viewing public:

I think that nothing but perfect finish ought to be allowed by artists; that they should not be content with anything that falls short of what the age acknowledges as essential to perfect work.

When pressed for a specific judgment he continued:

I have seen the pictures by Mr. Whistler which were produced yesterday in this court, and I think "Nocturne in Blue and Silver" is a work of art, but—[he added] a very incomplete one; an admirable beginning, but that it in no sense whatever shews the finish of a complete work of art. I am led to the conclusion because while I think the picture has many good qualities—in colour, for instance, it is beautiful—it is deficient in form, and form is as essential as colour.

When his verdict on "Battersea Bridge" (which the artist reputedly had painted in a day and a half) was called for, Burne-Jones continued: "The colour is even better than the other, but it is more formless, and as to composition and detail, it has neither." To the point-blank question as to whether he considered "Nocturne in Black and Gold" a work of art he replied: "No, I cannot say it is"; but in vindication of Whistler's efforts hastened to add: "I never saw a picture of night that was successful. This is only one out of a thousand failures which artists have made in their efforts at painting it." [4] And subsequently he made a particular gesture to give all credit possible: "There must have been great labour to produce such work, and great skill also." But Burne-Jones's honest failure to comprehend the purpose of the Impressionists forced him to conclude:

But I think he has evaded the chief difficulty of painting, and has not tested his powers by carrying it out. The difficulties in painting increase daily as the work progresses, and that is the reason why so many of us fail. The danger is this, that if unfinished pictures become common we shall arrive at a stage of mere manufacture, and the art of the country will be degraded.

Ruskin, who finally realized that "there *was* more difficulty" in his appearance "than in anyone else's," sent Burne-Jones a note of appreciation. But it did not keep the witness from regretting the part he had been forced to play: "I wish all that trial-thing hadn't been; so much I wish it, and I wish Whistler knew that it made me sorry—but he would not believe." And he wrote to Rossetti: "The whole thing was a hateful affair and nothing in a small way ever annoyed me more—however, as I had to go I spoke my mind, and I try not to think of it all more than I can help." [5]

Throughout his life Whistler battled for the aesthetic principles demonstrated in his paintings; and his highly nervous temperament led him into a series of bitter controversies of which the Ruskin lawsuit was merely the climax. Consistently, however, he received kindness at the hands of the Pre-Raphaelites and their associates. Madox Brown on one occasion, before Whistler received his belated recognition, issued a circular to all his own friends and patrons strongly urging them to purchase some of Whistler's etchings because he was "a great genius." At a tea-party at the Whistlers' in Chelsea Brown had witnessed the economic level to which the unappreciative British public had reduced the expatriate artist. Mrs. Whistler met him in the hall and begged him to go out and buy a pound of butter. "There was no money in the house. . . . The poulterer had cut off his credit, and Mrs. Whistler said she dare not send her husband, for he would certainly punch that tradesman's head." [6]

Whistler, of course, was eventually acclaimed as a major painter, in part because of the public acceptance of the French Impressionists; and rewards came in the form of commissions, decorations from several foreign governments, and memberships in artistic societies. From this later period only one episode need be recalled. Mr. Frederick Leyland, a rich Liverpool merchant, was one of the principal purchasers of Pre-Raphaelite art; and he likewise acquired Whistler's "Princesse du Palais de Porcelaine"—for which the model had been the sister of Marie Spartali Stillman. Whistler was now commissioned to decorate the Leyland dining room, and after many discussions and modifications, not always amicably agreed upon, the Peacock Room resulted. As the scheme expanded so too did Whistler's estimate of the expense. Misunderstandings led to a final disruption of relations between client and artist; and Whistler expressed his bitterness in an unkind caricature of Leyland which he called "The Gold Scab." The original Peacock Room was eventually purchased by Mr. Freer of Detroit, and is now to be found in the Freer Museum in Washington, D. C.

Whistler's cordial relations with the Pre-Raphaelites survived the crisis of Burne-Jones's unwilling defection at the time of the Ruskin lawsuit. Since Rossetti was always the dominant figure a final verdict concerning him might be taken as typical of Whistler's feeling for all of the English artists encountered in the P.R.B. circle. Some remark to the discredit of Rossetti was uttered in Whistler's hearing, and he replied: "You must not say anything against Rossetti. Rossetti was a king." [7]

THIRTEEN

The Arts and Crafts Movement

THE modern Arts and Crafts movement as distinct from the activities of the medieval craftsmen and guild members and of the workers in the continuing, unsophisticated, individual folk crafts, may be said for the sake of a specific date to have had its start in 1860 when William Morris built his famous "Red House" on the edge of London, and set about to design and produce all the decorations and furniture for his new home by his own hand. As "The Field of Art," edited by Russell Sturgis in *Scribner's*, put it in the 1890's concerning "the very active revival in decorative art which dates back some thirty or forty years"—"Nor is it less certain that this revival is largely due to the Pre-Raphaelites, or rather to the now famous house of Morris, Marshall, Falkner and Co., in which William Morris was the leading spirit." [1]

This simple personal apprenticeship in the industrial arts soon broadened to a popular interest in non-machine production of useful and presumably beautiful articles; and by the time of the First World War the *Studio* of London was able to issue a special number featuring the history and products of some fifteen schools of applied art in London itself, and an even larger number of training centers for the arts and crafts in the provinces.[2] And in the United States a comparable boom occurred.

Carlyle was the spiritual father of this development in

both countries.[3] A voice crying in the industrial wilderness of nineteenth-century England, he declaimed: "One monster there is in this world, the idle man." But the factory slave in the cotton-mill was not the ideal workingman, for his conditions of labor must be altered. "Soot and despair are not the essence of it: they are divisible from it." Since creative work is the chief end of man it should bear with it its own reward in the joy of creation. "He that can work," says Carlyle in *Past and Present,* "is a born king of something; is in communion with Nature, is a master of a thing or things, is a priest and king of Nature so far." Thus, instead of the machine's "cheap and nasty" products which inevitably are tainted with greed, there should be genuine, fit, and honest manufactures in the literal meaning of the term—the products of an individual, skillful, concerned workman, in which he feels personal pride and satisfaction.

John Ruskin was at this time a rich young man idling in Switzerland and Italy, employing his considerable literary skill in descriptions of natural phenomena illustrated by his own sketches. He was impressed by Carlyle's message. Largely through the influence of this "greatest of historians since Tacitus," as he thought him, Ruskin developed primarily into a sociologist concerned with the external aspects of art as they affected the economy of life. In *Modern Painters* he reasserted the essential worth of non-commercial products: that beautiful things are useful merely because of their beauty, and not because they can be pawned for money. Workers must be artists, and artists workmen. High art can spring only from high moral feeling. "You can have noble art only from noble persons." A nation's architecture can be great only if behind it are national fidelity and honor. De-individualized neo-Greek forms should yield place to the Gothic with its personal freedom of design and execution. Free workingmen must be educated upward, to plan and produce individual works of utility and beauty; they must no longer be mere manipulators of a machine. Modern artists must gain new vitality through direct handling of rough materials. Free hand-work must be looked on as the only good work. And, finally and fundamentally, art must be based, not on sensuous perception, not on intellectual appreciation, but on social usefulness.

Chief among Ruskin's admirers was William Morris, fifteen years younger, who had been attracted by both the ideas and the "splendid rhetoric" of the author of *Modern Painters* and *Stones of Venice*, the second of which was published as Morris was entering Oxford. This work kindled his concern in socio-artistic problems, and he looked on it as the first statement of his own ruling doctrine that "art is the expression of man's pleasure in labor." " 'On the Nature of the Gothic,' " he later declared, "seemed to point out a new road on which the world should travel." [4] Of a more intensive range than Ruskin, Morris devoted his subsequent career to the determination of the relationships between labor and art, and thus served unquestionably as the first practical exponent of the Arts and Crafts idea in its modern phase.

It need not surprise us that the "really most important side of art" for William Morris in 1893 was simply "the decoration of utilities." [5] For at the end of the machine-made nineteenth century "the great mass of civilisation" was, he claimed, "content to forego art almost altogether"; and the practitioners who had any impulse toward the fine arts had to choose between the production of pleasing but impractical—that is to say, unusable—objects which tended primarily to demonstrate the producer's dexterity, or the addition of "a certain amount of artistic beauty and interest to a piece of goods which would, if produced in the ordinary way, have no beauty or artistic interest." Since "organic art," that happy product of a craftsman unconscious of any definite style but "producing beauty instinctively," had died with the Middle Ages, the only duty of modern practitioners was a diligent cultivation of "the sense of beauty . . . skill of hand, and a niceness of observation, without which only a *makeshift* art" could be produced.[6]

Of the various American journals influenced by Morris in their reporting of the artistic scene, the one most closely allied to the Arts and Crafts movement was the *Craftsman*, the organ of the United Crafts of Eastwood, New York, an illustrated monthly whose life from 1901 to 1916 roughly encompassed the heyday of the crafts revival in the United States. Its motto is indicative of its scope: "In the interest of better art, better work, and a better and more reasonable way of living." Its pages not only serve to record crafts activities, but perhaps more significantly they offer further evidence of the lineal descent of the American crafts movement from William Morris and the British Arts and Crafts groups.[*]

The Foreword of the initial number of the *Craftsman* in October, 1901, indicates the direct blood-relationship of Gustav Stickley, the "Master of the Crafts," and the various members of his United Crafts organization—the key group in the American craftmanship renaissance—to their British Pre-Raphaelite forebears. After announcing themselves as a new association or guild of cabinetmakers and metal and leather workers, their spokesman declares:

The Guild has had but one parallel in modern times, and this is found in the firm organized in London, in 1860, by the great decorator and socialist, William Morris, together with his not less distinguished friends, Burne-Jones, Rossetti, and Ford Madox Brown, all of Pre-Raphaelite fame.

* For a discussion of this journal see Chapter XIV.

In particular the ideas of Morris are the very footing and foundation of the American enterprise:

The United Crafts endeavor to promote and to extend the principles established by Morris, in both the artistic and the socialistic sense. In the interests of art, they seek to substitute the luxury of taste for the luxury of costliness; to teach that beauty does not imply elaboration or ornament; to employ only those forms and materials which make for simplicity, individuality, and dignity of effect.

The Guild accepts "without qualification" Morris's proposition in the interests of the workman. "It is right and necessary that all men should have work to do which shall be worth doing, and be pleasant to do; and which should be done under such conditions as would make it neither over-wearisome nor over-anxious."

Another American observer of William Morris, the outspoken Russell Sturgis, pointed out the extremes to which this theory might lead, for on occasion Morris's art products were, he believed, "absurdly and self-consciously medieval in motive and treatment."

Indeed, to such an excess was this sham primitiveness, this neo-Gothic pose carried, that two or three years since, it seemed almost as if the Society of Arts and Crafts must perish beneath the burden. That Morris was sincere in his medieval adaptations there can be no doubt. He was no *poseur*, no sensation-monger, but a workman in dead earnest, with the financial prosperity of his shop, and no weak-kneed desire for notoriety, as incentive.

But with too many of those concerned with the crafts, "medievalism became a pose, a fad," and therefore its expression in specific works ultimately degenerated.[7] Nevertheless, in the course of its history the Arts and Crafts movement had wide and notable effect not only in England but likewise in the United States.

Landmarks in its development include the first Arts and Crafts Exhibition held in London in 1888, and the founding of the original American Society of Arts and Crafts in Boston in 1897. Ten years later the movement had spread so widely that the National League of Handicraft Societies of America was organized, with thirty-three chapters in twenty states. The Art Alliance of America came in 1914; and in 1916 the American Federation of Arts held its first exhibition of industrial arts in the National Museum in Washington. Two years later the New York Metropolitan Museum established an industrial arts department to cater to the popular interest in that field.[8]

A considerable number of art schools and institutions (some of course with no direct connection with the British Arts and Crafts movement) had been opened during this period to offer training in the "applied arts" to amateurs as well as to professional or commercial designers. The Pennsylvania Museum's School of Industrial Art, for example, the first school of its type, was started in 1876 after the Centennial Exhibition in Philadelphia had stimulated public interest in crafts by the extensive display of handmade European articles. The Rhode Island School of Design in Providence was founded in the next year. The Massachusetts School of Art was a result of that state's legislative Act of 1870 whereby every child in a tax-supported school was to be taught to draw. The Cleveland School of Art was begun in 1882. The famous Pratt Institute in Brooklyn offered courses in the practical arts as early as the mid-'80's. And so might be lengthened the list of institutions whose basic tenets included the aim of making commercial products more artistic through individual treatment on the part of the makers.[9]

Many private persons with no contact with these art centers also contributed to the momentum of the Crafts movement. Among these were untrained workers who developed their own independent skills often in a folk tradition without knowledge of, or reference to, the Arts and Crafts movement as such. This was true, of course, particularly in the Southern mountains or other rural or remote areas. Some organization of these folk elements is illustrated by the work of Mrs. Sarah Avery Leeds of Avery's Island, Louisiana, who energetically sponsored the weaving of cotton fabrics in traditional designs by Creole women. Too, Berea College in Kentucky pioneered in stressing sales of regional products to aid in supporting the students and the institution. And all over the country book-binders, rug-hookers, basket-weavers, and potters set up shop singly or in small groups to produce and market useful objects with some aesthetic appeal. But it is safe to say that the great mass of urban artists and craftsmen through membership in their popular associations were aware of the revival of handicraft traditions, and considered themselves as part of the larger movement.

In some instances successful producers expanded into the formation of commercial firms, usually small, which turned out goods considered artistic in their time. Some machine processes often were employed, but their output was considered "craft" products because they were made throughout by individual workmen who felt personal concern and pride in their creation.

In 1880, as a case in point, Mrs. Maria Longworth Storer opened on the outskirts of Cincinnati her Rookwood Pottery, which became a highly successful enterprise. At about the same time Hugh C. Robertson revived the famous Dedham pottery, a crackleware with blue in-glaze decoration. A Mr. Mercer of Philadelphia designed and marketed Moravian-style tiles. Henry Swan in his Wadham Hills workshop in New York State turned out adaptations of furniture in the

colonial, "Mayflower," and Dutch styles. The Joseph P. Mc-
Hugh Company of New York discovered a good market for
its "celebrated Mission furniture" in the Spanish style. Mary
Ware Dennett and her sister Clara Ware achieved some
recognition through the gilded Spanish leatherwork produced in their Boston studio. The Roycrofters under the
tutelage of the versatile and eccentric Elbert Hubbard flourished in East Aurora, New York. The Oneida Community
produced popular silverware and other goods. But of all the
many firms and organizations, the United Crafts of Eastwood, just outside Rochester, became the most notable for
their "modern" functional furniture and varied products in
glass, wrought iron, copper, brass, leather, and ceramics; and
in their monthly *Craftsman* they served as the loudest voice
of the Arts and Crafts movement. That there was throughout
some recognition of the original inspiration and ability of
William Morris is suggested by such items as the special
"Morris Memorial Room" of the Tobey Manufacturing Company in Chicago, created to display imported Morris goods
exclusively; [10] and by the wide use of original Morris materials in a great number of American mansions then extant.

The outstanding individual producer of craft goods, who
merited the epithet of "the William Morris of this century"
in America,[11] was Louis Tiffany, the son of the founder of
the famous jewelry house. One of the two distinctly American contributions to the art of stained glass—the other being
John La Farge's "opaline"—was Tiffany's "favrile" glass,
which he named from the obsolete English term "fabrile,"
meaning handmade. He first began to experiment with
stained glass in New York in the 1870's, and opened his
Tiffany Studios in 1878. By 1892 his products were in such
demand that he built the new furnaces of the Tiffany Glass
Company in Corona, Long Island. Here his technique of

combining molten glass already fused with different colors resulted in his "favrile" product of unusually brilliant glow and iridescence. This glass was widely used for windows for both churches and private homes, and was also the material for vases, lampshades, and mosaic decorations. Perhaps the most spectacular example of his craft was the monumental mosaic glass curtain in the National Theatre of Mexico City, which weighed seventy-two tons and illustrated the legend of the two lovers who were turned into the volcanoes, Popocatepetl and Ixtaccihuatl.[12] The Court House of Abington, Virginia, installed his memorial window "To the Brave Men of Washington County." The Cathedral of St. John the Divine contained an elaborate crypt mosaic, later transferred to Tiffany's own estate chapel on Long Island. The old Mellon mansion in Pittsburgh was enriched by a noted Tiffany window. The Benjamin Harrison Memorial in the Indianapolis First Presbyterian Church, and the Lincoln and Theodore Roosevelt windows in the Metropolitan Temple in New York were others of his very numerous works throughout this country. His execution of Maxfield Parrish's design, "The Dream Garden," for the Curtis Publishing Company in Philadelphia was also popularly received. In 1919 Mr. Tiffany created the Tiffany Foundation, to which he gave his Oyster Bay estate of eighty acres, his art collection, and his library, for the purpose of aiding and sponsoring promising young artists and craftsmen.

The original Arts and Crafts movement apparently came to an end in the period of the First World War. One qualified observer declared that it simply "petered out in 'mission' furniture and the activities of the amateur."[13] But a wider view might be that in our own generation the industrial designer has inherited the mantle of the older arts-and-craftsman; and that the Pre-Raphaelite insistence on the importance of color and logic of structure has borne fruit in the professional products of planned artistry, whether in the lines of tools, toys, kitchen utensils, bath fixtures, and new-model cars, or in the packaging of thousands of articles. It is significant to note that the Museum of Modern Art in New York City has recognized the "artistic" significance of design in utilitarian objects, with recent displays of "One Hundred Beautiful and Useful Articles." At the same time, although any sense of a central crafts "movement" has doubtless disappeared, the hand-looming of fine fabrics, the tooling of leather, the artistic binding of books, the weaving of rugs, and the individual production of ceramics, basketry, metalwork, and furniture certainly continue as a significant aspect of creative effort in this country. The Penland School of Handicrafts in the highlands of North Carolina, which has attracted students from fifteen foreign countries, is one of the most vigorous craft centers of our own day.[14]

The original Arts and Crafts movement often made an undesirable dichotomy of "art" and "life," and frequently assumed that beauty was something that could be voluntarily superimposed on the unpleasant practical. But sound craftsmanship was stressed; and the frank pertinence of the design and material, the emphasis placed on the craftsman himself, and the effort to simplify, humanize, and beautify one's surroundings, all justified the movement and the popular energy devoted to it. Indeed it is not impossible to make a case for the origin in Pre-Raphaelite principles of such contemporary concerns as twentieth-century city-planning, with its early stress on the "City Beautiful," on "Garden Cities" and "Greenbelts"; for the transition from Morris's "house beautiful" is recognizable, and the American *Craftsman* campaigned ardently for city planning and beautification. So, in widely varying applications, William Morris's central doctrines of simplicity, functional design, and recognition of the role of the workman as exemplified in the Arts and Crafts movement are of continuing pertinence in twentieth-century American life.

FOURTEEN

The Craftsman

THE *Craftsman*, published by the United Crafts of Eastwood, Rochester, New York, served as the chief journalistic medium of the Arts and Crafts movement in America. A
major function of this periodical was its clarification of the
influence exerted on craft workers in the United States by
their predecessors in England.

The term Arts and Crafts was coined by William Morris and his
associates in London . . . for the immediate purpose of defining
the nature of an exhibition that differed in one essential point
from the conventional exhibitions offered by the Royal Academy
and similar institutions. . . . The unique feature . . . was to be
found in the fact that it sought to eliminate distinctions in art, and
furnish an opportunity for the display of work in wood, leather,
glass, metal—in fact, any material adapted to artistic expression.

Furthermore, the label Arts and Crafts as applied to this
Exhibition of 1888 stood boldly for three things:

It was a protest against the narrow and commonly accepted definition of art; it was a protest against inutilities, the ugliness, the
sham and pretence of a great portion of the English industrial
product of that day; it was a protest against the deplorable industrial conditions which that product represented. . . . It sought to
demonstrate the value of art combined with honest workmanship
applied to useful service.[1]

As a matter of fact, the *Craftsman* asserted, the great
results ultimately accomplished by Morris and his helpers

grew out of the decoration of a single house, "the first family dwelling of the Master himself." Thence the work extended its "deep, restorative influence" until the look of "half the houses in London" was changed for the better, and "all over the kingdom" beauty replaced ugliness. With the example of Morris before them, the United Craftsmen therefore declared their intention to develop in America a national art by the people and for the people, and to unite in one person the designer and the workman. "This principle, which was personally put in practice by Morris, extended throughout his workshops; the Master executing with his own hands what his brain had conceived, and the apprentice following the example set before him as far as his powers permitted." [2]

The basic purpose of the *Craftsman* as announced, "to deal with the relations of art to labor," led to the editorial position clearly inspired by Morris, that "art will be regarded not as something apart from common and everyday existence, but rather as the very means of realizing life." Hence, as a matter of application, the initial number of the new magazine followed the leading articles on Morris as the master-craftsman by a discussion of "Simplicity in Household Furnishings," copiously illustrated by photographs of the United Crafts' own products: furniture and cabinet work in fumed oak, elm, ash, woven reed, and soft leather, with hand-wrought iron hardware. A complementary effort to define "Style and Its Requisites" proposed as the essential qualities in domestic equipment utility, structural honesty, and beauty of design derived from simplicity and frankness of function. The second month's issue of the *Craftsman* was devoted largely to a summary of the life and ideas of Ruskin, because of both the interest of his own theories of art and his influence on Morris. And the third number was focused on a survey of the medieval guilds in which the arts and crafts were pictured as ideally unified, performing "their opportune work in promoting the civic spirit and true socialism." [3]

With the historic origins and perspectives thus established, the *Craftsman* of course went on to present a wide variety of subjects, but the reader's attention was frequently called back to the English source of much of the journal's creed, by such articles as "A Visit to the Shop of William Morris," [4] "William Morris As I Remember Him," [5] or "William Morris the Man." [6] In one month's copy devoted almost entirely to the current Gothic Revival—"a style long misapprehended and stigmatized as barbaric"—he again was credited with an influential role. For that "impulse toward medieval art which began in Horace Walpole and Walter Scott, and culminated in Ruskin and Morris, was much more than an aesthetic movement—it was based on a desire for a simpler, truer, and more organic social life." [7]

Aside from associating the Arts and Crafts movement in America with its prototype in England, the *Craftsman* also performed some historic service as a sympathetic recorder of the general crafts activities in this country. In April 1902, for example (shortly after the magazine began publication), the Arts and Crafts Exhibition held at Springfield, Massachusetts, merited detailed comment. Among the numerous displays, such as baskets, metalwork, laces, pottery, bookbindings, tapestries and so on, the most interesting exhibits were the rugs produced by the village industries in the Connecticut River Valley. A contributor to the *Craftsman*, Mrs. Helen R. Albee of Pequaket, New Hampshire, was highly praised for her original color designs for hooked rugs: "The fine effects are obtained by the massing of dull yellows, dark blues and rich olive tones, the latter such as were used by the English Pre-Raphaelite painters." [8] Special mention was given by the *Craftsman* to various other artists who displayed

at the Springfield Exhibition, including the Misses Glantz-
berg for their looming of hereditary Swedish designs; Mr.
Volkmar of Corona, Long Island, for his unusual pottery;
Miss Ellen Starr of Hull House, Chicago, for her distinguished bookbindings; the Misses Allen of Deerfield for their
photographic studies, used by John La Farge as source material for some of his murals; and, in modest reference to themselves, the United Craftsmen, for their examples of cabinet-
work, a Morris chair, a hall settle, and a bride's chest. "From
this brief notice of the Springfield Exhibition," concludes
the editor, "an idea may be gained of its importance and significance for the development throughout our country of the
lesser arts."

A special room at this exhibition was filled with the works
of the Deerfield Arts and Crafts Society, which was later
honored by an extensive article entitled "From Merton Abbey
to Old Deerfield." Here the transition of crafts from British
to American hands is again stressed; and the prime source of
the craftsmanship revival is once more named as Morris and
his co-workers. In particular the London Exhibition of the
Arts and Crafts Society in 1888 was a key event, for "ever
since that time there has been an increasing interest . . .
here in America in societies of Arts and Crafts, so-called, for
the production of household decorations of good design and
of hand workmanship." The Deerfield Association in particular "has done most excellent service in this revival of the
old arts." Acknowledging British influences, the group
nevertheless "is no blind follower of Medieval Italians or
English Pre-Raphaelites." For as Morris and Ruskin spoke
lovingly of the thirteenth century, the Americans appropriately look back for inspiration to their own Colonial days,

particularly in the beautiful embroideries of the "Blue and White Society." [9]

The Exhibition of the Guild of Arts and Crafts of New York next received notice. After its organization with only four members in January 1900, the Guild developed rapidly until it occupied a number of permanent studios and work-rooms at 132 East 23rd Street; and its members produced and displayed competent examples of sculpture, woodcarv-ing, etching, needlework, basketry, leatherwork, bead designs, and photography, as well as work in other media. The Guild, whose motto was "to advance the union of the Arts of Design with the Arts of Production," now purposed to establish permanent sales and display rooms. At this invi-tational exhibit, the hammered brass and copper work of the Busck Studios so impressed the editor of the *Craftsman* that he ran several full-page photographs with his review article. Many other individual contributors were named, especially Mr. and Mrs. Douglas Volk of Lovel, Maine, who sponsored a summer craft-colony of spinners, dyers, and weavers to produce unusual tapestries.

The issue of the *Craftsman* for August 1902, bearing a cover design and motto from William Morris—"That thing which I understand by real art is the expression by man of his pleasure in labor"—contained a major article on the orig-inal Boston Society of Arts and Crafts, and its permanent exhibition in its quarters at 14 Somerset Street. The basic "breadth and soundness of its principles" were indicated by this representative section quoted from its Constitution:

This Society was incorporated for the purpose of promoting artis-tic work in all branches of handicraft. It hopes to bring Designers and Workmen into mutually helpful relations, and to encourage workmen to execute designs of their own. . . . It will insist upon the necessity of sobriety and restraint, or ordered arrangement, of due regard for the relation between the form of its object and its use, and of harmony and fitness in the decorations put upon it.

The Society's division of its personnel into three groups of amateur Craftsmen, recognized Masters, and non-practicing Associates was approved. Among the art objects currently on display the editor of the *Craftsman* was particularly enthusiastic about the glazed pottery from Dedham, Newburyport, and Tulane University, and the excellent exhibit of tiles from the shops of William R. Mercer of Doylestown, Pennsylvania, who supplied his wares for Mrs. John L. Gardner's "palace in the Fens." The fine books of the Merrymount Press were also notable.[10]

The westward expansion of the organized crafts movement is indicated by the *Craftsman's* report of the third public exhibition held by the Crafts Society in Minneapolis in January 1903. This small but energetic organization showed examples of their own varied products, and displayed as well effective leatherwork as coverings for chests, trays, screens, and desks from the studio of Charles Frederick Eaton and Associates in Santa Barbara, California. Other talented exhibitors of leathercraft were Mrs. Amelia Center of Chicago, and the Society of Arts and Crafts in Dayton, Ohio. Also of unusual interest was a large display of handmade jewelry of all types by craftsmen in Chicago, New York, Cleveland, and Winchester, Massachusetts. The ceramics section represented the work of numerous artists in Dedham, Colorado Springs, and the Rookwood Pottery in Cincinnati; and the basketry produced by the women at Hull House likewise was outstanding.

As a whole the exhibit was the finest that the Society has yet given, and the organization is to be congratulated for obtaining so many and such varied specimens from choice collections. . . . The influence of the work so accomplished will be most beneficial and far reaching.[11]

In the same number of their journal the United Craftsmen announced the first major exhibition of their own products, to be held first in the Craftsman Building in Syracuse, then to move intact to Rochester, where it would be sponsored by the Mechanics' Institute of that city. A detailed report of this show appeared as the leading article of the subsequent issue, with ten full pages of photographic illustrations. A "marked artistic success," it was considered "an adequate representation of the actual state of American handicraft." Furthermore, "it has excited sufficient interest and comment to make the organization that conceived and executed it a center for furthering and fostering the decorative and industrial arts." [12] Exhibitors of national and international reputation were invited to send samples of their work; and all items for the show, according to the catalogue, were "selected and approved according to the law set by that prototype of craftsmen, William Morris, who counseled wisely: 'Have nothing in your houses which you do not know to be useful, or believe to be beautiful.'"

The principles of the new art evinced by the "Handicraft Movement" were again set forth; in brief, "the prominence of the structural idea . . . the absence of applied ornament . . . the strict fitting of all work to the medium in which it is executed . . . and the development of all possibilities of color, texture and substance." As a then-novel method of presenting to the public the desired effect, the United Crafts arranged several specimen rooms completely furnished with their own products, among which a paneled dining-room with fumed oak and leather furniture and hand-loomed drapes caused the greatest comment. New exhibits from abroad were also on hand, including distinctive metalwork from Birmingham, and china and electric lamps from the Maison Bing, Paris. The composite result was an exhibition showing a definite advance over preceding shows, in that the objects displayed lacked any affectation in method or form, and were in the editor's opinion a spontaneous expression of "good and beautiful design," highly encouraging to the handicraft movement as a whole.

From this period onward for a decade new crafts groups and associations sprang up all over America. On the one hand viewing the newcomers with enthusiasm—as "encouraging signs of the times"—on the other the *Craftsman* was troubled by the lowering of standards and the poor quality of goods produced. The Rhode Island School of Design, the Industrial Art League of Chicago, the Guild of Arts and Crafts in San Francisco, the Richmond Sketch Club in Indiana, and various other groups in Pine Bluff, North Carolina, Muskegon, Michigan, St. Louis, and elsewhere, held exhibitions. But, commented the *Craftsman*, "it is to be regretted that the larger portion of the objects so exhibited are of bad or indifferent workmanship, made from illy-combined materials, and are anything but simple." Nevertheless, "all these enterprises must be regarded as prompted by the active, widely-prevailing desire to further the cause of art allied to labor." [13]

The *Craftsman* frequently used this easy technique of reporting exhibitions for comprehensive coverage of the crafts field; but in addition numerous articles were printed on individual workers or groups whose products seemed noteworthy. After the more obvious local veins were exhausted, explorations were extended to more exotic topics, such as the Acadians in Louisiana, Doukhobors in Canada, and the Ojibway, Hopi, and other Indian tribes. Typical subjects here included Eskimo and Mexican leatherwork, architecture in Yucatan, Peruvian silversmithing, Philippine basketry, native

Hawaiian homes, Maori woodcarving, the making of batik, Korean pottery, and a wide variety of discussions on Japanese art and design. Traveling in the other direction, the editor's fancy selected such topics as the Donegal weavers, the Hazlemere Industries in Surrey, the Royal Worcester Potteries, a Belgian smithy, locksmiths of old Nürnberg, Swiss woodcarving, Armenian silverworking, music and art in Finland, Russian lacemaking, and Greek encaustic portraits, all of which presumably were of some interest to American readers curious about the arts and crafts in other countries.

Although the vast variety of material encompassed by the *Craftsman* may seem confusing, it is possible to trace some general editorial trends. The central enthusiasm, as the name of the journal indicates, lay in sponsoring and reporting the Arts and Crafts movement in America. An expansion of this basic interest was the concern with interior decoration, in which the craft products might be used. Dozens of illustrated articles argued for the ostracism of Victorian knick-knackery, and the development of simple, pleasing, unostentatious, functional arrangements of furniture and furnishings in dining rooms, living rooms, dens, kitchens, and so on. From this point the advance was logical to the presentation of complete house plans and model homes, together with garden arrangements and landscaping to set them off to greatest advantage. Almost monthly a new "Craftsman Home" or "Bungalow" was presented in detail, often with considerable architectural ingenuity and effectiveness. Ultimately in the estate of Gustav Stickley, the founder and "Master" of the United Crafts, appeared a very successful working out of his own ideas; for the "Craftsman Farms" in the New Jersey hills were eminently attractive with their long, low, rambling buildings of timber and stone, and the beautifully but informally landscaped gardens and grounds. Here, too, after he had moved his headquarters from Rochester to a new Craftsman Building in New York City, Stickley opened a private crafts and agricultural school for fifty underprivileged boys from the metropolis.

From its concern with crafts, interior decoration, and house planning, in which always "the artistic is not the eccentric, or the unusual, but rather the thing which frankly and perfectly meets the requirements and respects the limits of its use and office," [14] the *Craftsman* opened out its pages to the wider horizon of public architecture. Individual churches and cathedrals were described and analyzed; various state capitols, public libraries, and business structures were criticized; modern concrete construction was discussed; and in general, contemporary architectural trends and problems were clarified for the journal's readers.

The final sequence of the editorial policy followed in close logic—advocacy of city planning and civic improvement. Particularly in the final years of the *Craftsman* was this true; and these more comprehensive articles tended largely to replace the earlier, more limited craft-reports. The catastrophe in San Francisco served as a spectacular focus for discussions of urban planning and rebuilding; but slum clearance in New York, civic improvement in Boston, the making of the "New Chicago," plans for beautifying Cleveland, Baltimore, Philadelphia, or Butte, Montana—"the ugliest town on earth"—all were reported in this journal. The "Garden City Movement" was sponsored enthusiastically, as were all other moves supported to eradicate the blighted areas of our huge urban centers.

Also in its latter period, perhaps reflecting the decline of public interest in the Arts and Crafts movement as such, the *Craftsman* stepped completely outside of its own designated field and became in effect a journal of social discussion. Thus it presented articles on agricultural crops and problems, such as irrigation and reclamation; conservation of natural resources, particularly the forest reserves; truancy, juvenile delinquency, and various institutions of correction or of social service, such as the Berry Industrial School in Georgia; public health and prevention of disease; the social influence of the new automobile, with the resultant "Romance of the Road"; and even such subjects as the economic value of birds and the virtues of brown vs. white bread. But more extensive than these general discussions were criticisms and surveys of the contributions of many painters, sculptors, musicians, and writers. A few of these were from other periods or cultures, such as Hiroshige, Botticelli, Manet, Arnold Boecklin, Rodin, and Edvard Grieg; but the majority were contemporary Americans, including such significant figures as Lorado Taft, Saint-Gaudens, Daniel Chester French, John La Farge, Mary Cassatt, John Sloan, George Luks, and William M. Chase. The contemporary English designer, illustrator, and craftsman, Walter Crane—whose popularity in America is indicated in the following chapter—was also discussed at length.

Finally, the thick pages of the *Craftsman* were rounded out with the presentation of various public figures and men of letters—particularly those concerned with social betterment: Jacob Riis, Ida Tarbell, Carducci, Ibsen, Tolstoy, Jane Addams, Woodrow Wilson—the spread is considerable; and literature is represented by Whitman, Mark Twain, Joaquin Miller, Lafcadio Hearn, John Burroughs, John Muir, Jack London, and others.

But although the ramifications are wide and the variations many, the basic theme of the *Craftsman* in its career as a whole is unquestionably that of the Arts and Crafts movement; and its chief journalistic service is the detailed recording of the personalities and products associated with the crafts revival. Throughout its course, also, the journal maintained a strict consistency of principle; for the founder of the crafts revival, William Morris, held his place on his pedestal as "the great model of the free workman: a man who in life and in art represents the principles to which the *Craftsman* and the association of which it is the organ stand fully pledged." [15]

FIFTEEN

Walter Crane: British Arts-and-Craftsman in America

WALTER Crane, a close associate of William Morris, was second only to him in the development of the Arts and Crafts movement in England, and was also a very popular figure in the American cultural circles of his time. Known variously as an illustrator of children's books, painter of classical and allegorical scenes, decorator, director of the Manchester School of Art, poet, and lecturer on art and on socialism, he enjoyed such a general reputation that, on an extended visit to the United States, he was given the opportunity to meet a surprising number of important people. His own account of his grand tour is interesting because it both mirrors the reactions of a sensitive Briton to the peculiarities of American life, and shows the extent to which British arts and crafts were incorporated in the nineteenth-century American art pattern.

In the summer of 1891, after Crane had exhibited his work at the Society of Fine Art in Bond Street, his friend and entrepreneur, Henry Blackburn—"the pioneer of illustrated art catalogues"—suggested that he send the unsold remainder of the exhibition to the "Boston Art Museum" whose director, General Loring, was a friend of his. With all details agreed upon, Crane forwarded his collection across the Atlantic, and arranged to follow it himself in early October.

After sitting for his portrait to the Pre-Raphaelite sympa-

thizer, Theodore Watts (later Watts-Dunton), Crane sailed
from Liverpool for Boston on the *Cephalonia,* in company
with his wife and two children—one son being already in
Florida visiting friends. In the course of the eleven-day passage he made the acquaintance of the head of the Classical
Department of the Boston Museum, Professor Edward Robinson, who soon introduced him to the best Brahmin society.
An earnest public defense of the Chicago strikers in the Pull-
man troubles immediately brought down on Crane's head the
wrath of the "gold-topped" Bostonians, and the cancellation
of a club dinner in his honor; but he was more than solaced
by a spontaneous friendship with Edward Bellamy, the author
of the best-selling *Looking Backward,* and his following of
young "Nationalists," and by the opportunity to address a
Congress of Architects which met in the still uncompleted
Boston Public Library by McKim, Mead, and White.

In Boston Crane also visited H. H. Richardson's Trinity
Church to view the windows designed by Burne-Jones and
partially executed in Morris's glass, and others done by John
La Farge. To his artist's eye the contrast was interesting; and
his honesty is refreshing:

The English glass looked a little flat and thin beside the deep tone
and more pictorial effects, thick glass, and heavy plating of the
American, and the light being so much stronger than we are
accustomed to, seemed to penetrate the colour and dilute it.[1]

Dr. and Mrs. Edward Emerson invited the visitors to
Concord, where the Cranes found it "most interesting" to see
Emerson's old home and neighborhood, and to visit Walden
Pond, carried thither in "two-wheeled, hooded buggies,
which bounded over logs, young trees, or any obstacle in the
rough woodland tracks, in apparently the most reckless way."
Horace Scudder, editor of the *Atlantic,* asked for an article,

which in due course appeared as "Why Socialism Appeals to Artists." Winthrop Scudder commissioned Crane to do the illustrations for the Riverside Press version of Hawthorne's *Wonder Book*, and introduced him to the governor of Massachusetts; and among the literary folk he met Julia Ward Howe, E. C. Stedman, "Mr. Bayley-Aldrich, the poet," and Mrs. Margaret Deland.

After quick trips to New York and Hartford to deliver an Arts and Crafts lecture, "Design in Relation to Use and Material," Crane was invited by the Boston architect, Peabody, to visit a large estate called "Vinland" in Newport, in order to inspect *in situ* a frieze which Crane had completed to order in London. Among the "costly villas or would-be palaces which were rising up along the coast in all sorts of weird architectural fashions, and almost with the rapidity of mushrooms," Crane found "Vinland" to be at least well designed and coherent in character. To stress its Scandinavian tone the owner had incorporated interior decorations by William Morris, "whose hangings and wall-papers were everywhere"; and a Burne-Jones window which depicted the pre-Columbian Norse explorers voyaging across the Atlantic. Crane's own frieze illustrating "The Skeleton in Armor" he found "very suitably placed above plain oak panelling" in the dining-room; and he also inspected several stained-glass panels which he had designed and which had been manufactured at Morris's works at Merton Abbey.

As the beginning of a comprehensive Western tour, the Britishers, after expressing surprise at the enthusiasm called forth in Boston by the celebration of Thanksgiving Day, entrained for Niagara Falls and thence for Chicago. There they were entertained at his "Edgewater" estate by an expatriate English decorative artist for whom Crane had done some panel designs, Mr. Pretyman. With him Crane was taken to inspect the already burgeoning site of the 1893 World's Fair, where Crane was interested not only in the architectural plans but in labor conditions, of the carpenters in particular. Since his own exhibit had arrived for showing in the Art Institute, he received several invitations to lecture, and was particularly pleased to meet Henry Demarest Lloyd, then editor of the *Tribune* and outspoken defender of labor.

In January both the artist and the exhibit moved on to St. Louis, traversing meanwhile "a flat agricultural country of maize fields." Since the head of the art school there was British, Crane reported that they were introduced to "a very pleasant circle of friends." Then with due exclamations over the expanse of prairie and desert and the height of the Western mountains, they arrived in February in Southern California. Los Angeles, Santa Barbara, and San Francisco called forth colorful comments; then the long trek eastward was begun.

In New York again Crane called on a decorative art firm headed by an Englishman, J. R. Lamb, and his two sons, one of whom had previously visited the Cranes in England. Frederick Lamb escorted his guest to Newark to view a large church window of Crane's design, showing St. Paul preaching in Athens. In the course of his visit he also addressed the Architectural League, where he met John La Farge, and designed a special wallpaper for exhibit at the forthcoming Chicago World's Fair. Their mutual interest in socialistic principles led to a meeting with William Dean Howells; Brander Matthews introduced his lecture at the Century Club; at the Players' Club Crane met Kipling for the first time; Albert Bierstadt, whose monumental canvases of western scenes he knew well, became an acquaintance; and the Moncure Conways entertained their old friends.

On a trip to Florida to meet their son Lionel, Crane continued working on his colored illustrations for the *Wonder Book,* and then returned to Philadelphia where his exhibition had moved from St. Louis. Here Crane was interviewed by Samuel Gompers, President of the American Federation of Labor; he was particularly interested in the crafts courses initiated at the new Drexel Institute, and assisted in the formation of an Art Workers' Guild, on the pattern of the group then flourishing in London. In Philadelphia, too, he was honor guest at a banquet inaugurating the new "Arts Club" building, which had been designed by a British architect; here he met his fellow-illustrator, Howard Pyle, whose work he had "so often admired in the magazines." After arranging for another exhibition in Brooklyn, Crane returned with his family to Boston, where they were entertained by General Loring. An interim in a studio on Nantucket gave him opportunity to fill a commission for two large panels for a World's Fair building, to work on an illustrated juvenile history of America for the Prang Company of Boston, and to make preliminary sketches for his later oil, "Neptune's Horses." By the end of July the Cranes were homeward bound, their only disappointment the death of Whitman which prevented a visit to that "unconventional and free spirit." [2]

Crane was thus a familiar figure in America in his own person; and his various widely circulated publications further advertised his name. His *Decorative Illustration,* for example, was reviewed in *Scribner's* in the "Field of Art" section; and Russell Sturgis seized this opportunity to deflate Crane's assertion that the current French productivity in the decorative arts stemmed directly from Morris and the British movement. "The evidence that these workmen are influenced by English examples can hardly be said to exist, Mr. Crane to the contrary notwithstanding." This was borne out by the fact that Morris and his workers designed almost exclusively for flat surfaces with little use of the human figure, while the French were dealing with embossed and sculptured forms. "There is almost nothing in the work of the Frenchmen to show that they have ever seen the English designs at all." [3]

Nevertheless, no such doubt exists as to the relationship between the British craftsmen and the American; and Crane himself stands out as a versatile, talented, and energetic exemplar of the Arts and Crafts movement in its international aspects.

SIXTEEN

The Ruskin Commonwealth

IN ALMOST every age certain idealists dissatisfied with the current social structure have felt the urge to set up new and presumably perfect communities. From the days of the pre-Christian Essenes, through the monastic Middle Ages, and on into the present, dozens of religio-economic schemes for the ideal society have been tried and abandoned. Two general types have appeared in the United States, especially during the nineteenth century: small Christian sects, frequently of European origin, which adopted a form of communism as the best means of maintaining personal equality; and non-religious groups, often led by rationalist or utopian social reformers bound on creating a new collective order in opposition to the encroaching forces of capitalism.

Many names are familiar among the seventy experiments that have appeared in this country: the Shakers, the Amana Society, the Rappites or Harmonists, the Owen-New Harmony group, John Humphrey Noyes's Perfectionists—better known as the Oneida Community—and various Fourierist settlements or phalanxes. Brook Farm and Fruitlands are well known because of their literary associations. Certain groups of Mormons, Mennonites, and the House of David also belong to the general list of community-experimenters. Even the inhabitants of Zion City and Father Divine's "Heavens" follow in the train. In some of these projects communism yielded to "joint-stockism," by which each participant engaged in communal living and production, but received individual wages supplemented by interest on his personal capital invested in the enterprise. Various shades of socialism evolved, most of which bore the imprint of François-Marie-Charles Fourier (1772-1837), abetted in America by Robert Owen and Albert Brisbane. Here co-operation was an essential feature of an "agrarian-handicraft economy." [1]

But the ideas of John Ruskin concerning "Christian Socialism" and the better way of life also had some currency. One particular community experiment, although generally unfamiliar, is of pertinence here because of its name and inspiration. This was the Ruskin Commonwealth which led a troubled but typical career for less than a decade at the turn of the century.[2]

Its founder was J. A. Wayland, first known for the publication of his journal, *The Coming Nation*, at Greensburg, Indiana, which rapidly rose to a circulation of 60,000 in its championship of the people's interests. With the funds thus acquired the editor organized his colony on the general doctrines of Ruskin and Morris—to apply pragmatically some of his own social theories—and served for a year as the president of its controlling stock company. The location for the new settlement was bought sight unseen for $2,500 and turned out to be an unprepossessing spot of one thousand acres on the outskirts of Tennessee City, Tennessee, to which the printing plant was immediately moved. Here a sawmill was constructed and the crude shacks of the pioneer builders of an ideal society arose.

In August 1894 the group numbered nineteen men with their families. Each head of a household now subscribed $500 for one share of stock in the "Ruskin Co-operative Association." But the physical situation was unfortunate, for the water supply was inadequate, the land unproductive, and the ticks and chiggers prolific. The sharp discomforts of winter drove the settlers during the following spring to a pleasanter but less accessible site at Cave Mills, six miles from the railroad. Here, with an influx of new members, money, and energy, the Commonwealth built a three-story printery, set up a communal steam-laundry, improved the sawmill, developed farming and cattle raising, made but had trouble selling various agricultural tools and implements, and constructed a store where transactions were largely by means of scrip or "hour-points." A kindergarten was organized, classes in music and drawing begun, a special instructor imported for industrial arts, and plans for a college formulated, to be known as Ruskin University, or alternately as the College of the New Economy.

This experimental community attracted considerable local attention; and on their first Fourth of July in the new Ruskin (to which the Post Office Department had changed the name of Cave Mills) the settlers entertained a thousand guests at a free barbecue, with dancing to the music of a Negro band in the coolness of one of the huge cave chambers (and a nice profit for the hosts from the concessions).

By fall the Community had in operation not only its central press, but machine shops, a hotel, an entertainment hall, and its lower schools. Communal rather than competitive labor resulted in enough leisure so that the adults as well as the children could attend and enjoy many of the training classes in the applied arts. The university, however, never got beyond the planning stage.

The Community apparently prospered (in spite of inefficiencies and some personal frictions) and by 1899 owned 1,700 acres of land with considerable livestock and farm machinery. The press published commercially as well as serving local interests and specialized in labor and trade journals, of which some thirty-six were for a time printed at Ruskin. In this general state of success and solvency, the sudden collapse of the whole enterprise was all the more unexpected. In July 1899, all the Commonwealth's property was disposed of at public sale and all debts were paid in full. The root of the evil was personal antagonism held by the older charter-members against the newcomers whose majority rule controlled the life of the colony. A participant in the experiment later asserted that its disruption was also due to the lack of any controlling religious principle and the absence of any strong central leader—Wayland had withdrawn in pique and disappointment at the end of the first year. Furthermore, some "free-love-anarchistic trouble," as he put it, hastened the final collapse; and no system of "mutual criticism" existed, as in the more famous Oneida Community, for the elimination of contentions and misunderstandings.

In spite of these intramural troubles, the majority of the members of the Ruskin Commonwealth decided to reorganize, and accepted the invitation to amalgamate with the American Settlers' Co-operative Association at Duke, Georgia. To make the move, almost 250 Ruskinians chartered a train for $3,500 to convey themselves, the press, and their portable property the six hundred miles to their new location. The welcoming Co-operative added only thirty-five members to the Commonwealth, but owned some eight hundred acres and a number of houses. The new combined colony soon expanded into a town of its own with post office, railroad station, stores, repair shops and the rest, and developed new crafts and crops. Leagues, clubs, libraries, lyceums, and musical organizations flourished, and for many months the new Utopia was happy and harmonious. "But, alas!" recalled the chastened historian of the group, "the demon of strife again entered Ruskin, and there was clapper-clawing without end." Soon many dissatisfied members withdrew, some to return to Tennessee, and others to join such organizations as the Fairhope Single-Tax Association in Alabama, which was based on the doctrines of Henry George. A lengthy article in the *Coming Nation* for April 6, 1901, disclosed the demoralized conditions in the colony, the numerous secessions of its members, and the financial quicksands in which it floundered. A few months later the property of the New Ruskin Commonwealth was sold at auction, and another Utopian venture had disintegrated.

SEVENTEEN

Vachel Lindsay and Ruskin: Preachers of the "Gospel of Beauty"

> Now let each child be joined as to a church
> To her perpetual hopes, each man ordained:
> Let every street be made a reverent aisle
> Where Music grows and Beauty is unchained.
>
> Let Science and Machinery and Trade
> Be slaves of her, and make her all in all,
> Building against our blatant, restless time
> An unseen, skillful, medieval wall. . . .
> FROM "On the Building of Springfield."

I N THAT inchoate, apocalyptical vision of the year A.D. 2018 known as *The Golden Book of Springfield,* Vachel Lindsay presents a hard core of thought pertinent to the mid-twentieth century: the achievement of a World Government, and its defense against an insurrection by an Asiatic bloc.* But his more local metempsychoses together with his mystic wanderings about the universe under the tutelage of "Lady Avanel," his Beatrice, have almost a Cabellian tone; for as the "Thistle of Dreams" grows up about her, "I am the breath of the prairie, I am only the West-going heart," she murmurs, "and by that authority I speak to you, and by that authority I sow the thistle." [1]

* Since this point has not been thoroughly grasped by general readers, it is interesting to note Lindsay's later comment: " 'The League of Nations, it must and shall be preserved'—Something like this is the implication beneath all the political poems and the implication beneath the prose work, *The Golden Book of Springfield.*" (Vachel Lindsay, *Collected Poems,* N. Y., 1927, p. 24.)

Mixed with this thin fabric of fantasy there is, however, a solider substance from which the New Springfield of the next century is to be builded. The new city's star-shaped double walls had been constructed "long ago" by Ralph Adams Cram, the famed exponent of Gothic architecture in the Cathedral of St. John the Divine, who carried on the medievalism defended by Ruskin and the Pre-Raphaelites in both England and America. In Springfield's own cathedral the creed—with Ruskinian overtones—had become one of universal social service—with such saints as Lincoln and Johnny Appleseed enshrined side by side with Prince Siddhartha, the Buddha; and "St. Friend" presided over his "Order of the Blessed Bread" by mixing prayers, sermons, and flour for the better sustenance of his parishioners' souls and bodies. His apprentice, an orphan Tibetan boy, had graduated from the bakery to the design of "exquisite and slender sunset towers"—which one gathers were, among other things, high glass-walled restaurants to enrich the ceremony of dining— "of the school of Louis H. Sullivan and Frank Lloyd Wright." [2] And further concern with "social art" in its forms of functional architecture and city planning was evidenced in the star-plan of boulevards and the clusters or groups of cottages laid out in a non-geometrical complex rhythm suggested by the curves of the petals of a violet.[3] In passing it is interesting to note that the dominant structure overlooking the whole city was the "Truth Tower," otherwise known as the "Edgar Lee Masters Tower," around which were spotlighted circles of lesser campaniles.

Under this circumstance one must regard with some reserve Masters's subsequent evaluations of his fellow Prairie Poet in the only major biography of Lindsay that has appeared. The least restrained judgment occurs after a list of Lindsay's better poems: "I take the responsibility of saying that they constitute the most considerable body of imaginative lyricism that any American has produced." [4] Nevertheless, Masters's opportunity for close personal association and extended correspondence with Lindsay, and access to his subject's voluminous private journals, give his account—which honestly admits the weaknesses in Lindsay's poetry and personality—a unique value. Considerable internal evidence of the influence of Ruskin and the British Pre-Raphaelites on Lindsay's work is here clarified by specific assertions of his biographer.

In *The Golden Book of Springfield,* for example, it is apparent that Lindsay was inspired by the social thought of both Ruskin and Morris, and an American seer; and Masters further comments: "In this book he undertook what Morris and Bellamy had done in their way—with the result that it is neither good sociology nor good prophecy." [5] And as Ruskin's aim had been, so too Lindsay's "hope was to shape men and a new state by an irresistible influence of art." [6]

To this end Lindsay set out on his major westward pilgrimage in May 1912; his invocation was: "Let me gird myself for my roadside priesthood, the teacher of the mysteries of beauty in the church of Beauty." Or in a more colloquial phrase: "I was," he said, "a special *idea* on legs." And the idea was largely Ruskin's.

Lindsay carried with him on his journey a big scrapbook in an oilcloth case containing his devotional objects together with copies of his own selected poems. Its title page bore the legend, "Gospel of Beauty," and his prologue: "I come to you penniless and afoot to bring a message. I am starting a new religious idea" [7]—which embraced not only the love of the beautiful but as his creed further asserted, the economic gospel of the "New Localism," wherein self-sufficient, happy communities would develop their own spontaneous arts and crafts and would "strive to make their neighborhood and home more beautiful and democratic and holy with their special art." [8] Within the board bindings of the scrapbook Lindsay next placed a picture of Ruskin with a photograph of his home at Brantwood and a reproduction of his water-color of the Castello Vecchio, and then a variety of other materials such as pictures of Tolstoy, Bryan, and a statue of the Buddha.

In the course of his rambles Lindsay noted in his journal that he not only was filled with "Ruskinian prejudices" but even dreamed of Ruskin himself—as well he might, since for years he had been a devoted student of Ruskin, Rossetti, Burne-Jones, Millais, and Morris.[9] His acquaintance with Ruskin's works dated, in fact, from his years at Hiram College in Ohio where he had explored Ruskin's writings "to the full." "Ruskin must be learned as a whole. . . . The great inspirations in him are the elements of his soul." [10] Later at the Art Institute in Chicago he had turned again to Ruskin and from him to D. G. Rossetti, whose poetry impressed him deeply. (On his western trip he quoted from memory "The Blessed Damozel" and some Swinburne and Tennyson for the benefit of his fellow wheat-harvesters; and once in Georgia he delivered a lecture on Pre-Raphaelite poetry.) Rossetti's painting likewise seemed a landmark; for during his struggles with art in Chicago Lindsay had confided to his journal: "Let your work be the first of its kind since Rossetti." [11] Occasionally, before giving up his travel on foot, Lindsay visited city libraries in the West to refresh his knowledge of the British figures. That they remained uppermost in his mind is indicated by the fact that in one of the "Proclamations" used to conclude his Adventures While Preaching the Gospel of Beauty Lindsay envisages the achievement of a people's religion and a new social equality through the ministrations of new priests and statesmen. But these alone "cannot ripen the land" without the aid of artists—"men as versatile as William Morris or Leonardo." These artists "shall fuse the work" of all the other shapers of the new state into a coherent whole; and over all will be the spirit of new "Ruskins with a comprehension of equality." [12]

In spite of wide divergence in their social background, the similarities between the careers and ideas of Ruskin and Lindsay seem extraordinary, some indeed superficial, but some fundamental. The American hated the commercial materialism of his country as Ruskin despised the machine civilization of nineteenth-century England. Each felt the inescapable urge to preach the "Gospel of Beauty"—to rear a "skillful, medieval wall" against the vulgarity of his own day. In Lindsay, indeed, this drive resulted in a literal Messianic complex; for as Christ began his "service of suffering" at the age of thirty, so too Lindsay had declared:

I have a world to save, and must prepare, prepare, prepare. Then it will be for me to save my world. I will constantly expect at thirty years of age I shall choose the chance of utter suffering, and the spending of self to which I am best adapted.[13]

Lindsay, under maternal impulsion, had had aspirations to be a practicing artist, to illustrate as well as to preach his doctrines. But four years at the Chicago Art Institute, additional study at the Chase School in New York with Robert Henri as critic, and a tour of the European galleries (where he admired particularly the Louvre collection of Italian Primitives), did not create artistic ability where none had existed. Even R. W. Gilder at the *Century*, who might have been expected to look sympathetically on any expression showing Pre-Raphaelite associations, turned down Lindsay's illustrations for "Aladdin's Lamp" and some poems which he had submitted. Nonetheless the effort to combine plastic art and poetry is typical of the Pre-Raphaelite pattern. Here Lindsay's dual expression not only suggests that of Ruskin as artist and writer, but on a much lower level parallels D. G. Rossetti's production of sonnets on his paintings, particularly in his "Verses of an Especially Inscriptional Character," which Lindsay says were "songs of my student days, written for my drawings." In both Lindsay and Ruskin, however, no sound, integrated theories of art evolved; and there is inevitably a feeling of misdirected effort and unrealized intentions. It may be more than a coincidence, too, that in their domestic lives both men experienced a fundamental difficulty in personal adjustment. As Masters put it: "Lindsay as a God-intoxicated man was of a mind too disorderly and ill-disciplined, and too like Ruskin . . . to take love as one of the comforting blessings of life." [14] And there is a tragic parallel in the fact that both Ruskin and Lindsay suffered an ultimate mental collapse.

Although these biographical similarities may be only fortuitous, the effect of Ruskin's thought on his American disciple is clear. As one looks back on Lindsay's role in the American scene he appears in part an eccentric entertainer, in part a visionary but courageous prophet. His contribution to American letters, though certainly not "the most considerable volume of imaginative lyricism" produced in this country, is in a sense unique. Although he cited Poe, Whitman, and Milton as the "final impulse" in creating his poetry, his dozen finest poems are fresh and individual, and strictly his own. But in the realm of his social thought, among the many influences shaping his mind Ruskin is the individual most easily identified and most consistently followed throughout Lindsay's career.

EIGHTEEN

Samuel Bancroft, Jr.: Collector Par Excellence

O NE OF the two finest collections of British Pre-Raphaelite art and manuscript materials in America * is now to be found in the Delaware Art Center, owned by the Wilmington Society of the Fine Arts, in Wilmington, Delaware, where it is known as the "Samuel and Mary R. Bancroft English Pre-Raphaelite Collection." The story of its formation and growth over a period of thirty-five years, the result of an American art connoisseur's admiration of the work of Dante Gabriel Rossetti in particular, furnishes an integral part of the account of the Pre-Raphaelite movement in the United States.

In connection with his large cotton-manufacturing enterprises in Delaware, Mr. Bancroft made frequent business trips to England; but in 1880 one such experience took on particular significance. "My first great interest in the combined art and poetry of Rossetti," he recalled some twenty years later,[1] "was excited one beautiful Sunday afternoon, on a visit to the house of my friend William A. Turner, in Pendleton, one of the manufacturing suburbs of smoky old Manchester; and I shall never forget my shock of delight at seeing hanging behind my host at tea table the first Rossetti

---

* The collection of Pre-Raphaelite paintings and drawings in the Fogg Museum at Harvard was referred to in connection with Charles Herbert Moore, above. A considerable body of MSS at Duke University has been described in Paull Franklin Baum, ed., *Dante Gabriel Rossetti, An Analytical List of Manuscripts in the Duke University Library* (1931).

picture I had ever looked at. It was one painted at his best period, in the plenitude of his power."

Among the guests was Mr. Bancroft's British cousin, an artist and architect who had admired the Pre-Raphaelites for some time. "For the moment," continued the American, "I lost all consciousness of my surroundings, and my cousin Alfred Darbyshire, who was one of the few men of my own age who knew Rossetti personally (and his art), woke me up by saying, in broad Lancashire, 'Aye, my lad, thy een are on th' right object!'" On Bancroft's eager query as to what it was, his interlocutor rejoined: "Nay, keep looking at it; it's one of the most beautiful things in England." The visitor turned to his host and said, "Will, if Alfred will not tell me what it is, you must." And Turner replied, simply, "It is Rossetti's 'Fiammetta.'" *

Several years elapsed before Samuel Bancroft had the opportunity to begin his own collection of the works of the much-admired Rossetti and his fellows. On the death of the Manchester industrialist, Bancroft purchased from his estate in 1887 the small oil called "Water Willow," which was a portrait of Mrs. William Morris painted by Rossetti in 1871 while he was living with the Morris family. Kelmscott Manor, which Rossetti and Morris owned jointly, may be seen in the background; but the central head dominates the canvas in which the dark brown of the hair contrasts richly with the deep green-blue of the setting.

From this modest beginning the Bancroft Collection made rapid progress. In 1892 the large Leyland Collection was broken up for sale in London, and the American succeeded in buying a number of representative P.R.B. works. Among these was Sir Edward Burne-Jones's monumental "The Coun-

* Mrs. William J. Stillman had posed for this study of Boccaccio's mistress. See p. 46, above.

cil Chamber," one of a series of four to illustrate "The Legend of the Briar Rose," a German version of the "Sleeping Beauty" tale.* But he was more pleased by two Rossetti canvases, which today seem to be of varying merit. The first of these is the familiar "Found," which was the subject of much discussion when it was undertaken in 1854 (but never completed). Here an honest country carter—with the head of Madox Brown—succeeds in finding his old sweetheart, now starving, desperate, and betrayed—posed by Fanny Cornforth against a completely literal brick wall and city-street background, with a very real white calf in an equally real two-wheeled cart. After Rossetti left it unfinished, Burne-Jones added some sky and wall; and details of the distant wharves and river scene were contributed by W. T. Dunn. Because of its stress on "anecdote" or literary content its appeal for modern critics has declined; and its chief value now is as a document in Rossetti's development, since it illustrates excellently the artist's early concern with the familiar P.R.B. principle of exact rendition of model and setting.† That he left it unfinished, to go on to other more subjective work, may also be significant in his evolution as an

* The original series included "The Sleeping Princess," "The Garden Court of Her Maidens," "The Council Chamber," and "The Sleeping Guards and the Prince Arriving." These were purchased by Lord Faringdon in England; and two years after completing them Burne-Jones began a second series on a larger scale, of which this is one. The canvas measures approximately four by eight and one-half feet.

† It was spoken of as a "great picture," by the British scholar A. C. Benson who said further: "It is certainly his most characteristic Pre-Raphaelite work, perhaps his greatest achievement, though it was never finished." (*Rossetti*, N. Y. and London, 1911, p. 25.)

The first curator of the Bancroft Collection, Mrs. Jessie Rockwell, has commented on the artist's use of color: "It is a wonderful example of Rossetti's use of colors to express emotions, as he used words,—the cool grayish tones with violets and blues in a comparatively high key,—all tragic notes." (Letter dated May 29, 1948.)

artist, although he did think enough of it to compose a matching sonnet.

But the major purchase in 1892 was one of Rossetti's finest and most popular works, the "Lady Lilith." Rossetti had painted this first in 1864 from Fanny Cornforth, and later made two smaller versions in water-color.* But in 1872-73 he painted out Fanny's features and used Alexa Wilding as his model instead. The resulting canvas suggests with startling force the sensuous and calculating beauty of "Adam's first wife"—"the witch he loved before the gift of Eve." First called "Body's Beauty," as was the complementary sonnet in *The House of Life* sequence, it pictures the Lady Lilith "subtly of herself contemplative" as she combs her long rich-auburn hair. The white-robed figure is seated against a background of climbing white roses, and although each rose petal may be meticulously reproduced, and the reflections from the silver candlestick photographically high-lighted, there is an otherworldly air in the features of the central figure which could come only from Rossetti's subjective interpretation of the model, and not from any slavish copying of the original: —"And still she sits, young while the earth is old." That Rossetti by this time was comparatively independent of his model is further shown by his presentation of the same sitter in "La Bella Mano," of 1875, in a manner so different that— except for the familiar line of neck and shoulder—it would be almost impossible to identify the models as the same individual.†

Another of the Bancroft purchases at the Leyland sale of 1892 was the oil, "Mary Magdalene," painted in 1877. Although not so well known or so spectacular as the "Lady

* One of these, known as the "Coltart Lilith," is in the New York Metropolitan Museum.

† It has been suggested that Marie Spartali Stillman might have been the model for this painting, rather than Alexa Wilding.

Lilith," it is considered one of the best of Rossetti's later works.

From a different source Samuel Bancroft also succeeded in acquiring a unique Rossetti item, an experiment in water-color method in which the artist used gold and umber on white paper. The resulting monochromatic sketch, of the actress-model Ruth Herbert, had been made in 1858 as a pre-liminary study for a larger oil portrait. The story of its acqui-sition was fondly recorded by Mr. Bancroft, and may now be found in his manuscript catalogue of his Pre-Raphaelite col-lection.

Again in Manchester in the summer of 1892, he heard from his cousin Alfred Darbyshire that a mutual friend, T. Wilton Gillibrand, had a Rossetti which he was willing to sell. This sketch had originally been donated by the artist to a charity sale benefiting a painter-friend, Henry James Holding, had been purchased in due course by Gillibrand, and was now sold by him "at the appraised price" to Bancroft. A few days later the two men met at lunch at the Brazenose Club, where the following passage took place. "Gillibrand turned to me," recalled the American, "and said with a comical grimace, 'Damn you, Bancroft, for a thieving Yankee!' On asking what I had stolen he said, 'Why, my little Rossetti girl. I didn't know how much I had fallen in love with her until you came and carried her off under my eyes, and now I wish I had bought her myself instead of letting her go to America, whence she can never come back to me.'" [2]

Another interesting find had been made just before this episode. Some time in the first or second year of the decade when Mr. and Mrs. Bancroft were traveling in England, he had heard through Fairfax Murray that Rossetti's old model and mistress, Fanny Cornforth, now Mrs. Schott, was living in London with her son Fred Schott. Against Murray's wishes, he succeeded in getting her address and called on her at least three times. Now only the relic of her former beauty, she was suspicious of the American's motives and for some time insisted that he was only a dealer trying to get some Rossetti mementos for resale. Fairfax Murray, in his turn, warned Bancroft against the probability of his being exploited by Fanny as a rich American, but eventually the visitor convinced her of his real admiration for Rossetti, and his desire to make only a private collection. Under these circumstances she was glad for a little needed income, although she still had some sentimental attachment to the various items she sold. Bancroft's trophies included a wide variety of objects, such as the original Rossetti seal and monogram, several little elephant statuettes—of pertinence, of course, because of Rossetti's playful pet names for and frequent epistolary references to his "Dear Elephant." A number of old photograph albums contained irreplaceable pictures of the Rossetti family and a wide circle of friends. But most treasured of all were the extended series of Rossetti's own letters to Fanny,[3] often illustrated with whimsical marginal pen-sketches, and several dozen of the original manuscripts and clean copies in Rossetti's hand of his various ballads and sonnets.[*]

All of this material Samuel Bancroft added to the growing collection in his spacious home, Rockford, on the outskirts of Wilmington. By the end of 1892 his holdings were so extensive that, at the request of his friend Harrison Morris, who was the director of the Philadelphia Academy of Fine Arts, Mr. Bancroft agreed to send a number of Pre-Raphaelite paintings and other materials to the Academy for an exhibition, which opened on December 8 catalogued as "Examples

[*] A complete list of the Bancroft MSS of sonnets and ballads, including later acquisitions from the publishing house of Dent, is given in Appendix II. This list was kindly supplied by Mrs. Jessie Rockwell.

of the English Pre-Raphaelite School of Painters, including
Rossetti, Burne-Jones, Madox-Brown and others, together
with a Collection of the Works of William Blake." This was
the second major showing of British Pre-Raphaelite art in
the United States, the first having been arranged more than
thirty years before by William Michael Rossetti and his col-
laborators, in New York City.

The Blake collection was borrowed largely from Herbert
H. Gilchrist of London and Charles Henry Hart of Philadelphia, and a few Pre-Raphaelite water colors and drawings
from Charles Eliot Norton who, Bancroft had previously
noted, possessed "a few choice but small specimens." (Moncure Conway, who also had a small collection, apparently
was not asked to contribute.) A single Rossetti oil, a version
of the "Beata Beatrix," was loaned by the president of the
Chicago Art Institute, Mr. Charles L. Hutchinson. But the
vast majority of the items came from the Rockford collection,
and, for the edification of serious students of art, the exhibit
included extended series of the artists' preliminary studies
and sketches, and the Holyer photographic reproductions of
almost all the major works by Rossetti not available in this
country. In the more than one hundred catalogued entries
the most outstanding were, of course, the works already
mentioned, such as "Lady Lilith," "Found," "Mary Magdalene," an autotype from the original cartoon for "La Bella
Mano," and "Water Willow." A preliminary study for the
"Head of one of the Attendant Ladies in 'Dante's Dream'"
carried the note: "The sitter was Mrs. W. J. Stillman, then
Miss Spartali"; and a sketch for the "Head of Dante": "The
sitter was Mr. W. J. Stillman, art-critic and author." Mr. Bancroft had also acquired some of the preliminary studies for
the "Fiammetta" which had first awakened his admiration of
Rossetti, although he never succeeded in buying the finished

work. The water-color of Ruth Herbert was among the exhibits, as was the large Burne-Jones opus, "The Council Chamber." Frederick Shields was represented by his moving sketch, "The Dead Rossetti," dated Easter Monday, 1882, drawn as the artist unrestrainedly wept over the body of his dead friend. Ford Madox Brown's illustration of Byron's "The Corsair," was listed next to a water-color by Mrs. Dante Gabriel Rossetti; and Rossetti's and Bancroft's friend, Fairfax Murray, appeared as an artist in his own right with several portraits of children, an illustration for a Morris poem, and a design for a stained-glass window.

With his interest in the Pre-Raphaelites thus publicly demonstrated by the 1892 exhibition, Samuel Bancroft continued to build up his collection of paintings, sketches, manuscripts, letters, and personal mementos as they became available in public sale or by private arrangement; and he likewise assembled one of the finest private libraries in this country dealing with nineteenth-century English art and artists. The most memorable of his later additions was "La Bella Mano," painted by Rossetti in 1875 and acquired from W. Cuthbert Quilter in 1909. After his death in 1915 Mrs. Bancroft bought other outstanding canvases such as "Veronica Veronese," notable for the treatment of the model's green velvet robe and chestnut hair which matches the exact shade of her violin; this painting Mrs. Bancroft purchased in 1923 through Thomas Agnew and Sons, London, from the estate of Fairfax Murray. The same firm made possible the acquisition of Rossetti's water color, "Hesterna Rosa," a couple of years later. In 1931, Mrs. Samuel Bancroft, Jr., together with her son, Joseph Bancroft, and her daughter, Mrs. John B. Bird, offered this entire body of material to the Wilmington Society of Fine Arts as a memorial to its collector. The site for the construction of a new art center was also provided. Since

Mrs. Bancroft died before the building was completed, when the Pre-Raphaelite paintings, papers and books were moved from Rockford to the new Delaware Art Center in 1938, it was thought fitting that the material should be known as the Samuel and Mary R. Bancroft Pre-Raphaelite Collection.[4] As recently as 1947 the Wilmington Society of the Fine Arts added to the Bancroft Collection a water-color, "Mary in the House of John," which, after being bought in London by Miss Mary Garrett of Baltimore, eventually came into the possession of Bryn Mawr College. The first curator of the collection, Mrs. Jessie C. Rockwell, has done much to aid the public appreciation of both pictorial and manuscript materials.

Perhaps by coincidence, Marie Spartali Stillman, the girl who had posed for Rossetti's study of "Fiammetta" which aroused Samuel Bancroft's first fine enthusiasm for the British Pre-Raphaelites, later became his good friend and frequent correspondent; and through this connection the Stillmans' daughter Effie was commissioned to make a large portrait statue known as the "Bayard Memorial," now standing on the Park Drive, facing the Delaware Art Center. The various letters exchanged between the Bancrofts and Mrs. Stillman add a number of illuminating comments concerning the latter days of W. J. Stillman, the continuing reputation of Rossetti, and the personal relationships among the surviving members of the Pre-Raphaelite group.

When the Stillmans finally met Mr. Bancroft in England in the fall of 1900 he was already familiar to them by name. Fairfax Murray was a mutual friend, and Bancroft had already called on the Stillmans' architect son, Michael,[*] at

* Presumably named after the Stillmans' good friend, William Michael Rossetti. Michael Stillman and his wife Florence were proprietors for a time of the "Kelmscott Decorating Co.," at 134 East 25th St., New York (c. 1907).

his New York office, of which visit the latter "was not a little proud." Several years earlier, Bancroft had also purchased one of Mrs. Stillman's pictures. Following Mr. and Mrs. Bancroft's visit at their large estate, Deepdene, in Frimley Green, Surrey, he made a peculiarly appropriate gesture of appreciation, to which Mrs. Stillman replied:

It was indeed a delightful surprise to receive from you thro' Effie's hand the beautiful sonnet to Fiammetta in Rossetti's handwriting! Knowing how you treasure these relics of Rossetti, I feel all the more touched at your kindness in ceding this to me. Pray accept my warmest thanks. . . . We thought it so good of you to come so far to see us. We regretted your staying so short a time. . . .[5]

As a New Year's gift Mr. Bancroft sent the Stillmans a copy of Elisabeth Luther Cary's new book on the Rossettis. Marie Stillman's comments in reply reflect her sympathetic understanding of Dante Gabriel's character and eccentric genius:

I can understand . . . that anyone with a New England conscience can scarcely grasp the nature of the artistic temperament and its impulses always indulged in, its want of responsibility. For my own part Miss Cary seems to explain away any qualities short of heroic in Rossetti and to make too many excuses for deficiencies. We ought to accept a man of genius—and such a genius—with all his faults—and be thankful—neither criticise nor explain. Those who knew and loved him in those bright days when he was quite himself were under the spell of his splendid and imperious personality. . . . I suppose it is almost impossible to describe such a personality and give any approximate idea to anyone who had not known him in those best days.[6]

Reference to her own career as a painter is implicit in her thanks to Samuel Bancroft for his praise of her "Love's Messenger" (posed by her daughter Effie against the background of the Villa Borghese in Rome). As early as 1894

Bancroft had purchased another of her water colors, "Love Sonnets," (painted from the artist's blonde Italian maid in Rome) from the New Gallery in Regent Street; and he soon completed arrangements for this second composition. Both of these clearly belonged, as did the rest of her work, to the Pre-Raphaelite tradition, for as the British critic Percy Bate has pointed out: "The accomplished lady early fell under the personal influence of Rossetti, and it is not a matter of surprise that her work, such as the beautiful 'Persefone Umbra' or 'Love's Messenger,' betrays his inspiration." [7] Mrs. Stillman, herself, however, in a note to Bancroft mentions another primary influence:

It is always most flattering to me to be taken for a pupil of Burne-Jones, for of course I have loved his work of all periods as few others have, and he was always most helpful and good to me when I was in need of advice about my work, especially those latter years; but it was Madox-Brown who encouraged me to paint and I can never feel sufficiently grateful for his having given this immense interest to my life.[8]

Another of Mrs. Stillman's water colors which Mr. Bancroft wished to buy was her "Magic Garden," but this had already been purchased by Mr. T. E. Stillman, after display at Curtis and Cameron's. From time to time she sent him photographic reproductions of others, such as "Villa Landor Gardens" and "Upon a Day Came Sorrow Unto Me," but there are no other examples of her work in the Bancroft Collection. He was of course interested in her career, and congratulated her on the disposal to Boston purchasers of the "Wedding from the *Vita Nuova*" and "Kelmscott Manor." Also on occasion he was helpful in arranging a Philadelphia exhibition and sale of her works at Doll and Richards's and put in a good word for her concerning a commission from

Vassar College for a stained-glass window design.* She was appreciative of his concern, and after his purchase of "Love's Messenger" modestly wrote: "Lisa and Effie [her daughters] have told me about your pictures, so I feel rather anxious to think of my poor handiwork in such splendid company." [9]

Shortly after the Bancrofts' first visit to Deepdene, Stillman sent as a gift for the Rockford collection an autographed photographic copy of a sketch which Rossetti had made of him. Mrs. Stillman explained:

It was William who sent you a photo of the head Rossetti did from him, he thought you might like to have it as R. considered it one of his best drawings. The head in Miss Cary's book (Study for Dante) was done from the model Alexandro. D.G.R. made a study from William and said unless he would cut his beard off he could not use the head. I did not consent to this so the professional was called in. . . .[10]

Since in the finished version of "Dante's Dream" Mrs. Stillman herself appears as the figure at the right of the composition, it is perhaps regrettable for sentimental reasons that the substitution was made. But the sketch in question presents a bearded countenance of such serenity and benignity that Rossetti's title, "Study for the Head of Christ," is not inappropriate; it is of added importance since the artist himself ranked it so high among his productions. Another portrait of Stillman, by the artist Rouse, had been in the possession of Ruskin until the latter's death, and was then sent to Stillman who included it as the frontispiece in his autobiography.[11]

That Stillman's health was a matter of grave concern to his

* Other water-colors included "Bloom Time," 1876; "Dante with Beatrice," 1891; "Antigone," undated; and the "Enchanted Garden," 1889. In all probability the last is identical with the work referred to by Mrs. Stillman as the "Magic Garden." These have all been reproduced in the Copley Prints series, or by the American Water Color Society.

"Messenger of Love," by Marie Spartali Stillman

Portrait of Marie Spartali Stillman by D. G. Rossetti

family was indicated as early as January 1901, when Mrs. Stillman reported in a letter to Mr. Bancroft that he had been suffering from bronchitis and gout. After a slow recovery he was again in bed in March with "a bad relapse after such a long attack." His wife wrote: "The Doctor thinks him decidedly better but I cannot convince myself that he is out of danger, he is so weak. . . ." In June she reported:

I was glad to say that William is improving in health each week; today with the help of crutches he walked to the end of the passage to spend a few hours in a fresh room. He has suffered terribly and recovery at his age is slow. I shall now dread the winter more than ever on account of the risk of bad weather to his health.—We still have a professional nurse, and Lisa and Effie and I are also fully occupied with our invalid. . . .[12]

Under these circumstances his death in early July was comparatively unforeseen. Upon reading the announcement in the New York paper for which Stillman had once acted as art critic, Bancroft at once wrote:

The sad news from Deepdene which came to us through the Evening Post's notice of your husband's death on Monday night last, was unexpected after the last accounts of his convalescence. . . . All we can do is to tell you of our sympathy, which you know you have, and to express our grief at your loss. The corn was ripe to the harvest.[13]

Several weeks later, Mrs. Stillman acknowledged his note:

Many thanks for your kind words of sympathy. I ought to have written long ago to say how touched I was by your thought of us in our sorrow, but I have been overwhelmed with business to attend to, as for months I had been too cruelly preoccupied to see to anything. Notwithstanding the long illness, death came on us almost unexpectedly. My husband seemed to be recovering when a relapse occurred which was fatal.

It is well that he should not have had to drag on an invalided existence, but for me it is of course a changed world. Already so many friends have gone, and now this dearest of all companions and friends. . . .[14]

Only a few months before Stillman's death, their old friend, William Michael Rossetti, had published a volume of heterogeneous documentary material entitled *Prae-Raphaelite Diaries and Letters* which he dedicated to the Stillmans. Since some of the contents seemed to deal with very personal and perhaps inconsequential data, the book was not too popular among some of the remaining members of the Pre-Raphaelite circle. It caught the eye of Samuel Bancroft in America, and he could not refrain from commenting to Mrs. Stillman:

I have burrowed a bit into W. M. Rossetti's new book, and in spite of your being the Dedicatee, I must tell you what a friend of mine in N.Y. said of his work (I mean W.M.R.'s) of the past few years. "It is like the Hawthorne children. When they ran dry one would say to another,—'Come, let's dig up father!' W.M.R. had both brother and father-in-law to exhume, and he has now gone outside the family!" [15]

She was amused, and in due course responded:

I laughed much at what you told me. . . . Feeling as I do about such matters of publishing people's private letters, and having expressed myself very frankly on the subject to W.M.R., I was surprised at his wishing to dedicate the vol. to William and me. William wished us to accept the dedication—so that is why my name is there, and I felt touched at the way it was done much as I disapprove of such books. This one is such a salad of things the public cannot care about. . . .[16]

But William Michael was not easy to repress; and he insisted on another public declaration of his admiration for Mrs. Stillman, a few years later in his own *Reminiscences*. His affection for her was increased by the fact that his wife, the daughter of Madox Brown, had also been very fond of her:

Marie [Mrs. Stillman] had from an early age a great love and aptitude for pictorial art. She studied under Madox Brown along with his son and two daughters, and was the most intimate and most beloved of all Lucy's female friends, both before and after marriage. I will not here renew my panegyric of this most gracious, gifted, and amiable lady: she neither needs it nor likes it. My daughter and I continue to enjoy the privilege of her friendship.[17]

Over this period, following the death of Stillman, Mr. Bancroft continued corresponding not only with Mrs. Stillman but also with her daughter Effie, concerning the matter of the Bayard statue in Wilmington. As early as 1900 the citizens of that city wished to have a memorial made to honor a famous son, the Hon. Thomas F. Bayard, Senator and first U.S. Ambassador to England after that diplomatic post was raised from a ministry. Several sculptors were invited to submit models, among them Effie Stillman, who previously had produced a marble memorial tablet for the Calcutta Cathedral and a bronze relief for Bath College. After an exasperating series of delays and extended arguments among the committee members, Bancroft wrote:

July 29th, 1902

My dear Miss Effie:

I have been so disgusted with the whole management of the matter . . . that I have made up my mind as follows—If I remember rightly you told me that you would make the statue for £1,400, or $7,000. Now, if you still are of the same mind, and feel that you can do it justice, you may write to Mr. England, as Secretary of the Association, that an American friend of yours and of Mr. Bayard, if the Ass'n will accept your statue and will furnish the pedestal and setting, has offered to donate the statue to them. He, and they, are not to know who the donor is. If it comes out in later years, without any agency of mine, I don't care. . . .

At the same time he also gave Effie a commission for a small medallion portrait of himself. Mrs. Stillman was immensely pleased, too, and reported that if Effie wished aid and advice Augustus Saint-Gaudens had offered to help her if the work were done in America.* After several years of work she finally delivered the finished statue, which was mounted on a pedestal designed by her brother Michael, and unveiled in June 1907. Ironically, the special invitation to the sculptor had gone astray in the mails, and Effie Stillman felt quite hurt at what appeared to be a serious oversight. Bancroft assured her:

I am delighted with it and the verdict is general that it is a success, artistically and otherwise. Tom Bayard told me that when the veil fell from it the likeness "gave him a shock,"—it was so perfect and so strong.[18]

Over the years following Stillman's death his wife returned with added energy to her art work as a means of consolation. She spent much time with her aged parents on the Isle of Wight, traveled often to Rome, Venice, and Florence to escape the English winters, visited Mrs. William Morris and painted the gardens at Kelmscott, and was a frequent visitor to the National Gallery. She exhibited her work and enjoyed moderate sales in Boston, New York, and Philadelphia; and in 1904 and again in 1908 she experienced the hospitality of the Bancrofts' home. Letters to them gradually became fewer, and in 1913 Mr. Bancroft wrote to Michael for recent news of the family. He replied that his sister Effie had died in 1911; that his mother had recently suffered a broken arm, but had recovered rapidly and was living happily in London with her daughters Lisa and Bella and their families. Michael himself had prospered in his profession as architect, and

* Saint-Gaudens also acted as something of a patron in relation to young Michael Stillman, who was reported by his mother in 1905 as "still in Cornish [Vermont] overlooking Mr. St. Gaudens' work. I hope he has learned many practical lessons during the winter. . . ."

invited the Bancrofts to visit him at his new home in Essex Fells. Samuel Bancroft himself died only two years later, on April 22, 1915.

The Samuel and Mary R. Bancroft English Pre-Raphaelite Collection as it now stands is unique in its comprehensiveness. In addition to the Pre-Raphaelite paintings and sketches, it contains some forty-five manuscripts of Rossetti's poems, ninety letters written by him and others of the group, all of the editions of Rossetti's poems brought out by himself or his brother William, the proof sheets of the 1870 edition as corrected by Rossetti, and several first editions of Christina Rossetti's poems. The *Germ*, the *Oxford and Cambridge Magazine*, and Stillman's *Crayon* are on the shelves, together with a superb art reference library and wide collection of criticisms, memoirs, and letters concerning figures prominent in the later nineteenth century. But more important than the material canvases and manuscripts is the fact that the Bancroft Pre-Raphaelite Collection serves as the record and memorandum of Anglo-American artistic sympathies and warm human relationships.

—and Others

W ALTER CRANE, the English artist and craftsman whose work was so well received in this country, once attempted to analyze the components of the British Pre-Raphaelite movement. His definition, so inclusive as to be almost amusing, suggests at least the complexity of the so-called Pre-Raphaelite attitude: "It was primitive and archaic on one side; it was modern and realistic on another, and again, on another, romantic, poetic and mystic, or again, wholly devoted to ideals of decorative beauty." [1]

Most of these variant aspects were exemplified in the work of the central figures of the American Pre-Raphaelite developments already described. But further random associations may be found, both personal and literary, which indicate the extent of English and American relationships within the frame of Pre-Raphaelite reference.

In general the traffic was in the westward direction, but a number of American men and books reached the Britishers on their home shores. Buchanan Read, W. J. Stillman, Joaquin Miller, Charles Herbert Moore, John La Farge, Whistler, and others, as we have seen, knew individually the men of the Brotherhood. But in addition, by benefit of his works alone, Edgar Allan Poe was one of the most admired Americans.

Rossetti's acclaim of Poe is widely known. The most famil-

iar incident concerns the origin of "The Blessed Damozel."
After reading "The Raven" Rossetti believed that Poe had
exhausted the possibilities of expressing the grief of a lover
left on earth, and determined to reverse the conditions in a
sort of "counterstatement" to describe the sorrow of the one
in heaven. Beyond this simple thematic frame, however, there
is no discernible stylistic influence. "The Raven" continued
to be one of Rossetti's favorite poems, and frequently he
recited it, together with selections from Browning and Tennyson, for the pleasure of the assembled Brothers. He also
enjoyed "Ulalume," though of this work he composed a
burlesque, in the words of William Michael—"now lost, I am
sorry to say. I forget what may have been the subject of this
parody of Poe's strangely haunting poem." [2] As late as the
1880's, when Dante Gabriel was on the verge of physical
collapse, Hall Caine recalled that in their cottage in the Vale
of St. John, Rossetti would break the monotony of his sleepless nights by declaiming not only his own works but "repeat-
edly, also, Poe's 'Ulalume' and 'Raven.' Even yet I can hear
the deep boom of his barytone rolling out like an organ that
seemed to shake the walls of the little room." [3]

Most of Rossetti's friends shared his feeling. The news of
Poe's death—at that time believed to be suicide—had come to
them one evening while gathered at Coventry Patmore's, and
had profoundly depressed them all. Shortly afterward Patmore at Woolner's read a number of Poe's tales aloud, "to his
own great satisfaction," as W. M. Rossetti reported it. "He
considers Poe the best writer that America has produced." [4]
Christina Rossetti, on her brother's recommendation, agreed
that "Arthur Gordon Pym" must be "beyond measure interesting," and looked forward to reading it. [5] But among the
various enthusiasts for the prose tales young Edward Burne-
Jones at Oxford was the most outspoken. "One thing I am

most ashamed to mention," he wrote to his father, "viz. the spell that man Poe throws around me. His book of horrors is by me now. I know how contrary to all rules of taste are such writings, but there is something full of delicate refinement in all that hideousness." He comments individually on a half dozen tales: the "Fall of the House of Usher" is "very grand, almost my favorite"; "The Gold Beetle" [*sic*] is "a beautiful story"; and others are "marvelously startling." He assures his father, however, that although Poe at present is "lord of the ascendant," the "charm is temporary." But "in spite of this forecast of indifference," commented Burne-Jones's biographer, "Edward's estimate of Poe's work always remained high, and a harsh and inaccurate memoir published after Poe's death gave him acute distress. . . . I remember his joy in 1874 on the appearance of Mr. Ingram's edition of Poe's works, with a 'Life' which refuted these accusations, and how he hastened to get the book." [6] An earlier edition of Poe's poems, made in 1857 for Routledge by William Allingham, also indicated the practical interest of the Pre-Raphaelites.

Through the eyes of this same Irish poet we are given an intimate glimpse of Hawthorne. Allingham, who served as Customs-House Officer for several years in his native town of Ballyshannon, published a volume of verse in 1850; and in 1854 he gave up his official duties in order to settle permanently in London. En route he visited his fellow government-servant and man of letters.

I called on him at his Consul's office, a dirty little busy place on the line of the docks, and was very kindly received. He happened to have heard my name. He is about forty-six years old, middle-sized, hair dark, forehead bald, features elegant though American, cheeks shaved, eyes dark. He is very bashful in manner, and speaks little and in a low tone. He has not yet had time to visit

London, but intends to do so some time in Spring, when I hope
to see more of him. He looked oddly out of place in Liverpool. . . .[7]

An entry in Hawthorne's *English Notebooks* yields a complementary report:

There came to see me the other day a young gentleman with a
moustache and a blue cloak (of rather coarse texture) who
announced himself as William Allingham, and handed me a copy
of his poems. . . . His face was intelligent, dark, rather pleasing,
and not at all John Bullish. . . . We talked awhile in my dingy
and dusky cònsulate, and he then took leave. His manners are
good, and he appears to possess independence of mind. On looking over his poems, I find some good things among them.[8]

A few weeks later Hawthorne sent to the American publisher
Fields a review copy of Allingham's *Poems* with a note urging suitable publicity; and in the following year he transmitted to Ticknor copies of *Day and Night Songs* with the
comment that he hoped Allingham could establish a reputation in America. In 1861 Hawthorne's publishers brought out
an edition of the Irish poet's works.

Before he left his Liverpool consulate for Italy, Hawthorne
in 1856 belatedly made the thirty-mile trip to Manchester
where he was entertained by Francis Bannoch, poet and busi-
nessman, one of his closest friends in England. In the process
of seeing the few sights offered by this "dingy and heavy
town" the two men dropped into the art firm of the Messrs.
Agnew. There Hawthorne saw his first example of Pre-Raphaelite painting, and his remarks characterize his philosophy
of art:

There was a new picture by Millais, the distinguished Pre-
Raphaelite artist, representing a melancholy parting between two
lovers, or a husband and wife. The lady's face had a great deal of
sad and ominous expression; but an old brick wall, over-run with

foliage, was so exquisitely and elaborately wrought, that it was hardly possible to look at the personages of the picture. Every separate leaf of the climbing and clustering shrubbery was painfully made out; and the wall was reality itself, with the weatherstains, and the moss, and the crumbling lime between the bricks.

Then his evaluation:

It is not well to be so perfect in the inanimate, unless the artist can likewise make man and woman as lifelike—and to as great a depth too—as the Creator does.[9]

The famous Manchester Exhibition of the following year was the focus for some of Hawthorne's most explicit comments on art in general and the Pre-Raphaelites in particular. After his term as consul expired, he settled with his family in the suburbs of that city ("ugly as only the British know how to make it") from the end of July until early September; and during the summer he visited the exhibits a dozen times, as his fellow-American, John La Farge, did in the course of his European jaunt. Untrained and unsure of himself as an art critic, Hawthorne began his tours with diffidence: "Nothing is more depressing than the sight of a great many pictures together." After his first visit he had only faint praise: "Viewed hastily . . . it is somewhat sad to think that mankind, after centuries of cultivation of the beautiful arts, can produce no more splendid spectacle than this." But on closer acquaintance, some pleasure was finally aroused by Hogarth, whose work clarified Hawthorne's belief that pictures are "all excellent in proportion as they come near to ordinary life." Sir Thomas Lawrence was graceful but tricky; Reynolds was "not quite genuine"; Copley was "gifted" but ineffective; Turner's "light-colored pictures" were so much "painted gingerbread."—"Hogarth is the only English painter, except in the landscape department; there is no other (unless it be some of the modern pre-Raphaelites) who interprets life to me at all."

Deft transcription of the natural object was not for Hawthorne's New England conscience a sufficient end of art. Further observation of P.R.B. paintings convinced him of their double worth, and he soon declared:

> The only modern pictures that accomplish a higher end than that of pleasing the eye—the only ones that really take hold of the mind (and they do it with a kind of acerbity, like unripe fruit)— are the works of Hunt, and one or two other painters of the pre-Raphaelite school. They seem wilfully to abjure all beauty, and to make their pictures disagreeable out of mere malice; but, at any rate, for the thought and feeling which are ground up with the paint, they will bear looking at, and disclose a deeper value the longer you look.

Although every detail in the compositions seems to be "taken directly out of life and reality," the results are strangely "stiff and unnatural"; and the objects appear to be pasted upon the canvas. "Accomplishing so much, and so perfectly," Hawthorne meditates, "it seems unaccountable that the picture does not live. . . . Perhaps these artists may hereafter succeed in combining their truth of detail with a broader and higher truth. . . . Nature has an art beyond these painters."

Hawthorne does not mention the Rossettis; and his associations with any other P.R.B. artists were slight. At the Exhibition one day he saw Woolner at a distance, "a small, smug man, in a blue frock and brown pantaloons," showing Tennyson around the galleries; but Hawthorne was too reticent to introduce himself. By the end of the summer he felt himself sufficiently a connoisseur to settle on the old Dutch Masters as the greatest artists, because they seemed to exceed the Pre-Raphaelites in the depth of their work: "It is strange how spiritual, and suggestive the commonest household article—an earthen pitcher, for example—becomes when represented with entire accuracy. These Dutchmen get at the soul of common things, and so make them types and interpreters of the spiritual world." Ironically, however, Hawthorne still clung to the Puritan suspicion of beauty, as his valedictory comment on the Exhibition so clearly shows: "Doubtless, I shall be able to pass for a man of taste, by the time I return to America. It is an acquired taste, like that for wines; and I question whether a man is really any truer, wiser, or better, for possessing it." [10]

In London shortly thereafter Hawthorne visited Marlborough House to see Turner's pictures, without much satisfaction. "I mean to buy Ruskin's pamphlet at my next visit, and look at them through his eyes." He had previously fortified himself with a library copy of *Modern Painters;* but this work, together with a visit to the National Gallery, failed to affect his opinion that "a picture ought to have something in common with what the spectator sees in Nature."

After missing him twice at the British Museum, Hawthorne met Coventry Patmore in January 1858, just a few days before his departure for Italy. As usual, he noted the encounter in his journal:

We had read his Betrothal and Angel in the House with unusual pleasure and sympathy, and therefore were very glad to make his personal acquaintance. He was a man of much more youthful aspect than I had expected, looking younger than his real age, which he told us is thirty-four . . . a man very evidently of refined feelings and cultivated mind, but, it seemed to me, not exhibiting altogether the air of an English born-and-bred gentleman.

The two authors expressed admiration of each other's works; and Hawthorne remarked that (thanks in part to Buchanan Read's efforts) his new friend's popularity seemed greater in the United States than in England. Patmore replied "that it was already so, and he appeared to appreciate highly his American fame, and also our general gift of quicker and more subtle recognition of genius, than the English public." The two men on parting made plans to meet in Italy, since Read had invited Patmore to visit him there.[11]

On March 14 Hawthorne dined with Read in Rome; and although Patmore could not arrange a trip that promptly, another Englishman in the group served to prompt Hawthorne's final judgment on the Pre-Raphaelites. The British sculptor Gibson, long an habitué of Rome, discoursed on his own classical principles—to discover the spirit of the Greeks and to apply it to his own work—and concurrently condemned "the Pre-Raphaelite modern school of painters," an attitude sure to strike Read himself because of his earlier associations with them in London. As for Gibson's classical leanings, Hawthorne commented in his notebook:

A doctrine fair enough, I should think, but which Mr. Gibson can scarcely be said to practice. . . . The difference between the Pre-Raphaelites and himself is deep and genuine, they being literalists and realists, in a certain sense, and he a pagan idealist. Methinks they have hold of the best end of the matter.[12]

In England again, another peripatetic American, Emerson, met some of the Pre-Raphaelite circle through Allingham, sometime after that poet's initial encounter with Hawthorne. When Emerson and his daughter were visiting London, this reader of the *Essays* escorted them on a sightseeing tour to Milton's tomb, the Tabard Inn, and the grave of an ancestor, William Emerson, "who lived and died an honest man, 1695." Allingham's diary continues: "I show E. my little green edition of his *Eight Essays*, which I have long carried in my pocket; he looks carefully at my pencil marks. His daughter says, 'That's just what father likes to see, hints of real opinions. . . .' E. asks what my marks mean—'What is +500?' (Sin is but defeat.) A: 'That the statement is 500 times questionable.' After a short discussion E. said smiling, 'I agree with the author.' " As a token of his high opinion of his Irish friend, however, Emerson offered to make a selection of his poems for publication in America; [13] and he also transcribed in his journal Allingham's "Morning Thoughts."

Emerson knew another figure on the near-fringe of the Brotherhood, William Bell Scott, a native of Edinburgh and once master of the School of Design at Newcastle. D. G. Rossetti had written him to praise some early verse, and when Scott visited London in 1847 he became acquainted with the Rossetti family and remained an associate of the Pre-Raphaelites for some years. A major religio-didactic allegory entitled *The Year of the World* (one section of which largely paraphrased the *Bhagavad-Gita*) Scott had sent to Emerson, on the presumption of his interest in Indian philosophy. On its arrival Emerson had written:

. . . . I received on Saturday your book, with the kind note accompanying it. I certainly did not read the poem through at one sitting, but I found that it concerned me very much. . . . It was a great satisfaction to find the Bhagavat Geeta [sic], which I unwillingly left in my library at Concord, here fairly and wonderfully understood in England. . . .[14]

When Emerson visited Newcastle on his lecture tour he inquired for the author. "This brought us together," wrote Scott, "and I found a lovely and noble American nature—a man of a type I had never met before, a man to honour and yet to be at home with at once, a wise and childlike nature who wanted no recognition or sympathy, modest, and yet altogether self-contained. . . ." [15] As one result of this meeting, when Emerson went on to Edinburgh he sat for a portrait to William Bell Scott's brother David, the canvas eventually finding its way to the village library at Concord. On another visit twenty years later, Emerson made a point of calling twice on William Bell Scott, then living in Chelsea. Scott proudly reported these visits to his American correspondent, Moncure D. Conway; and in this letter he passes on Emerson's succinct verdict on Pre-Raphaelite poetry:

The one thing I specifically remember of his talk . . . was in reply to my asking him why the Rossettis received *comparatively* little attention in America. His answer I have never forgotten and never will, though at the time it hit my love and admiration for DGR's poetry rather hard, yet the more I thought over it, the truer it appeared. His answer was this: "We like our own period and what is vital in these days about us, especially in poetry, but the Rossetti work is not touching us—it is exotic. . . ." [16]

Emerson was also cognizant of the activities of the American Pre-Raphaelites. He had heard of W. J. Stillman first through his journal, the *Crayon,* and had met him briefly in Boston late in 1854. On May 5, 1855, William Emerson had written to his brother that he had seen three numbers of this new magazine and had found material of interest: an extract from an account of Emerson by George Gilfillan (a Scot known for his *First Gallery of Literary Portraits,* whom Emerson had visited in Dundee [17]) and three papers by the American sculptor, Horatio Greenough. Emerson cautiously replied: "If you please, & continue to please, you shall send them to me, these three; I am not prejudicing thereby my right & duty to subscribe still to the work, if I will & can." On May 15 he acknowledged their receipt and added: "The passages from Greenough are excellent." [18]

The Adirondack Club served as the means by which Emerson and Stillman became close friends. While the expedition of 1858 was in the process of organization, Emerson sent a note to Lowell: "I was setting forth an hour ago to find Mr.

Stillman & yourself as heads of the Adirondac [sic] party; but learning just now that Mr. S. does not live in Cambridge, & that it was doubtful if you were at home, I shall check my social zeal till Saturday." [19] Stillman later informed Emerson that he would precede the other members and that Lowell was to convey all necessary instructions. Stillman also suggested that Emerson need bring no gun, since a large assortment would be available.[20] Longfellow, who had been urged by Stillman to join the party, parried: " 'Is it true that Emerson is going to take a gun?' he asked me. 'Yes,' I replied. 'Then I shall not go,' he said; 'somebody will be shot.' " [21]

With all details well in hand, the Adirondack Club proceeded to the deep woods. The entry in Emerson's journal for August 2, 1858, written at their headquarters on Follansbee's Pond, declared: "It should be called Stillman's henceforward, from the good camp which this gallant artist has built, and the good party he has led and planted here for the present at the bottom of the little bay which lies near the head of the lake." [22] Stillman commemorated the occasion by a very photographic oil painting (given by Judge Hoar to the Concord Public Library), in which Emerson is pictured standing alone in thought between two groups of his companions: in the first, Agassiz, Dr. Jeffries Wyman, and Dr. Estes Howe with John Holmes watching the dissection of a fish; and in the other, Stillman himself giving instructions in handling the rifle to Lowell, Dr. Binney, Horatio Woodman, and Judge Hoar.

Emerson's high pleasure in the primeval forest is evident in his familiar verse-record, "The Adirondacs, A Journal Dedicated to my Fellow Travellers in August, 1858." It is particularly fitting that this should include a tribute to "Stillman, our guides' guide, and Commodore,/Crusoe, Crusader, Pius Aeneas. . . ." [23] On the spot in his forest notebook Emerson was moved to more elaborate laudation of their "chief," in which he celebrates both his personal qualities and artistic abilities:

> Gallant artist, head and hand,
> Adopted of Tahawus grand
> In the wild domesticated,
> Man and Mountain rightly mated,
> Like forest chief the forest ranged
> As one who had exchanged
> After old Indian mode
> Totem and bow and spear
> In sign of peace and brotherhood
> With his Indian peer.
>
> Easily chief, who held
> The key of each occasion
> In our designed plantation,
> Can hunt and fish and rule and row,
> And out-shoot each in his own bow,
> And paint and plan and execute
> Till each blossom became fruit;
> Earning richly for his share
> The governor's chair,
> Bore the day's duties in his head,
> And with living method sped.
> Firm, unperplexed,
> By no flaws of temper vexed,
> Inspiring trust,
> And only dictating because he must.
> And all he carried in his heart
> He could publish and define
> Orderly line by line
> On canvas by his art.
>
> I could wish
> So worthy Master worthier pupils had—
> The best were bad.[24]

Whitman, as well as Emerson and Hawthorne, had some personal connections with the Pre-Raphaelites, particularly through W. M. Rossetti's English edition of his works. The presumed line of contact was devious. A book-pedlar took a copy to England where it was first discovered by Thomas Dixon, the "working cork cutter of Sunderland," who enjoyed a certain fame as the "Working Man" addressed in Ruskin's letters in *Time and Tide*. Dixon reported his find to William Bell Scott in Newcastle, who at once sent the volume to W. M. Rossetti.[25] And as Charles Rowley, a Manchester Ruskinite and friend of the Pre-Raphaelites put it: "William Rossetti launched this great modern spirit upon us." [26]

While William Michael gladly accepted credit for the first English edition of Whitman, he pointed out that others had preceded him in sympathetic reviews, in particular George Henry Lewes, as early as 1856. But he himself had known the *Leaves of Grass* "almost as soon as it was published." He had read it "with great delight: not supposing that it is impeccable in taste, or unassailable in poetic or literary form, but finding in it a majestic and all-brotherly spirit, an untrammelled outlook on the multiplex aspects of life, and many magnificent bursts of sympathetic intuition allied to, and strenuously embodying, the innermost spirit of poetry." [27] He wrote a strong defense of Whitman for the *Chronicle;* and when Mr. Camden Hotten, the publisher of Swinburne's poetry, invited him on the basis of this article to make a selection of Whitman's *Leaves* he agreed. This appeared in 1868, with a second edition in 1886.

In June 1869 Madox Brown handed to Mrs. Anne Gilchrist a copy of Rossetti's *Selections from Walt Whitman.* The Rossetti family had known the Gilchrists for almost a decade; and when Mr. Gilchrist died of scarlet fever in 1861, leaving unfinished his *Life of Blake*, the Rossetti brothers, impressed with her "strong sense—common sense and mental acumen combined," had helped his widow to complete and publish the work. Now, in 1869, Anne Gilchrist picked up the Whitman volume with feelings "partly of indifference, partly of antagonism," but was immediately fascinated. "Since I have had it, I can read no other book; it holds me entirely spellbound," she wrote to the editor.[28] Rossetti thereupon lent her the complete works which she read "without shock"; and although she found "some things to demur to" she wrote him a number of letters "in a truly fervent and exalted strain." The gist of these, Rossetti noted in his *Reminiscences*, "was published later on in an American periodical named the *Radical*, and, to my judgment, nothing better has ever been said about Walt Whitman." [29] This article, "A Woman's Estimate of Walt Whitman (from Late Letters by an English lady to W. M. Rossetti)," appeared in May 1870, and owed much of its final form not only to Rossetti's original suggestion to publish but also to his specific aid in shaping the manuscript.

The well-publicized story of the subsequent relationship between Whitman and Mrs. Gilchrist is extraneous here; but some of Rossetti's incidental correspondence with the principals is informative. His own contemporary evaluation of Whitman is explicit in a letter of July 13, 1869, to Mrs. Gilchrist:

All you say about Whitman delights me beyond measure: it is the earnest of the boundless enthusiasm he will one day excite, & continue exciting for ages—tho' where to find the other woman who wd. be true-hearted and brave enough to express herself with the decision & perfectness of perception wh. I find in your letters I know not for yet awhile. I quite agree with you about the glorious music that Whitman commands. . . .[30]

Whitman, in turn, expressed his heartfelt thanks to his English supporters in a note to Rossetti: "Nothing, nothing in my life, or my literary fortunes, has brought me more comfort and support every way—nothing has more spiritually soothed me—than the warm appreciation of friendship of that true, full-grown woman." [31]

Rossetti had written extensively to Whitman at the time his English edition was in progress; and as late as 1876 he said to Swinburne: "I continue in active communication with Whitman." Before Mrs. Gilchrist went to America both she and William Michael had been instrumental in collecting cash contributions and aiding subscription lists for *Leaves of Grass*. Robert Buchanan, Dante Gabriel's critical opponent of "The Fleshly School," had also furthered the campaign, but under the circumstances W. M. Rossetti did not wish to collaborate with him. To Swinburne, he added, concerning a second drive to aid Whitman: "He [is not] 'miserably poor' (Buchananice), but will be extremely glad to have English book purchasing recruits beaten up." [32]

Rossetti's hand was also felt in directing Mrs. Gilchrist's course in America. With her son Herbert, then about twenty years old, she sailed for New York in August 1876. Her primary objective was to visit Whitman; but she also entertained Joaquin Miller at tea; and on a later visit to Boston she delivered Rossetti's letters of introduction to Charles Eliot Norton, Thomas Wentworth Higginson, Horace Scudder, and others.[33] In New York she had some memorable visits with Richard Watson Gilder; and a letter from Rossetti implies that she also knew W. J. Stillman and was interested in the fact that he had visited Whitman some time before.

William Michael Rossetti was thus the *deus ex machina* of the Gilchrist-Whitman friendship, and with his edition of the poems and fine fervor for their author he did much to shape Whitman's reputation in England.

Dante Gabriel did not share his brother's feeling for this poet. Shortly after Longfellow's *Hiawatha* had appeared, he exploded in a note to Allingham: "How I loathe *Wishi-washi*,—of course without reading it. I have not been so happy in loathing anything for a long while—except, I think, *Leaves of Grass*, by that Orson of yours. I should like just to have the writing of a valentine to him in one of the reviews." [34] D. G. Rossetti likewise derived some innocent pleasure from an anecdote at the expense of "the good old bard," who came to visit him in England. Hall Caine tells the story. Longfellow was courteous and kind in the last degree, but had made the error of believing that Rossetti the painter and Rossetti the poet were different men. On leaving the house he said: " 'I have been very glad to meet you, Mr. Rossetti, and should like to have met your brother also. Pray tell him how much I admire his beautiful poem, "The Blessed Damozel." ' " [35]

Although brother William missed Longfellow, he considered another American man of letters, Moncure D. Conway, a good friend. This liberal leader and Unitarian clergyman, who was to write more than seventy books (including several novels as well as biographies of Emerson, Hawthorne, Carlyle, and Tom Paine), first met him about 1863 in the house of William Bell Scott. "He interested me in various ways," Rossetti wrote in his *Reminiscences*, "not least as being a Virginian who had espoused the Abolitionist cause, and who had for conscience' sake, on the outbreak of the War of the Secession,* migrated from the United States to Eng-

---

* It is interesting that D. G. Rossetti's sympathies with the Northern cause led him to plan a ballad on the death of Lincoln, in which he intended to offer a tribute to John Brown. This work was never carried out. William Michael's little-known *Democratic Sonnets*, however, included three entitled "John Brown," "The Slaves Freed," and "Lincoln."

land to diffuse his principles." [36] Conway's conversation was "open-minded and telling," against the background of his wife's "placid but by no means phlegmatic amiability," and W. M. Rossetti felt that they were all on very pleasant terms. Conway later helped to arrange American publication of some of his friend's works.

Conway also numbered Allingham and Walter Crane among his British acquaintances. In 1867 while on a tour of the South Coast he sent a note warning Allingham of an impending visit and of the writer's intention to persuade him to go to America. When they met in September they talked much of Emerson, whose *Essays* both men admired. A memorable dinner at the Conways' later in the winter, where the playwright Tom Taylor was among the guests, was also duly noted in Allingham's diary.[37] Walter Crane met Conway a year or two later, and was impressed by his "independence of thought and high character." The expatriate felt quite at home among his English friends, and saw Crane often, at the Combe Bank estate of an art patron, Dr. William Spottiswoode, at dinners of the "New Vagabonds" club, and elsewhere. When the Cranes made their art pilgrimage to America in the '90's they were delighted to visit their "old friends the Moncure Conways at their New York home, facing the Central Park." Conway's continuing relationship with the general Pre-Raphaelite group was perhaps best shown on the occasion of Madox Brown's death in 1893; as mentioned by both Crane and W. M. Rossetti, Conway was invited to deliver the funeral eulogy at his grave in Highgate Cemetery. He also made a small collection of Pre-Raphaelite art, among which a prized study was D. G. Rossetti's "Head of Christ" for which W. J. Stillman had been the sitter.[38]

Such details as these are fragments important only to the

larger scheme, but are suggestive of the extent to which certain American writers and their works were known to the Pre-Raphaelites of nineteenth-century England.* There remains the obverse of the question, to inquire briefly how Ruskin and the British P.R.B.'s affected other individuals in this country who clearly did not belong to a "school," but who reflected something of the Pre-Raphaelite tone in their own contributions to economic and social planning, the visual arts, and poetry.

The social concepts of Ruskin and Morris continued to have some currency. A typical application of "Christian Socialism" in the nineteenth century is to be found in the activities of a Congregational clergyman in North Abington, Massachusetts, the Rev. Jesse H. Jones, "who owed his chief inspiration to Ruskin." [39] After reading *The Crown of Wild Olive*, which was published in the United States in 1866, he "aspired to the role of the Ruskin of America." [40] His economic and social philosophy drew not only from this particular source, but was also related to Fourierism with its concern in experimental communities. His basic creed as a minister embraced

---

* During the Civil War decade and after, other casual Anglo-American literary contacts of course occurred. Elihu Burritt, for example, called on the Rossettis in September 1867. William Michael in writing of the event felt the need to identify the visitor: "I am not quite sure whether the name of Elihu Burritt is now much remembered in England. He was an American, a man of some mark, often called 'the literary blacksmith.'" This erudite craftsman, editor, and pacifist produced "a very agreeable impression" upon Christina in particular; and William regretted that work on his own edition of Whitman kept him from meeting this other American. (See W. M. Rossetti, ed., *Rossetti Papers 1862 to 1870*, N.Y., 1903, p. 241.)

Christina's reaction to the work of a fellow-poet in the United States, expressed some time later, is also interesting: "There is a book too I might have shown you, if I had remembered," she wrote to her brother, "Poems by Emily Dickinson, lately sent me from America—but perhaps you know it. She *had* (for she is dead) a wonderfully Blakean gift, but therewithal a startling recklessness of poetic ways and means. . . ." (W. M. Rossetti, ed., *Family Letters of Christina Georgina Rossetti*, N.Y., 1908, pp. 176–177.)

the social responsibilities of the church, in particular toward the working class. He therefore set up a comprehensive program in which he founded the Christian Labor Union in Boston in 1872 to educate the workers and aid in labor reforms; he actively promoted the eight-hour day, urged public ownership of the means of production, and argued for co-operative factories and stores. The Christian Labor Union also published a monthly journal, *Equity*, with Jones as editor, to publicize its doctrines. Before it failed for lack of support in 1875 it defended the Erie Railroad strike of 1873 as a major step toward the new status of labor.

A popular critic of our own day, Van Wyck Brooks, likewise felt an early compulsion in the ideas of Ruskin and Morris. These two with Nietzsche and Tolstoy, were for him the great prophets of the nineteenth century. At the inception of his career Brooks was described as "a Ruskin come alive in New York in 1915, a sensitive, dynamic, brilliant young American who had found his standards in the great Victorian critics of materialism." [41] His attack on acquisitive society, *America's Coming of Age,* makes the parallel more applicable than do his subsequent accounts of specific literary figures.

About the time modern architecture in this country was evolving through the spectacular innovations of such men as Louis Sullivan and Frank Lloyd Wright (who have been spoken of as "children of Ruskin" [42]), the so-called Art Nouveau saw its brief crescendo and rapid decline. This decorative art was to be identified particularly through its stylized treatment of a restricted group of natural forms: long sensitive curves expressed in tenuous, swirling, delicate stems and fronds, swaying flowers, and sinuous human figures, often with elaborate drapery. Its chief heyday was in France, as the title indicates; but in its original development it owed something to the British Pre-Raphaelites. Burne-Jones in particular evolved a prototype in his famed "Tree of Life" mosaic, and William Morris worked out for many of his printed pages a frame-design of the involuted and convoluted figures that came to typify the Art Nouveau from about 1890 to 1905. His wallpapers and tapestries likewise indicated the trend that would come. His associate Walter Crane went farther in his own illustrative work, and (in spite of his definition of Art Nouveau as a "decorative illness") had a "period" that might be labeled by the new name. Aubrey Beardsley's illustrations in the 1890's offer the most familiar instances in English art. In this country Vachel Lindsay's own sketches for his *The Candle in the Cabin* (1926) make a belated and eccentric application of the Art Nouveau curve-motif. Many examples of "fine" printing of the turn of the century might be discovered which show obvious relationship to their European sources. In particular the Roycroft Press in East Aurora, New York, purveyed this brand of typography in its numerous offerings. Various ceramic manufacturers adopted designs in bas-relief that were essentially of Art Nouveau origin; among them the Rookwood Company in Cincinnati produced perhaps the most popular work. The same types of decorations were used not only for flat surfaces, including large wall areas, but were adapted frequently to metal work and grills, as in screens, stair railings, and doors; and many structures still stand in which evidences of the Art Nouveau are visible. Paradoxically, the furniture which evolved as part of this program was essentially "straight-line"—which may have been in part the result of Morris's simple craft styling; at any rate, the designers of the "modern" furniture of our own era owe some debt to these predecessors. The Art Nouveau is thus of some historic significance; for as the German authority on art and architecture, Nikolaus Pevsner, suggests, it is probable that the whole modern movement in design springs from three roots: primarily from the new engineering architecture of the nineteenth century which employed steel, glass, and concrete; in addition, from William Morris's Arts and Crafts movement; and finally from the Art Nouveau.[43]

This same critic believes that the term may be applied also to the type of "decadent" literature produced by such men as Verlaine, Rimbaud, Mallarmé, and Oscar Wilde. But rather than pursuing this tangential problem further, it might be well to consider certain American writers in whom a more direct relation to Ruskin and the Pre-Raphaelites is visible. Similarities may be comparatively easy to recognize, but any final assertion of direct influence is more problematical.

Sidney Lanier knew Ruskin's works and admired them both for the ornate quality of his style in descriptive passages and for the attack on materialism which in his own verse served as a major theme. Ruskin's use of language seemed intoxicating, a prose transformed: "Here is Poetry escaped from his palace, bathing, crazy with delight, in the sea and the air and the sunshine. . . . What a man, a right, true, godlike man is this. . . ."[44] Ruskin's strong individuality in expression had created a popular suspicion of his "ruddy-cheeked style when the general world writes sallow-skinned"; but, declared Lanier, in such an attitude "we are guilty of a gross wrong. . . ."[45] In his early account of Florida he quoted at length from *Modern Painters* Ruskin's tribute to the pine, written "in the noble days before his mournful modern insanity."[46] The almost painful tone of jocularity in another prose work, "The Three Waterfalls," does not conceal numerous literary echoes from *Stones of Venice* and other sources; and Lanier makes his narrator declare explicitly:

As an adorer of scenery, I have been particularly weak on waterfalls. How much sweet bread, full nourishing to the soul, has Ruskin cast into the waters of the Fall of Schaffhausen! I appreciate Ruskin.[47]

It is indicative of his tastes, too, that although Lanier made only passing reference to D. G. Rossetti, he included William Morris and "Miss Rossetti" in a selected list of eighteen British, Continental, and American writers "that have claimed and secured the attention of the age."

Lanier's reformist poetry, especially "The Symphony" of 1875, springs from his own bitter resentment of the grossness of the post-Civil War commercialism. Although the similarity to Ruskin's message may be only coincidental, it does not seem completely so when Lanier speaks of him in a letter of 1870 as "one of our noblest souls"; [48] and it is known that Lanier expressed admiration of *Unto This Last* as a social protest.[49] "Lanier takes Ruskin's view," we are told by one of the pioneer critics of the poet.[50] This statement is suggestive rather than exact; but after Lanier visited Wheeling, West Virginia, on a tour with his orchestra he wrote a sharp-toned letter of righteous indignation certainly akin to the mood of Ruskin. "The hell-colored smoke of the factories" moved him to compose "The Symphony" to attack selfish commercialism and to plead for humanitarian concern for the depressed classes:

> "O Trade! O Trade! would thou wert dead!
> The time needs heart—'tis tired of head:
> We are all for love," the violins said.[51]

Josephine Preston Peabody (Mrs. Lionel S. Marks) was a Dresden-China romanticist with a hint of a similar social consciousness, who was once exhorted by Edwin Arlington Robinson "to drop 'philosophizing' and twittering at infinities and to write about things objective." [52] An avowed foe of the newer realism, she achieved international recognition and some popularity as the author of the Stratford-on-Avon prize play, "The Piper," in 1910 against three hundred fifteen competitors. This somewhat prettified treatment of the old Hamelin legend (which was produced in New York in 1911) made the Piper into a poet who led the children away from a world of egocentric confusion into a realm of quiet beauty. Because he found only "lies, greed and cruelty, and dreadful dark" among men, he snatched away the innocents:

> Those radiant things that have no wish at all
> Save for what is all-beautiful. . . .

Hamelin town is indeed the symbol of the whole corrupt society:

> It stands for all, unto the end of time,
> That turns this bright world black and the Sun cold,
> With hate and hoarding;—all-triumphant Greed
> That spreads above the roots of all despair,
> And misery, and rotting of the Soul! [53]

But after a too-facile repentance the once-benighted burghers are of course allowed to reclaim their lost children; and the Piper wanders on over the wide world where "there's so much piping left to do." This is perhaps representative of the tone of much of her work in the poetic drama.

A recent history of American poetry has stated without elaboration that in addition to other origins, "one is certain" that Miss Peabody's ideals embraced "those of the Pre-Raphaelite Brotherhood." [54] She herself in a letter to Horace Scudder named the basic trio of Homer, Shakespeare, and the Bible as her favorite reading, and added the names of Spenser, Keats, Shelley, Browning, Emerson and Lowell.[55] It is possible, however, to find in her work evidence of some familiarity with Rossetti and others of the P.R.B. Scudder, for example, recommended to her at the start of her career

the verse of Christina Rossetti, "The Goblin Market" in particular. She enjoyed it greatly, and with almost the first roy-
alty check from her own work she purchased the volume of
Christina's poems. But a more specific result of reading some
of Dante Gabriel's lines is recorded in her journal:

I asked them if they had ever noticed the suggestion of shape
form in these sound combinations. . . . They had not, so I told
them, as I am much interested in it—about first seeing it in these
words of Rossetti's—"slim-curved lute." They so perfectly expressed the shape of a lute—the *im* sound being flat and straight
(for the neck), the outward curve of the *ur*, the inward curve *u*.
It sounds fantastic, but it is true. To me the short vowel sounds
are straight.[56]

She also discussed Rossetti's verse structure with Scudder,
who pleased her by recalling details of a dinner that poet had
given for him years before. It seems probable, therefore, that
some of Miss Peabody's care for the exact or the exotic word
derived from her admiration of Pre-Raphaelite poetry.

In the now-familiar pattern she, too, incorporated plastic
art with her poetic expression. She turned to amateur sketching and modeling, especially in the years before her death
in 1922, partly for their therapeutic value, but perhaps primarily for the enlargement of spirit which she felt in the creative process. "That whimsical insistence of Rossetti's that
'*all* men should be artists, certainly,' at some time, was, I
believe, the truly *wisest* thing that he ever said or saw." Then
she continued:

And not merely as a statement of high faith in the three dimensions of mind that are ours to occupy . . . but as a truth that
contains more than we can dream of healing, enlightenment, and
the creation of a new self-knowing self.

The copying of Burne-Jones's sketches, and life-classes at the
Copley Society in Boston created in her "a wildish, Dionysiac

inspiration"; and this approach to the fine arts provided "delicious, new, absorbing Objective *Work with hands*—and artistic, of a kind I have *craved* all my life." [57]

In spite of her poetic-artistic-domestic preoccupations Josephine Peabody broadened her interests to include certain social problems such as those lightly treated in "The Piper." She was a pacifist and a supporter of suffrage for women and the rights of labor; to these causes she devoted energy in the form of speeches and articles. In 1909, after a visit to England, she became an associate of the Fabian Society.

Although the once-popular "Marlowe," "Fortune and Men's Eyes," "The Piper," and "The Wolf of Gubbio," are no longer read, their author remains as a delicate, sensitive figure, not completely unlike the models so cherished by the Pre-Raphaelite artists themselves.

Sara Teasdale, too, suggests Christina Rossetti's lyricism throughout her own lines. It is more than a coincidence that at the time of her death in 1933 she was working on a critical study of her sister poet. The same subtlety in expressing nuances of feeling is in both; but in the Anglo-Italian this emotion was sublimated to one of religious devotion and mysticism, while in the American the love was warmly human. Sara Teasdale is perhaps "classical" in the restraint of her more mature work, but as a lyricist with an intuitive awareness to life, she is also the inheritor of the romantic tradition.

There were for her, however, more direct lines of contact with Ruskinian-Pre-Raphaelite activities. Vachel Lindsay had dedicated his *Adventures While Preaching the Gospel of Beauty* to her; and her sympathetic estimate of his purpose and character is expressed in her verse, "In Memory of Vachel Lindsay," written just before her own death.

"Deep in the ages," you said, "deep in the ages,"
And, "To live in mankind is far more than to live in a name."
You are deep in the ages, now, deep in the ages,
You whom the world could not break, nor the years tame.

Fly out, fly on, eagle that is not forgotten,
Fly straight to the innermost light, you who loved
    sun in your eyes,
Free of the fret, free of the weight of living,
Bravest among the brave, gayest among the wise.[58]

Sara Teasdale also expressed a small part of the popular
poetic concern with the Middle Ages which had shown itself
in the *Idylls* of Tennyson, the paintings and poetry of Rossetti
and Morris, the Oxford Movement, and the Gothic Revival.
In America, Richard Hovey, Edwin Arlington Robinson, and
Ezra Pound in due course—and in widely varying treatment
—recurred to the Arthurian legend or other medieval materials as points of departure. Sara Teasdale's "Guenevere," "A
Ballad of Two Knights," and "The Princess in the Tower" do
not in themselves discover the poet as a belated Pre-Raphaelite. But they, and other early poems such as "At Tintagil" and
"Galahad in the Castle of the Maidens" (suggested by a
painting by Edwin Austen Abbey), indicate some bond with
the Pre-Raphaelite spirit.*
Iseult by the long waterways watched the wintry moon
above Tintagil:

By casements hung with night, while all your women slept
You turned toward Brittany, awake, alone,
In the high chamber hushed, save where the candle dripped
With the slow patient sound of blood on stone.

---

* Miss Teasdale's collection of poetry for children, *Rainbow Gold* (New
York, 1924) contains several selections from William Allingham, Christina
Rossetti, Lanier, and Lindsay. The illustrations by Dugald Walker are
directly in the Pre-Raphaelite–Art Nouveau tradition.

The ache of empty arms was an old tale to you,
And all the tragic tunes that love can play,
Yet with no woman born would you have changed your lot,
Though there were greater queens who had been gay.[59]

Or as Galahad returns victorious "with a victor's right," a modest maiden will not look on him:

The other maidens raised their eyes to see
And only she has hid her face away,
And yet I think she loved him more than they,
And very fairly fashioned was her face.
Yet for Love's shame and sweet humility,
She could not meet him with their queenlike grace.[60]

The longest of the Arthurian poems, "Guenevere," presents the figure of a pathetic and chastened woman, who is at once the symbol of all women caught in the mesh of similar circumstance:

I was a queen, and I have lost my crown;
A wife, and I have broken all my vows;
A lover, and I ruined him I loved:—
There is no other havoc left to do. . . .

I was a queen, and he who loved me best
Made me a woman for a night and day,
And now I go unqueened forevermore. . . .

All this grows bitter that was once so sweet,
And many mouths must drain the dregs of it,
But none will pity me, nor pity him
Whom Love so lashed, and with such cruel thongs.[61]

Although it is usual to think of Richard Hovey only as the poet of those who afoot and lighthearted follow the open road to Vagabondia, there may be more serious implications in his carefree verse. The biographer of Bliss Carman, his frequent collaborator, has asserted that it was far more than

The Adirondack Club," by W. J. Stillman

Vachel Lindsay

this to the authors, for it was actually their joint protest against the money-minded, materialistic, unimaginative America of their generation.[62] Thus Hovey may have ante-dated by a decade such a figure as Vachel Lindsay in his exhortation toward a more satisfying and artistic way of life. Hovey, too, had studied art at one period in his career before devoting himself completely to poetry. But he did not pre-sume to illustrate his own books as Lindsay tried to do. The designs and end papers of the *Songs from Vagabondia* series were by Tom Buford Meteyard, a fellow Bohemian whose decorations suggest rather mechanically something of Morris combined with the Art Nouveau.

But it is primarily as a shaper of the Arthurian legend that Hovey may be considered here. As with Teasdale this does not make him *per se* a Pre-Raphaelite; but the Brotherhood, together with Tennyson, had furnished a Victorian precedent of obvious suggestivity. In the posthumous *The Holy Graal and Other Fragments* the poet's wife presents the "Schema" of the projected triple trilogy, *Launcelot and Guenevere: A Poem in Dramas*. Each of the three parts was to contain a masque, a tragedy, and a romantic drama. "The Quest of Merlin," "The Marriage of Guenevere," and "The Birth of Galahad" completed Part I; "Taliesin," and the unfinished "The Graal," fell in Part II, together with the unwritten "Asto-lat"; and the work was to have been concluded by "Fata Morgana," "Morte d'Arthur," and "Avalon," which was termed a "Harmonody."

Hovey was of course familiar with the Arthurian literature, but was motivated by a differing interpretation of character. Mrs. Hovey elaborates:

Our time has given us three Gueneveres: the Guenevere of Ten-nyson, who sinned, and came to repentance and remorse; the Guenevere of Morris, who appeals to the tenderness of the human

heart, who explains and asks human sympathies; and the Guenevere of Hovey, who only loves, who never sins, who never
repents.[63]

Hovey's heroine is thus the "truly tragic" one, for she symbol-
izes womanhood at the point of civilization where the might
of an overpowering social and economic system destroys the
individuality of those "furthest developed in emotional and
intellectual power." Within the tale itself Arthur was to serve
as the ultimate source of tragedy through his "ignorance of
human hearts and psychic forces." But the whole ambitious
cycle was by implication a social commentary and stricture:

The "Poem in Dramas" was undertaken less to excuse or explain
Launcelot's act or Guenevere's, or to show Arthur's very natural
psychic blindness of a good and trusting nature, than to impeach
the social system that had not yet—and has not yet—gone far
enough in evolution to become a medium in which all lives can
move at all times and in all respects in freedom. This surely is
the ideal.[64]

Love thus is the central theme, with an implicit criticism of
contemporary society. Bliss Carman commented on this interpretation of the Arthurian cycle: "To Richard Hovey it
afforded a modern instance stripped of modern dress." [65]

In Edwin Arlington Robinson's total work his Arthurian
group of *Merlin, Lancelot,* and *Tristram* has been publicized
out of due proportion. These modern psychological analyses
owe little to the nineteenth-century treatments, except perhaps inversely. It is possible that "the Arthurian cycle gave
him an opportunity to test his wit and the astringent merits
of his style against the highly gifted, loose and brilliant met-
rical variations through which Tennyson in the disguise of
Galahad had sought the Holy Grail." [66] Robinson also makes
a negative approach to Pre-Raphaelite balladry, as the
"admirable Mr. Killigrew" in "Captain Craig" so aptly demon-
strates. He

"Has latterly committed what he calls
A *Ballad of London*—London 'Town,' of course—
And he has wished that I pass judgment on it."

The presumed opus is quoted at some length, of which a stanza will suffice:

" 'And you—you go to London Town?'
(Breezes waved the feather)—
'Yes, I go to London Town.'
(Ah, the stinging feather!)—
'Why do you go, my merry blade?
Like me, to marry a fair maid?'—
'Why do I go? . . . God knows,' he said;
And they rode on together."

Captain Craig then observes, by way of commentary:

" 'Pardie!'
You call it, with a few conservative
Allowances, an excellent small thing
For patient inexperience to do:
Derivative, you say,—still rather pretty.
But what is wrong with Mr. Killigrew?
Is he in love, or has he read Rossetti?—" [67]

This deft thrust need not indicate a failure to appreciate the positive qualities of Pre-Raphaelite poetry, however; for even in Volume I of Stillman's *Crayon* one finds a so-called "humorous effusion" entitled "Ye Laye of Ye Cat, &c. A Pre-Raphaelite Ballad," which is a well-meant burlesque beginning:

Oh who will build a goodly ship,
To sail o'er the salt, salt sea?
And who will ride o'er the world so wide,
For an Angora cat for me? . . .[68]

And Bayard Taylor in his day had coined the name "Cimabuella" to apply to a pseudo-Raphaelite feminine type that appeared in New York society.

In a survey of more recent poets it may fairly be asserted that Stephen Vincent Benét was for a time under the influence of Browning and William Morris; [69] and that Robinson Jeffers was once stirred by a reading of Dante Gabriel Rossetti's poems.[70] But the only contemporary figure who seems to bear any extensive relationship to the men and ideas of the Pre-Raphaelite Brotherhood is Ezra Pound, as he began his multi-faceted poetic expression. Having written essays on the Provençal poet Arnaut Daniel, Cavalcanti, Villon, and other early figures in *The Spirit of Romance*, "he arrived in London in 1910 as a belated member of the Pre-Raphaelite Brotherhood." [71]

This allegiance was a temporary and a partially misleading one. The accuracy, precision, and definiteness of description which T. E. Hulme identified in Pound's verse were akin to such characteristics in Pre-Raphaelite poetry. But where the Brotherhood seemed to translate themselves back into the mood of the Middle Ages, Pound freely adapted medieval materials to his own original and modern treatment. In a major respect, however, Pound gladly acknowledged his indebtedness to Dante Gabriel Rossetti.

Their common contact was in the poetry of the original Dante and his period. With the dedication, "Whatever is mine in this book is inscribed to my wife. D.G.R., 1861," Rossetti issued as his first book *The Early Italian Poets*, with its two sections, "Poets Chiefly before Dante," and "Dante and His Circle." A later editor of this work stresses its pioneer position:

When Rossetti made his translations, accurate texts of these early Italian poets were not yet available, and the critical investigation of their works and the circumstances under which they wrote . . . had hardly begun. It is less remarkable that he should sometimes have been mistaken in the dates to which he assigned individual poems, or the poets to whom he attributed them, than that he should thus wonderfully have succeeded in making certain aspects of a whole epoch in Italian literature intelligible to English readers.[72]

In Part II of this collection Rossetti translated some nineteen sonnets, a half dozen *ballate*, and four *canzoni* by Cavalcanti. In 1912 Ezra Pound issued *Sonnets and Ballate of Guido Cavalcanti*, with the dedicatory lines: "As much of this book as is mine I send to my friends Violet and Ford Madox Hueffer,"—the author of a critical study of Rossetti.[73] Included in this work was a longer list of thirty-five sonnets, a madrigal, and fourteen *ballate*. Its relative importance is suggested by R. P. Blackmur's paradoxical comment: "Mr. Pound is at his best and most original when his talents are controlled by an existing text. . . . His best work is his best translation." [74]

In his Introduction, Pound objected to some of Rossetti's readings of the original, and quite properly took advantage of an added half century of scholarship and his own vast erudition in medieval matters; but he graciously expressed his pleasure in the work of his predecessor, and, in expiation of possible etymological errors, added: "One man cannot be expected to see everywhere at once."

Pound's awareness of Rossetti is also demonstrated in one section of "Hugh Selwyn Mauberley (Life and Contacts)." This poem entitled *"Yeux Glauques,"* which may be translated "Sea-green Eyes," has been called by Yvor Winters "a lugubrious lament for the passing of Pre-Raphaelitism" cast in the vein of romantic irony.[75] It merits quotation:

> Gladstone was still respected,
> When John Ruskin produced
> "Kings' Treasuries"; Swinburne
> And Rossetti still abused.

Foetid Buchanan lifted up his voice
When that faun's head of hers
Became a pastime for
Painters and adulterers.

The Burne-Jones cartons
Have preserved her eyes;
Still, at the Tate, they teach
Coph'etua to rhapsodize;

Thin like brook-water,
With a vacant gaze.
The English Rubaiyat was still-born
In those days.

The thin, clear gaze, the same
Still darts out faun-like from the half-ruin'd face,
Questing and passive. . . .
"Ah, poor Jenny's case" . . .

Bewildered that a world
Shows no surprise
At her last maquero's
Adulteries.[76]

By way of gloze: the literal reference is of course to the painting by Burne-Jones entitled "King Cophetua and the Beggar Maid," whose subject matter came to him by way of Tennyson's poem of 1842, in turn based on an old Border ballad celebrating the love of an African king. The canvas was completed in 1884; and "poor Jenny," rather than denoting any specific model, must here evoke the "Jenny" of Rossetti's long poem—"so pure,—so fall'n!"—whose case the poet presents with tolerant, gentle irony. Thus, by extension, "poor Jenny," the spirit of Pre-Raphaelitism, gazes with her sea-green eyes, bewildered, perhaps, at a world passing from classic amorality or innocence to materialistic corruption and aesthetic insensibility. In this interpretation it is "a lament," but not necessarily a "lugubrious" one. Or as Babette Deutsch views the whole "Mauberley" group: "Here is Pound's lasting rage at the mob-minded money-lusting crew that holds the world in fee." [77]

Of all of Pound's startling eclecticism, be it in relation to Greek and Roman, Oriental, Anglo-Saxon, Provençal or Italian materials, we need concern ourselves here only with his treatment of the Italian. For as we have seen, some of his earliest and perhaps best work was inspired by Rossetti; and following the title-page of his *Sonnets and Ballate of Guido Cavalcanti* he wrote:

> I have owned service to the deathless dead,
> Grudge not the gold I bear in livery.

To make the reference clear and direct, he added in his Introduction: "In the matter of these translations and of my knowledge of Tuscan poetry, Rossetti is my father and my mother." [78]

APPENDIXES AND NOTES

APPENDIX I

THE WINTHROP COLLECTION IN THE FOGG

MUSEUM OF ART

THE *Art News* edition of Jan. 1–14, 1944, was devoted chiefly to describing the Winthrop Collection. An article, "Winthrop Collection Goes to Fogg," in the *Art Digest* of Nov. 1, 1943, is also informative.

Grenville Winthrop, a retired lawyer, died in January 1943, and by the terms of his will left to the Fogg Museum at Harvard his entire collection of art objects. He had built up his holdings throughout his lifetime largely by the activities of his dealers and agents who ranged over the world and brought back their findings to his home in Lenox, Massachusetts. He had expressed on several occasions—first to his friend Paul J. Sachs, and later to Presidents A. Lawrence Lowell and James B. Conant—his intention of making this bequest. The final gift numbered nearly 4,000 separate items, including paintings, sculpture, drawings, prints, furniture, and objects in porcelain, jade, and bronze.

Paul Sachs writes concerning the donor: "Mr. Winthrop was the particular bright exemplar in our country of the true connoisseur, the knowing amateur. His instinct and sense of quality account for his astonishing success. Through long practice and by constant comparison, he had trained his sensitive eye and with courageous enthusiasm strengthened his rare judgment." (*Art News*, 42:9, Jan. 1–14, 1944). He had many friends among artists and art critics, notably Royal

Cortissoz and Paul Manship, and Daniel B. Updike of the Merrymount Press.

Mr. Winthrop assembled his comprehensive private collection with brilliant eclecticism and catholic taste. In sculpture his acquisitions ranged from Chaldean and Egyptian materials to Aztec heads, Gothic statuary, Houdon marbles, and bronzes by Rodin. His rare assortment of Chinese pieces in jade and bronze was enriched by numerous stone Buddhas and bas-reliefs.

In paintings Mr. Winthrop owned a small but distinguished group of Flemish primitives, and representative works by Tintoretto, El Greco, and Goya. His neo-classic French section received perhaps his major attention, with some forty drawings by Ingres, and important works by David. Among other French figures his tastes ranged from Chardin, Fragonard, Proudhon, Gericault, Delacroix and Daumier, through the Barbizon School and Puvis de Chavannes, Renoir, Seurat, Berthe Morisot, and Redon. American artists included Copley, Stuart, West, the Peales, Inness, La Farge, Homer, Cassatt, Whistler, and Sargent, with considerable modern sculpture. English art was represented by Gainsborough, Lawrence, and Turner; and his Blake materials alone numbered over fifty water-colors. Of particular pertinence here, however, is the group of Pre-Raphaelite works, which in this country is rivaled only by the Bancroft Collection in the Delaware Art Center.

There is an extensive selection of preliminary sketches and studies in pencil, ink, chalk, crayon, charcoal, and water-color by most of the Pre-Raphaelites; these are of value especially to students concerned with the technique and actual studio methods involved. But the number of finished pictures is impressive, and indicates the enthusiasm which Mr. Winthrop felt for P.R.B. art. The work of Madox Brown, on the edge of the group, may be seen in his strong "Self-Portrait," and "La Rose de l'Infante," painted in 1876 as a portrait of the little daughter of Mr. and Mrs. W. J. Stillman. The most popular canvas by George Frederick Watts, who was of the P.R.B. circle, but not of the Brotherhood, is his sentimental "Sir Galahad." Other oils dealing with classical or Biblical subjects are "Orpheus and Eurydice," "Ariadne," the "Creation of Eve," and "Denunciation of Adam and Eve."

Of the work of the four central figures of the Brotherhood, Hunt's "Triumph of the Innocents," and "Miracle of the Holy Fire," are excellent examples of his finely worked finish and concern with minute detail. Burne-Jones's watercolor on canvas, "Venus Epithalamia," has an added interest as the artist's wedding gift to his close friend Marie Spartali, on the occasion of her marriage to Stillman. From her hands it passed to Fairfax Murray's and thence to the Winthrop Collection. The six water-color panels of the "Days of the Creation" were a major acquisition; and other works by Burne-Jones in the same medium are "Day," "Night," "Helen of Troy," and "Depths of the Sea." His oils include "Pan and Psyche," "Danae and the Brazen Tower," "Flamma Vestalis," and the "Portrait of Sara Norton." A number of water-colors by Millais are also to be found, usually studies for or replicas of larger treatments in oil. The series of "Six Parables," "The Proscribed Royalist," "The Huguenot," "A Lady with a Greyhound," and "The Ransom" are among the most familiar.

The works of Dante Gabriel Rossetti form the nucleus of the Pre-Raphaelite collection. Among the dozen or more sketches and compositions in pen and ink, charcoal, crayon and chalk several stand out: his early treatment of "Il Saluto di Beatrice," in a frame of his own design (1850), "Faust and Margaret in Prison," "Aurea Catena (The Lady of the Golden Chain)," and several portrait heads of Mrs. William Morris.

His chief water-colors are "A Christmas Carol," "Giotto Painting Dante's Portrait," a version of "Beata Beatrix," and "Lucretia Borgia." Oil paintings are "My Lady Greensleeves," titled from an old English ballad, and modeled in 1863 probably by Fanny Cornforth; "Il Ramoscello," 1865, the portrait of a girl holding an ilex branch; "A Sea Spell," dated 1877, for which he wrote a matching sonnet; "La Donna della Finestra," for which Mrs. Morris was the sitter in 1879; and, finally, the picture which is perhaps Rossetti's best known and most prized work, the original version in oil of "The Blessed Damozel," which was completed in 1877 to illustrate his own poem composed three decades earlier.

APPENDIX II

LIST OF ROSSETTI MSS IN THE BANCROFT
COLLECTION

Alone
Also a Tale is Told (from "Aella," a tragic poem by
    Thomas Chatterton)
Beryl Song
Excellent Ballad of Charity
Fiammetta
Filii Filia
For Answer
Found
From Dawn to Noon
Funeral of the Duke of Wellington
Heart's Haven
Heart's Hope
Hero's Lamp
Jenny (an early draft)
John Keats
La Bella Mano
Life the Beloved
Love and Deceit
Love and Hope
The Love-Lamp Sonnet XXXV (printed The Lamp's
    Shrine)
Lovelight Sonnet XXVIII (printed Soul-Light)
Love's Fatality Sonnet LIV

Love's Last Gift
The Minstrel's Marriage Song
The Moonstar
My Lady's Gifts
On the Site of a Mulberry Tree; Planted by Wm.
   Shakespeare; felled by the Rev. Gastrell
Percy Bysshe Shelley (also on the reverse of La Bella
   Mano)
A Prayer
Raleigh's Cell in the Tower
Rose Marie
The Soul's Sphere Sonnet LXII
Spheral Change
Sunset Wings
Thomas Chatterton
Through Death to Love
Venus Victrix Sonnet XXXIII
The Wedding Ballad
Youth's Antiphony Sonnet XIII

APPENDIX III

TWO MINOR AMERICAN PRE-RAPHAELITE
PAINTERS: JOHN W. AND J. HENRY HILL

ONE OF the comparatively few artists in the 1860's singled out by the *New Path* because of their Pre-Raphaelite tendencies was John William Hill. Almost two decades after the end of that magazine Charles Herbert Moore, then at Harvard, wrote an "Artist's Memorial" at the time of Hill's death which indicated Moore's continuing praise and appreciation of this painter.[1] From this and other sources it becomes clear that Hill, otherwise a forgotten figure, was an exponent in America of Ruskinism and the early principles of the English P.R.B.

Hill's father, John Hill, had been a London engraver, one of the first experimenters in aquatint. Four years after his son's birth in 1812 the elder Hill went alone to Philadelphia in hope of better fortune, and sent for his family to join him there in 1819. Not long after their arrival he took them to New York, where one of his chief works was the engraving of W. G. Wall's *The Hudson River Portfolio*, assisted by his wife in the printing and by his two elder daughters in coloring the plates.

Surrounded by all this activity, it was only natural for the younger Hill to try his own hand at drawing. In 1825 at the age of thirteen he had produced a detailed sketch of a dahlia, which in Moore's judgment showed "care and skill," and, given some suitable direction, he might have produced some

259

worthwhile work. But at this stage his preceptors, "instead of assisting him to observe the characteristic lines, the true colors, and the beautiful variations of light and shadow . . . merely suggested the various mannerisms and mechanical tricks of the most conventional landscapists." [2] His dexterity was further sharpened by an extended series of drawings which the New York State Geological Survey later hired him to make, but this sort of assignment stressed primarily the mechanical rendition of subject matter.

In 1836 the Hill family moved out of the city to Nyack Turnpike, where they bought land and built a house; here the elder Hill died in 1850. John William meanwhile had served a seven-year apprenticeship to his father, built himself a house nearby, married, and now considered Nyack Turnpike as his permanent home in spite of the considerable travel incident to his artistic pursuits.

Following his employment by the State for a year, he was commissioned by a private firm, the Smith Brothers, to make drawings of all the principal cities from Halifax to Havana (doubtless the first "Cities of America" series). While he was at work in Portland, Maine, a resident recommended to him the first volume of Ruskin's *Modern Painters*, which he immediately bought and read with close attention. "It was," declared Moore, "the means of opening a new world to him." Although he had to continue his contract with Smith Brothers, he took a short side trip into the White Mountains for experimental sketching in the direct realistic manner. After his return home there was a gradual change in his technique and approach, as Ruskin's ideas continued to simmer, and about 1855 "he appears to have become firmly possessed with the conviction that he ought to try to paint Nature just as he saw it." [3]

His first piece of work under the new impulse was a small

oil of an old thatched sawmill in strong light and deep shadow. Pleased with the result, he continued working in the open air through the summer of 1856, and produced a series of studies in both oil and water color of the near-by Hackensack River valley. With a particular fondness for close views of the river with its water plants and overhanging trees, he built for himself a platform on stakes in the middle of the channel, where he worked eight or nine hours a day. In the fall he journeyed into the Catskills to sketch mountain streams, spending the following winter in New York. Here the attention of the public was first drawn to him by the showing of some of these faithful nature-studies in the spring exhibition of the National Academy of Design.

Thus encouraged, he redoubled his efforts in the summer of 1857, trying now particularly to lighten the tone and increase the brilliancy of his color, continuing meanwhile his concern in rendering multitudinous detail. He went to the White Mountains again, and then to Cape Elizabeth on the Maine coast. A resulting view of Mt. Washington he sold to an art collector in Troy, New York, and a vigorous Maine scene to a patron in Brooklyn. Working always at the actual location, he was concerned not only with the more grandiose aspects of nature, but also with the simpler and more limited details—birds, flowers, grass, and weeds. Some of his least assuming sketches from this period are of crab-apples and wild grapes, and a deserted dory on a grassy, sandy beach, against which leans an empty lobster-pot.

Hill's portrait by his son, John Henry Hill, shows him as a benign old gentleman with muttonchop whiskers, direct, piercing eyes, and a forehead traversed by deep wrinkles. In spite of the generous patronage of a few enthusiasts, he found little public response to his works, and in his latter years was remembered as an "earnest old gentleman" padding about with a huge portfolio under his arm, trying to support himself by distasteful solicitation of sales from door to door.

But among his followers Hill was considered a real though unappreciated artist, and Charles Herbert Moore concludes his eulogy:

> Among the names of those in America who have striven to cultivate the art of painting aright there is none more worthy of honor than that of John W. Hill. Indeed for sincerity of purpose and laborious faithfulness of devotion during a long life, he has had, so far as our knowledge extends, no peer.

Not only a means of livelihood, art was for Hill as for Ruskin "one of the most serious and important of human pursuits," with a "deep moral significance." To him it seemed that "all true beauty and right pleasurableness of art must be based upon a foundation of veracity. It was, therefore, his first and constant care . . . after his principles had become settled, to be true to Nature." [4]

The New York *Times* carried an obituary of Hill which also indicated his artistic stature in the minds of some of the critics of the period.[5] Concerning his landscapes this notice asserted: "His rendering of mountain and hill forms was subtle, firm, and strong. I know of no American in which the grandeur of mountain masses in the distance, the tenderness and mystery of outline . . . were so rendered." [6] His superiority to his fellows was marked, and "although he was in sympathy with the professed ideas of the little band of artists rather awkwardly termed pre-Raphaelite, I am not aware that any of his work betrayed the crudeness which was the fault of much of theirs." Then this reviewer concludes: "Prediction in matters of art is not safe, but I am much in error if Mr. Hill's work does not live long after him, and grow in repute and estimation as the knowledge of art in the United States advances."

A similar appreciative notice in the New York *Tribune* stresses Hill's Pre-Raphaelite sympathies.[7] Hill, declared the writer, "was one of the leaders in the so-called Pre-Raphaelite school . . . in this country—a handful of artists, most of them very young, who advocated a strict following of nature, in contradistinction to academic rules and teachings, and who carried out their principles with great earnestness and—considering how young they were and what unmannerly opposition they met with—with surprisingly little wilfulness or extravagance." With the transplanted young Englishman, Thomas Charles Farrer, the reviewer continued, Hill stood out among the practicing artists in applying Ruskin's ideas and those of the British Brotherhood; and in spite of his late conversion and his lack of technical training, Hill settled down to "patient indefatigable study" of nature and produced effective "color memoranda" of all that he saw that interested him. Although he suffered public neglect Hill continued to paint and preach his doctrines and had ultimately "a strong hold upon many of the best among the younger artists of his time, and did a yeoman service in breaking down the old conventionalism, and building up a healthier public sentiment as to the true relation between art and Nature."[8]

Nine years after J. W. Hill's death, his son, John Henry Hill, published a folio memorial volume which contained eleven full-page reproductions of Hill's best work, with some ten smaller sketches throughout the text. The larger ones include "Old Boat on the Seashore," referred to above, and "Moonlight on the East River at New York," both etched by the elder Hill; and J. Henry Hill's etched reproductions of his father's pencil drawing, "Sunnyside, Irvington"; an oil study, "Old Saw Mill," his first successful work in his new style; and the following water colors: "Sunset in the Hackensack Valley," "Along the Hackensack," "Crab-Apples and

Wild Grapes," "The Hudson from the Palisades," "Coast Scene at Newport," "Sand Dunes at Long Island," and "Creek at Mattituck, Long Island."

The smaller "type illustrations," pen sketches by J. Henry Hill from his father's original water colors, include such scenes as the artist's home, his old church with its burial ground, an old Dutch house, the Turnpike bridge, the Hackensack meadows, a calm mill pond, and views of the Hudson River and Lake George.

J. Henry Hill

In February 1864, the *New Path* (which carried no pictorial material in its pages) made the following announcement:

The want of proper illustration of what we so often allude to as "faithful study from nature" has so long been felt that the proprietors of this journal propose to publish a series of 10 photographs from drawings and paintings by men of the Realist School, provided a sufficient number of subscriptions are received to warrant the undertaking. . . .

These were to be sold by Brentano's at $6.00 for the set of ten, which was barely over the cost of production. After considerable juggling of the list of contributing artists, the final series as announced in the June number, was heavily weighted in favor of members of the "Society for the Advancement of Truth in Art." T. C. Farrer, the active founder of the group, was represented by three pencil sketches, a sepia drawing, and one painting; and Charles Herbert Moore offered one drawing in pencil and one in ink. Of the three remaining places to be filled by carefully selected artists working in the *New Path's* pattern one, significantly, was given to J. Henry Hill.

John Henry Hill, the son of John William, was thus a member of the third generation to carry on the family's artistic tradition. Painting concurrently with his father, and exhibiting works often side by side with his, the younger Hill worked in close sequence of idea and treatment. In 1867 he published his *Sketches from Nature*, with twenty-five plates based on material from his portfolios which he had "drawn upon the copper at intervals between more persistent and serious work." [9]

This folio volume was addressed didactically not only to lovers of art and nature, but to those wishing to become artists. To the latter group he suggests: "The best instruction for beginners in landscape art is to be found in the *Elements of Drawing* and *Modern Painters*, both by John Ruskin, which contain all the information necessary for those who have sufficient industry and love of nature to persevere as artists in the right track." And to all artists, amateurs or practiced, who might be working with natural objects and seeking "to impress upon their fellowmen the infinite beauty of God's handiwork in this world of ours,"—a further message:

To all such I would say, drawing a single flower, leaf, or bit of rock thoroughly well is something better worth doing than conjuring up pictures in the studio without a bit of accurate drawing to account for their evident pretentions. Do not be in the least hurry to get on; take simple things to work from, and if anyone tells you that it is a pity to waste so much time upon such uninteresting subjects, do not mind them, for the great power of Titian may be seen in drawing a wreath around the head of one of his figures, and the skill of Veronese is displayed in tracing patterns among folds of drapery. [10]

His Pre-Raphaelite concern with "the simple things" is evident in his accompanying descriptions of the various etchings. He points out carefully the difference in foliation and silhouette between elms and chestnuts; explains that the shadows on three thrush's eggs are cast by fibers around the edge of the nest; comments, concerning his careful sketch of a "black-capped titmouse," that one should not waste his time on stuffed specimens; calls attention to the highlight on a single nailhead in the sketch of a ruined, thatch-covered hut; identifies such specific plants as thimble-berry and yellow water-lily; mentions the pleasant contrast between the red sandstone of some bridge piers and the green foliage beside them; explains why a clump of cedars is so weather-beaten; and in general suggests that verisimilitude is his chief aim in reproducing natural phenomena, for, as he says, "most of the subjects in this book are literal views from nature." He regrets, of course, the lack of color in the reproductions, but suggests that "the study of natural form in black and white" can still be "very essentially instructive."

In addition to the subjects just mentioned, Hill also included his meticulous treatments of such simple subjects as burdock leaves, an old stone oven, boulders in a creek bed, some boys fishing, and cows standing in meadow shade. "Wide-angle" subjects might be suggested by his sketches of Mt. Washington and Bald Mountain in Maine, Niagara Falls, and "Moonlight on the Androscoggin." But his greatest charm and talent, if one is to judge from the not too satisfactory reproductions, lay in discovering unpretentious and often unnoticed sources of beauty—"Haystacks at Northumberland, N. Y.," "Wild Flowers of the genus *Bidens*," or "Old Whaler at New Bedford, Mass."

In contrast to his father, the younger Hill exemplified greater personal freedom in interpreting his subject materials. As a minor mechanical technique, for example, he typically does not square out the details into the corners of his composition, either in the sky or in the foreground, but vignette-like centering of attention on the main object of his work concentrates the viewer's eye on it. "Bald Mountain" (Plate # 6) serves as an excellent example; "Mt. Washington" is framed by a conveniently perfect arch of wild blackberry briar, which yields an oval design; and the "Cedars on the Coast" are so placed that they form a near-perfect curve in the center of the composition.

Except in the pages of the *New Path* the younger Hill did not receive as much public recognition as did his father; but together they serve, in spite of their transient fame, as figures representative of the course of the Pre-Raphaelite movement in this country.

NOTES

CHAPTER I. THE PRE-RAPHAELITE MOVEMENT IN AMERICA:
AN INTRODUCTION

1. William Michael Rossetti, ed., *The Germ, A Facsimile Reprint,* London, 1901, Introduction, p. 7.
2. R. W. Macan, F.R.S.L., Introduction, *Essays by Divers Hands, Transactions of the Royal Society of Literature,* London, 1933, XII: v.
3. Russell Sturgis, "The Pre-Raphaelites and Their Influence," *Independent,* 52: 181–183 (Jan. 18, 1900) and 246–249 (Jan. 25, 1900).

CHAPTER II. THE BRITISH BROTHERHOOD

1. Agnes Mongan, "Introduction," *Paintings and Drawings of the Pre-Raphaelites and Their Circle,* Cambridge, 1946, p. 7.
2. John Guille Millais, *The Life and Letters of Sir John Everett Millais,* N. Y., 1899, 2 vols., I: 49.
3. *Ibid.*
4. W. M. Rossetti, *Prae-Raphaelite Diaries and Letters,* London, 1900, pp. 205–206.
5. W. M. Rossetti, *Dante Gabriel Rossetti: His Family Letters, with a Memoir,* Boston, 1895, 2 vols., I: 135.
6. W. J. Stillman, *The Old Rome and the New and Other Studies,* Boston, 1898, p. 111.
7. Cf. Harry Quilter, *Preferences in Art, Life, and Literature,* London, 1892, pp. 40–45.
8. Millais, *op. cit.,* I: 223.
9. William Bell Scott, *Autobiographical Notes,* N. Y., 1892, 2 vols., II: 53.
10. W. Holman Hunt, *Pre-Raphaelitism and the Pre-Raphaelite Brotherhood,* London, 1906, 2 vols., II: 490.
11. Millais, *op. cit.,* II: 2.
12. Sturgis, *op. cit.,* p. 182.
13. Editor of *Art Journal,* "Sir John Everett Millais," *Presidents of the Royal Academy,* London, 1906, p. 1.
14. Sturgis, *op. cit.,* p. 182.
15. Millais, *op. cit.,* I: 52.
16. *Ibid.,* pp. 54–55.

17. W. M. Rossetti, *Dante Gabriel Rossetti: His Family Letters*, pp. 135–136.

18. The best brief discussion of the British Pre-Raphaelites which I have seen is by Laurence Housman, F.R.S.L., "Pre-Raphaelitism in Art and Poetry," *Transactions of the Royal Society of Literature*, 12: 1–29 (London, 1933).

19. John Ruskin, *Pre-Raphaelitism*, N. Y., 1877, p. 19.

20. Cf. Louis Judson Swinburne, "Rossetti and the Pre-Raphaelites," *New Englander*, 8: 1–42 (July–Sept. 1885).

21. Gabriel Mourey, *D. G. Rossetti et les Préraphaélites Anglais*, Paris, 1910, p. 7, tr.

22. Arthur Pope, "Preface," *Paintings and Drawings of the Pre-Raphaelites and Their Circle*, Harvard, 1946, p. 3.

23. Madox Brown, for example, saw "something fine" in a Masaccio in the National Gallery; he also admired Albrecht Dürer of the Flemish school but reported only "bad Rembrandts." See W. M. Rossetti, *Prae-Raphaelite Diaries and Letters*, p. 148.

24. Irene Sargent, "William Morris," *Craftsman*, 1: 35 (Oct. 1901).

25. W. M. Rossetti, *Prae-Raphaelite Diaries and Letters*, pp. 13–14.

26. W. M. Rossetti, *Fine Art, Chiefly Contemporary*, London, 1867, p. 176. Italics supplied.

27. William Knight, *Six Lectures on Some Nineteenth-Century Artists*, Scammon Lectures, Art Institute of Chicago, 1909, p. 120.

28. Housman, *op. cit.*, p. 12.

29. Cf. T. Earle Welby, *The Victorian Romantics 1850–1870*, London, 1929, p. 8.

30. Stillman, *op. cit.*, p. 96.

31. Two significant studies of this basic problem are: Herbert Read, *Art and Industry*, N.Y., 1938; and Nikolaus Pevsner, *Pioneers of the Modern Movement from William Morris to Walter Gropius*, London, 1936.

32. The most familiar versions are: Francis Bickley, *The Pre-Raphaelite Comedy*, London, 1932; Frances Winwar (Grebanier), *Poor Splendid Wings*, N.Y., 1933; and William Gaunt, *The Pre-Raphaelite Tragedy*, London, 1942. Evelyn Waugh has a more specialized study in *Rossetti, His Life and Works*, London, 1928.

CHAPTER III. BUCHANAN READ AND THE ROSSETTIS

1. Cf. Isaac Clayton Keller, "Thomas Buchanan Read," *University of Pittsburgh Bulletin*, 29: 1–9 (Jan. 1933).

2. Margaret Howitt, ed., *Mary Howitt, an Autobiography*, London, 1899, pp. 70–72.

3. W. M. Rossetti, ed., *Dante Gabriel Rossetti—His Family Letters*, Boston, 1895, 2 vols., I: 88–89.
4. *Ibid.*, pp. 89–90.
5. *Ibid.*, pp. 73–74.
6. H. Allingham and D. Radford, eds., *William Allingham, A Diary*, London, 1908, p. 59.
7. Howitt, *op. cit.*, pp. 74–75.
8. Henry C. Townsend, *A Memoir of T. Buchanan Read*, Philadelphia, 1889, p. 90.
9. *Ibid.*, p. 110.
10. *Ibid.*, p. 111.
11. John R. Tait, "Reminiscences of a Poet-Painter," *Lippincott's Magazine*, 19: 317 (March 1877).

CHAPTER IV. W. J. STILLMAN: "THE AMERICAN PRE-RAPHAELITE"

1. See Chapter V for detailed data on this periodical.
2. See W. J. Stillman, *The Autobiography of a Journalist*, 2 vols., 1901, *passim*. It is of interest to note that the *Atlantic Monthly* printed the first two chapters of this work as its leading article, "Autobiography by W. J. Stillman," in January 1900 (85: 1–16).
3. Stillman, *op. cit.*, I: 116.
4. *Ibid.*, p. 114.
5. *Ibid.*, pp. 122–130.
6. *Ibid.*, pp. 136–137.
7. *Ibid.*, pp. 138–139.
8. *Ibid.*, p. 140.
9. *Ibid.*, p. 220.
10. *Ibid.*, p. 298.
11. *Ibid.*, p. 299.
12. *Ibid.*, p. 300. Stillman suggested to Christina on one occasion that she broaden the scope of her poetry to include the subjects of politics or philanthropy, but she said it was not in her. See *Family Letters of Christina Georgina Rossetti*, p. 31.
13. *Ibid.*, p. 308.
14. *Ibid.*, p. 317.
15. *Ibid.*, pp. 312, 320.
16. Charles Eliot Norton, ed., *Letters of John Ruskin to Charles Eliot Norton*, Boston, 1904, 2 vols., I: 98–99.
17. *Ibid.*, p. 101.
18. Stillman, *op. cit.*, p. 336.
19. *Ibid.*, p. 373.
20. *Ibid.*, II, 466.
21. In W. M. Rossetti's contribution to the *Crayon* dated June 20,

1856, he reports a water-color by "Miss Barbara Smith" hung in the Royal Academy exhibition. This coast scene was "full of *real* Pre-Raphaelitism, that is to say, full of character and naturalism in the *detail.*" (3: 245, Aug. 1856.)

22. Stillman, *op. cit.*, II: 468–469.

23. *Ibid.*, p. 470.

24. George Birkbeck Hill, ed., *Letters of Dante Gabriel Rossetti to William Allingham, 1854–1870*, N. Y., 1898, p. 290.

25. W. M.. Rossetti, ed., *Dante Gabriel Rossetti: His Family Letters,* Boston, 1895, I: 286–287.

26. Violet Hunt, the daughter of Holman Hunt, in *The Wife of Rossetti* (N.Y., 1932, p. xxii), says that Elizabeth Siddal first influenced Rossetti in taking drugs, and that Stillman merely confirmed him in the habit "with a neater and more modern remedy."

27. Stillman, *op. cit.*, II: 469.

28. W. M. Rossetti, *Dante Gabriel Rossetti: His Family Letters,* I: 287–288.

29. Gordon Hake, *Memoirs of Eighty Years*, London, 1892, pp. 192–193. Dr. Hake notes (p. 225) that Rossetti made a portrait sketch of him and another of Stillman.

30. W. M. Rossetti, *op. cit.*, I: 243, 257.

31. Cf. Evelyn Waugh, *Rossetti—His Life and Works*, London, 1928, pp. 206, 211.

32. Stillman, *op. cit.*, II: 472–473.

CHAPTER V. THE CRAYON: THE FIRST AMERICAN PRE-RAPHAELITE JOURNAL

1. Frank Luther Mott, *A History of American Magazines*, Cambridge, 1938, II: 193.

2. *Ibid.*, passim.

3. Stillman, *The Autobiography of a Journalist*, I: 217.

4. *Ibid.*, 165–167.

5. *Ibid.*, p. 178.

6. *Ibid.*, pp. 219–221.

7. *Ibid.*, p. 222.

8. *Ibid.*, p. 223.

9. *Ibid.*, pp. 224–225.

10. "Sketchings," *Crayon*, 8: 133, (June 1861).

11. "Feeling and Talent," 1: 17 (Jan. 10, 1855).

12. "Sketchings," 1: 75 (Jan. 31, 1855).

13. "Duty in Art," 1: 49 (Jan. 24, 1855).

14. "Sketchings," 1: 107 (Feb. 14, 1855).

15. "Artistic Licenses," 1: 258 (Apr. 25, 1855).

16. "Common Sense in Art," 1: 81 (Feb. 7, 1855).

17. "The Nature and Use of Beauty," 3: 1–4 (Jan. 1856).

18. *Ibid.*, 3: 34 (Feb. 1856).

19. *Ibid.*, 3: 194 (July 1856).

20. "Sketchings," 3: 123 (Apr. 1856).

21. William Linton, "A Summary of Modern Colors," 3: 300–303 (Oct. 1856).

22. "Pre-Raphaelitism," 1: 219 (Apr. 4, 1855).

23. *Ibid.*, 220.

24. "Pre-Raphaelitism and Its Lessons," 1: 241–242 (Apr. 18, 1855).

25. The *Crayon* also enjoyed the services of a Paris correspondent, one P. Mantz.

26. W. M. Rossetti, "Art News from London," *Crayon*, 1: 263–265 Apr. 25, 1855). It is interesting to note that Christina Rossetti apparently did not think too highly of her brother's American vehicle. On August 18, 1858, she wrote to him at Freshwater, a vacation spot: ". . . Did you thank us for that *Crayon?* Sometimes a very mean instalment of occupation is acceptable at the seaside. . . ." (W. M. Rossetti, ed., *Family Letters of Christina Georgina Rossetti*, N. Y., 1908, p. 26.)

27. *Ibid.*, p. 263.

28. W. M. Rossetti, "Art News from London," *Crayon*, 1: 327-328 (May 23, 1855).

29. "The Hope of Art," 2: 32 (July 18, 1855).

30. "The Two Pre-Raphaelitisms," 3: 225-228 (Aug. 1856).

31. *Ibid.*, pp. 289–292 (Oct. 1856).

32. *Ibid.*, p. 290 (Oct. 1856).

33. *Ibid.*, p. 321 (Nov. 1856).

34. *Ibid.*

35. *Ibid.*, p. 356 (Dec. 1856).

36. "Sketchings," 1: 283 (May 2, 1855).

37. "Correspondence," 2: 310 (Nov. 14, 1855).

38. W. J. Stillman, *Autobiography of a Journalist*, I: 225-226.

39. In subsequent issues he dealt also with the treatment of landscape by Lowell and Street.

40. *Crayon*, 1: 73 (Jan. 31, 1855).

41. Stillman, *op. cit.*, p. 229.

42. A section from Simms's later *Cassique of Kiawah* first appeared in the *Crayon* as "Southern Coast Scenery" (4: 346-348, Nov. 1857).

43. Stillman, *op. cit.*, p. 228.

44. *Crayon*, 5: 95 (April 1858). In the preceding number Durand had presented an exegetical editorial on Pre-Raphaelitism.

45. "The Nature and Use of Beauty," 3: 2 (Jan. 1856).

46. Stillman, *op. cit.*, p. 227.

47. Stillman's later writings were divided between his interests in art and in contemporary events. *The Acropolis of Athens* (1870) —"the beautiful Greek album," as Christina Rossetti called it— is notable for the excellence of twenty-five of his own photographs, presented in folio size with descriptive notes. *Poetic Localities of Cambridge* (Boston, 1876) is another series of his fine camera studies illustrating various passages from the New England poets. A nostalgic Preface recalls this period of his career. He likewise wrote the text for *Old Italian Masters Engraved by Timothy Cole* (1892), and for *Venus and Apollo in Painting and Sculpture* (1897). Some penetrating criticism appears in his essays, *The Old Rome and the New, and Other Studies* (1898). And his concern in the Cretan insurrection, the Balkan problems, and the unification of Italy, is mirrored in several historical works on those problems.

CHAPTER VI. BRITISH PRE-RAPHAELITE ART IN AMERICA: 1857 EXHIBITION

1. W. M. Rossetti, ed., *Ruskin: Rossetti: Pre-Raphaelitism, Papers 1854 to 1862*, London, 1899, pp. 178-179.

2. *Ibid.*, pp. 180-181.

3. *Ibid.*, p. 182.

4. This was not Hunt's major treatment of this subject, which was hung in Keble College, Oxford, but was his smaller replica of that composition.

5. *Ibid.*, p. 182.

6. *Ibid.*, p. 185.

7. *Ibid.*, p. 189.

8. *Ibid.*, pp. 188-189. Italics his.

9. *Ibid.*, pp. 197-206.

10. Some Pre-Raphaelite pictures were also exhibited at the Boston Athenaeum in 1858. The *Crayon* commented in its April issue: "Although the exhibition is a decided success, I do not think that Bostonians take very kindly as yet to the works of the Pre-Raphaelite School."

CHAPTER VII. THE AMERICAN BROTHERHOOD: "THE SOCIETY FOR THE ADVANCEMENT OF TRUTH IN ART"

1. *The New Path*, 1: 11 (May 1863).

2. Editor, "The Work of the True and the False Schools," *New Path* 1: 84-88 (Nov. 1863).

3. *New Path*, 1: 11. See also comments from the contemporary press, reprinted on the inside covers of the *New Path*, May to September, 1865.

4. The bound copies in the Library of Harvard College bear the inscription: "1870, Jan. 18 / Gift of / Henry W. Longfellow / of Cambridge"—who evidently had been a reader of the magazine. Investigation reveals it to have been a twelve- to sixteen-page pamphlet, a monthly at ten cents per copy or one dollar per year. The price later was raised to fifteen cents and one dollar fifty; then to twenty cents and two dollars, because of "the greater cost of printing" during the Civil War. The first six numbers were sold only by the members, but subsequently Brentano's, 708 Broadway, acted as agent.

With Volume II (May 1864) the magazine became independent financially of the original sponsors, but with the same editorial policy was published by James Miller, 522 Broadway. Following the number for July 1864, no more issues appeared until April 1865. In August of that year a general appeal for financial aid was made; and with the December number the *New Path* ceased publication.

The actual "Society for the Advancement of Truth in Art" disbanded on Feb. 27, 1865, according to one of its members, Peter B. Wight. See his "Reminiscences of Russell Sturgis," *Architectural Record*, 26: 124 (Aug. 1909).

5. "A Letter to a Subscriber," *New Path*, 1: 114 (Jan. 1864). Concerning this pugnacious attitude of the review the *Independent* commented: "This keen-edged periodical brilliantly attacks the vulnerable points of American art and artists." (Quoted on inside cover of *New Path*, 1865.)

6. *New Path*, 1: 11-12. Unsigned article, probably by Clarence Cook.

7. *Ibid.*, 2: 2-3 (May 1864). Ruskin's "Mont Blanc Revisited" and Rossetti's "The Blessed Damozel" were also reprinted in the magazine.

8. "Pictures and Studies," *New Path*, 2: 47 (July 1864).

9. Thomas Charles Farrer, "A Few Questions Answered," *New Path*, 1: 17 (June 1863).

10. *Ibid.*, p. 14. Italics supplied.

11. Farrer, *op. cit.*, p. 14.

12. C.H.M. [Charles Herbert Moore], "Fallacies of the Present School," *New Path*, 1: 62-63 (Oct. 1863).

13. *Modern Painters*, Sterling ed., Boston, n.d., II: 210. See also

Charles H. Moore's much later discussion, "John Ruskin as an Art Critic," *Atlantic Monthly* 86: 438-450 (Oct. 1900).

14. W. M. Rossetti, *Fine Art, Chiefly Contemporary*, London, 1867, p. 174 *n*.

15. "The Limits of Medieval Guidance," *New Path*, 1: 158-159 (April 1864).

16. M., "The Office of the Imagination," *New Path*, 1: 77–78 (Nov. 1863).

17. J. S., "Art as a Record," *New Path*, 1: 39-40 (Aug. 1863).

18. "A Letter to a Subscriber," *New Path*, 1: 117 (Jan. 1864).

19. J. S., "Naturalism and Genius," *New Path*, 1: 70 (Oct. 1863).

20. *New Path*, 2: 136 (Aug. 1865).

21. J. S., *op. cit.*, pp. 66-68.

22. Quoted, with pleasing candor, on the inside of the front cover, May 1865.

23. "Letter to a Subscriber," *New Path*, 1: 117 (Jan. 1864).

24. "Introductory," *New Path*, 1: 3 (May 1863).

25. "The Essential Difference between the True and the Popular Art Systems," *New Path*, 2: 33 (July 1864).

26. "An Important Gothic Building," *New Path*, 2: 17-32 (June 1864).

27. *Stones of Venice*, London and N. Y., 1904, pp. 179, 267.

28. W., "What Has Been Done," *New Path*, 1: 52-59 (Sept. 1863).

29. "Our Furniture: What It Is and What It Should Be," *New Path*, 2: 55-56 (April 1865).

30. *Ibid.*, pp. 55-62; and 2: 65-72 (May 1865).

31. W. M. Rossetti, *Fine Art, Chiefly Contemporary*, pp. 171-172.

CHAPTER VIII. THE P. R. B. IN THE U.S.A.: CHARTER MEMBERS

Thomas Charles Farrer: Link Between the Brotherhoods

1. Cf. E. T. Cook, *The Life of John Ruskin*, London, 1911, 2 vols., I: 379.

2. Cf. Mantle Fielding, *Dictionary of American Painters, Sculptors and Engravers*, Philadelphia, n.d., p. 116. This source states that Farrer first came to the United States in 1858.

3. Elisabeth Luther Cary, *The Rossettis: Dante Gabriel and Christina*, N. Y. and London, 1902, p. 46.

4. *Ibid.*, p. 49.

5. Thomas Charles Farrer, "A Few Questions Answered," *New Path*, 1: 13-16 (June 1863).

6. *Ibid.*, p. 17.

Clarence Cook: Pre-Raphaelite Journalist

1. Letter quoted from *Independent*, in *Crayon*, 2: 313 (Nov. 14, 1855).
2. *Art and Artists of Our Time*, 3 vols., N. Y., 1888.
3. *International Studio*, 12: Supp., ii (Nov. 1900).
4. A later printing was issued in 1886, attesting to the popularity of the work.
5. Clarence Cook, *The House Beautiful*, N. Y., 1878, pp. 147-148.
6. *Ibid.*, p. 61.

Clarence King: Scientist, Writer, and Patron of the Arts

1. *Clarence King Memoirs*, N. Y., 1904, pp. 190-192 and 129-130.
2. *Ibid.*, p. 312. King's book was published in Boston in 1872, after having been serialized in part in the *Atlantic Monthly* in the previous year.
3. "Report of Mr. Clarence King, Geologist in Charge of the Geological Exploration of the Fortieth Parallel," in *Report of the Chief of Engineers*, Washington, 1873, II: 1206-1207.
4. Henry Adams, *Esther*, Robert E. Spiller, ed., N. Y., 1938, pp. 19-20.
5. Additional details may be found in my article, "Clarence King—Scientist and Art Amateur," *Art in America*, 32: 41-51 (Jan. 1944).

Peter B. Wight: Architect in the Pre-Raphaelite Pattern

1. *Architectural Record*, 58: 513 (Nov. 1925). Resolution by the Chicago Chapter of the American Institute of Architects.
2. Elisabeth Luther Cary, *The Rossettis: Dante Gabriel and Christina*, London and N. Y., 1902, p. 47.
3. *Ibid.*, p. 48.
4. *National Academy of Design: Photographs of the New Building*, N. Y., 1866.
5. *Ibid.*, p. 10.
6. Editorial, "Our Mission," *Fireproof Magazine*, 11: 3 (July 1907).

Russell Sturgis: "Principal Popularizer of Architectural Knowledge in America"

1. "Reminiscences of Russell Sturgis," *Architectural Record*, 26: 123-131 (Aug. 1909).
2. *Ibid.*, pp. 130-131.
3. Montgomery Schuyler, "Russell Sturgis," *Architectural Record*, 25: inside front cover (Feb. 1909).
4. See Anon., "Russell Sturgis's Architecture," *Architectural Record* 25: 405-410 (June 1909). In New York he also designed such

structures as the Flower Hospital and the mansion of Theodore Roosevelt's father.

5. Wight, *op. cit.*, p. 127.

6. "Poet and Artist," *Scribner's Magazine*, 35: 767-768 (June 1904).

7. "Art Criticism and Ruskin's Writings on Art," *Scribner's Magazine*, 27: 509 (April 1900).

8. *Ibid.*, pp. 510-512.

9. "Artists with Theories, Convictions, and Principles," *Scribner's Magazine*, 40: 125-128 (July 1906).

10. Russell Sturgis, *The Technique and Principles of Visual Art*, Chicago, The International Art Association, 1900, p. 69.

11. Wight, *op. cit.*, p. 130.

12. New York, 1906, I: 373.

13. New York, 1909, II: 245.

14. Anon., "Russell Sturgis," *Outlook*, 91: 373-374 (Feb. 20, 1909).

15. Montgomery Schuyler, "Russell Sturgis," *Scribner's Magazine*, 45: 635-636 (May 1909).

Charles Herbert Moore: Disciple of Ruskin

1. A very carefully annotated and informative catalogue, *Paintings and Drawings of the Pre-Raphaelites and Their Circle*, was issued for the event.

2. C.H.M., "Fallacies of the Present School," *New Path*, 1: 63 (Oct. 1863).

3. "John Ruskin as an Art Critic," *Atlantic Monthly*, 86: 438-450, *passim*.

4. *Letters of John Ruskin to Charles Eliot Norton*, Boston and N. Y., 1905, 2 vols., II: 135-136.

5. *Ibid.*, p. 141.

6. *Ibid.*, p. 144.

7. Arthur Pope, "Charles Herbert Moore," *DAB*, XIII: 116-117.

8. *Development and Character of Gothic Architecture*, N. Y. and London, 1899, p. 428.

9. *Ibid.*, p. vii.

10. *Ibid.*, p. 8.

11. *Ibid.*, p. 21.

12. *Ibid.*, p. viii.

13. *Ibid.*, p. 424.

14. *Character of Renaissance Architecture*, N. Y. and London, 1905, p. 1.

15. *Ibid.*, p. 4 ff.
16. *Ibid.*, pp. 65, 250.

CHAPTER IX. JOAQUIN MILLER AND "THE MASTER," D. G. ROSSETTI

1. Cf. Harr Wagner, *Joaquin Miller and His Other Self*, San Francisco, 1929, p. 68.
2. Joaquin Miller, "Bits from My Journal," *Joaquin Miller's Poems* (Bear Edition, San Francisco, 1917), I: 100.
3. T. Wemyss Reid, *The Life, Letters and Friendships of Richard Monckton Milnes*, London, 1890, 2 vols., II: 276-278.
4. See, for example, Martin Severin Peterson, *Joaquin Miller, Literary Frontiersman*, Stanford Press, 1937; and Julian Hawthorne, *Shapes that Pass*, Boston, 1929.
5. W. M. Rossetti, ed., *Family Letters of Christina Georgina Rossetti*, N. Y., 1908, "Appendix," p. 207.
6. Miller, *op. cit.*, p. 102.
7. The English edition contained "Arizonian," "With Walker in Nicaragua," "The Californian" (later called "Joaquin Murietta"), "Ina," "The Tale of the Tall Alcalde," "Burns and Byron," and "The Last of the Taschastas." In the subsequent American edition "Kit Carson's Ride," "Myrrah," and "Even So" were added.
8. W. M. Rossetti, "Songs of the Sierras," *Academy*, 2: 301-303 (June 15, 1871). Christina Rossetti also owned a personal copy of *Songs of the Sierras* and loaned it to her friends. See *Family Letters of Christina Rossetti*, p. 34.
9. Miller, "Recollections of the Rossetti Dinner," *op. cit.*, pp. 107-116.
10. Juanita J. Miller, *My Father, C. H. Joaquin Miller, Poet*, Oakland, 1941, p. 54.
11. Cf. Peterson, *op. cit.*, pp. 72-73.
12. W. M. Rossetti, ed., *Family Letters of Christina Georgina Rossetti*, p. 211.
13. *Academy*, 13: 4601 (May 25, 1878).
14. Peterson, *op. cit.*, p. 145.
15. Stuart P. Sherman, ed., *The Poetical Works of Joaquin Miller*, N. Y., 1923, p. 304.
16. Peterson, *op. cit.*, p. 145.

CHAPTER X. RICHARD WATSON GILDER: POET AND ART PATRON IN THE GILDED AGE

1. W. J. Stillman, *The Autobiography of a Journalist*, Boston, 1901, 2 vols., II: 466.

2. Rosamond Gilder, ed., *Letters of Richard Watson Gilder*, Boston and N. Y., 1916, p. 56.

3. *Ibid.*, pp. 59-60.

4. *Ibid.*, p. 47.

5. New York, 1875.

6. *Scribner's Monthly*, 7: 42-43 (Nov. 1873). Sonnet XLVI, "Parted Love" in *The House of Life*, may have influenced Gilder's poem:

> What shall be said of this embattled day
> And armed occupation of this night
> By all thy foes beleaguered,—now when sight
> Nor sound denotes the loved one far away?
> Of these thy vanquished hours what shalt thou say,—
> As every sense to which she dealt delight
> Now labors lonely o'er the stark noon-height
> To reach the sunset's desolate disarray?
>
> Stand still, fond fettered wretch! while Memory's art
> Parades the Past before thy face, and lures
> Thy spirit to her passionate portraitures:
> Till the tempestuous tide-gates flung apart
> Flood with wild will the hollows of thy heart,
> And thy heart rends thee, and thy body endures.

7. Gilder, *op. cit.*, p. 47.

8. *Ibid.*, p. 404.

9. *Ibid.*, p. 66.

10. Rosamond Gilder calls the organization the "Academy of Fine Arts," but all of Saint-Gaudens's references are clearly to the "National Academy of Design."

11. Gilder, *op. cit.*, p. 80.

12. Homer Saint-Gaudens, ed., *The Reminiscences of Augustus Saint-Gaudens*, N. Y., 1903, 2 vols., I: 186-187.

13. *Ibid.*, pp. 188-189.

14. *Ibid.*, p. 164.

CHAPTER XI. JOHN LA FARGE

1. Royal Cortissoz, *John La Farge, A Memoir and a Study*, Boston, 1911, p. 67.

2. He moved from Columbia to St. John's College, Fordham, and thence to St. Mary's College at Emmitsburg, Maryland.

3. Cortissoz, *op. cit.*, pp. 70, 109.
4. *Ibid.*, pp. 91-93.
5. *Ibid.*, p. 98.
6. Cecelia Waern, *John La Farge, Artist and Writer*, London, 1896, pp. 12-13.
7. Cortissoz, *op. cit.*, p. 38.
8. Waern, *op. cit.*, p. 13.
9. *Ibid.*
10. *Ibid.*, p. 16.
11. Cortissoz, *op. cit.*, pp. 86-87.
12. *Ibid.*, p. 186.
13. Waern, *op. cit.*, p. 27.
14. Cortissoz, *op. cit.*, p. 122.
15. *Ibid.*, p. 259.
16. *Ibid.*, p. 184.
17. Waern, *op. cit.*, p. 52.
18. *Ibid.*, pp. 50-51.
19. Henry Adams, *The Education of Henry Adams* (Modern Library ed., N. Y., 1931), p. 371.
20. John La Farge, *Considerations in Painting*, N. Y., 1895, pp. 74-75.
21. *Ibid.*, pp. 197, 256.

CHAPTER XII. WHISTLER: BURNE-JONES: RUSKIN—ART ON THE LEGAL SCALES

1. H. Allingham and D. Radford, eds., *William Allingham, A Diary*, London, 1908, p. 100.
2. G. Burne-Jones, *Memorials of Edward Burne-Jones*, N. Y. and London, 1904, 2 vols., II: 188.
3. *Ibid.*, p. 86.
4. *Ibid.*, pp. 87-88.
5. *Ibid.*, pp. 88-89.
6. Ford Madox Hueffer, *Memories and Impressions*, N. Y., 1911, p. 33.
7. *Ibid.*, p. 33.

CHAPTER XIII. THE ARTS AND CRAFTS MOVEMENT

1. *Scribner's Magazine*, 23: 253 (Feb. 1898).
2. Charles Holme, ed., *Arts and Crafts, A Review of the Work Executed by Students in the Leading Art Schools of Great Britain and Ireland*, London (*The Studio*), 1916.
3. Cf. Oscar Lovell Triggs, *Chapters in the History of the Arts and*

Crafts Movement, Chicago (Bohemia Guild of the Industrial Art League), 1902, p. 5.

4. *Ibid.,* p. 60.

5. Arts and Crafts Exhibition Society, *Arts and Crafts Essays,* with preface by William Morris, London, 1899, p. xiii.

6. *Ibid.,* pp. x-xii.

7. Russell Sturgis, "The Field of Art," *Scribner's Magazine,* 23: 253 (Feb. 1898).

8. Cf. Rilla Evelyn Jackman, *American Arts,* Chicago, 1928, pp. 26-27.

9. See R. L. Duffus, *The American Renaissance,* N. Y., 1928, *passim.*

10. Cf. Rho Fisk Zueblin, "The Production of Industrial Art in America," *Chautauquan,* 36: 622-627 (Mar. 1903).

11. Jackman, *op. cit.,* p. 32.

12. *Ibid.,* p. 31.

13. W. S. Rusk, "Arts and Crafts Movement," *Encyclopedia of the Arts,* N. Y., 1946, p. 77.

14. See "Enriching Work of Penland Makes Crafts Live for Many," *Christian Science Monitor,* Jan. 24, 1953.

CHAPTER XIV. THE "CRAFTSMAN"

1. Ernest A. Batchelder, "The Arts and Crafts Movement in America: Work or Play," *Craftsman,* 16: 544-549 (Aug. 1909).

2. "Foreword," 1: i-iii (Oct. 1901).

3. Irene Sargent, "The Guilds of the Middle Ages," 1: 2 (Dec. 1901).

4. Eltweed Pomeroy, 1: 43-48 (Feb. 1902).

5. Arthur Stringer, 4: 126-132 (May 1903).

6. George Wharton James, 7: 412-420 (Jan. 1905).

7. "Foreword," 1: iii (Mar. 1902).

8. Editorial, "An Arts and Crafts Exhibition," 2: 49 (Apr. 1902).

9. Jane Pratt, 5: 183-191 (Nov. 1903).

10. "The Boston Society of Arts and Crafts," 2: 258-259.

11. Katherine Louise Smith, "An Arts and Crafts Exhibition at Minneapolis," 3: 377 (Mar. 1903).

12. Irene Sargent, "A Recent Arts and Crafts Exhibition," 4: 69 (May 1903).

13. Editor, "Recent Exhibitions of Arts and Crafts Societies," 5: 315-316 (Dec. 1903).

14. Editorial, "The Influence of Material Things," 1: vi (Jan. 1902).

15. "Foreword," 3: vii (Oct. 1902).

CHAPTER XV. WALTER CRANE: BRITISH ARTS-AND-CRAFTSMAN IN AMERICA

1. Walter Crane, *An Artist's Reminiscences,* N. Y., 1907, p. 369.
2. *Ibid.,* pp. 361-409.
3. Russell Sturgis, "English Movements in Decorative Art," *Scribner's Magazine,* 23: 255 Feb. 1898).

CHAPTER XVI. THE RUSKIN COMMONWEALTH

1. Charles Nordhoff, *The Communistic Societies of the United States,* N. Y., 1875, is an early account of American communities. Among the many studies in the field, V. F. Calverton's *Where Angels Dared to Tread,* Indianapolis and N. Y., 1941, is a recent popular but comprehensive treatment.
2. A sympathetic survey, Ernest S. Wooster's *Communities Past and Present,* which was published by the Llano Colony in Louisiana in 1924, serves as the basis for the following discussion; this should be balanced against a disillusioned firsthand report on general inefficiency and mismanagement written by an ex-member: J. W. Braam, "The Ruskin Co-operative Colony," *American Journal of Sociology,* 8: 667-680 (Mar. 1903).

CHAPTER XVII. VACHEL LINDSAY AND RUSKIN: PREACHERS OF "THE GOSPEL OF BEAUTY"

1. Vachel Lindsay, *The Golden Book of Springfield,* N. Y., 1920, p. 315.
2. *Ibid.,* p. 173.
3. *Ibid.,* p. 84.
4. Edgar Lee Masters, *Vachel Lindsay, A Poet in America,* N. Y., 1935, p. 314.
5. *Ibid.,* p. 276.
6. *Ibid.,* p. 267.
7. Nicholas Vachel Lindsay, *Adventures While Preaching the Gospel of Beauty,* N. Y., 1914, p. 15.
8. *Ibid.,* p. 16.
9. Masters, *op. cit.,* pp. 112-113.
10. *Ibid.,* p. 68.
11. *Ibid.,* p. 118.
12. *Adventures While Preaching the Gospel of Beauty,* p. 184.
13. *Ibid.,* p. 75.
14. Masters, *op. cit.,* p. 301.

CHAPTER XVIII. SAMUEL BANCROFT, JR.: COLLECTOR PAR EXCELLENCE

1. Samuel Bancroft, Jr., "Rossetti and the Pre-Raphaelite Brother-hood, and Their Influence on Late English Art," MS of a speech delivered Feb. 6, 1901. Wilmington Society of the Fine Arts. A partial quotation from this MS is made in Paull Franklin Baum, ed., *Dante Gabriel Rossetti's Letters to Fanny Cornforth*, Baltimore, 1940, "Foreword," p. xi.

2. MS "Catalogue of Paintings and Photographs of the Collection of Samuel Bancroft, Jr.," note signed "S.B. Jr."

3. See Paull Franklin Baum, "The Bancroft Manuscripts of Dante Gabriel Rossetti," *Modern Philology*, 39: 47-68 (Aug. 1941). Dr. Baum had edited the most significant of the items: *Dante Gabriel Rossetti's Letters to Fanny Cornforth*, Baltimore, Johns Hopkins Press, 1940.

4. Cf. Jessie C. Rockwell, "Foreword," *The Samuel and Mary R. Bancroft English Pre-Raphaelite Collection*, Wilmington, Del., n.d.

5. Letter dated Nov. 23, 1900.

6. Letter dated Jan. 31, 1901.

7. Percy Bate, *The English Pre-Raphaelite Painters*, London, 1901, p. 115.

8. Letter dated Sept. 19, 1903.

9. Letter dated June 4, 1901.

10. Letter dated Feb. 1, 1901.

11. Letter from Michael Stillman to Bancroft, Aug. 10, 1904.

12. Letter dated June 4, 1901.

13. Letter dated July 12, 1901.

14. Letter dated Aug. 13, 1901.

15. Letter dated Oct. 22, 1903.

16. Letter dated Oct. 26, 1903.

17. W. M. Rossetti, *Some Reminiscences*, N. Y., 1906, 2 vols., II: 492.

18. Letter dated Aug. 26, 1907.

CHAPTER XIX.—AND OTHERS

1. Walter Crane, *Ideals in Art*, London, 1905, p. 14.

2. W. M. Rossetti, ed., *Prae-Raphaelite Diaries and Letters*, London, 1900, p. 289.

3. Hall Caine, *My Story*, N. Y., 1909, p. 186.

4. W. M. Rossetti, *op. cit.*, p. 236.

5. W. M. Rossetti, ed., *Family Letters of Christina Georgina Rossetti*, N. Y., 1908, p. 7.

6. G. Burne-Jones, *Memorials of Edward Burne-Jones*, N. Y., 1904, 2 vols., I: 88.

7. H. Allingham and D. Radford, eds., *William Allingham, A Diary*, London, 1908, p. 69.

8. Randall Stewart, ed., *The English Notebooks by Nathaniel Hawthorne*, N. Y. and London, 1941, p. 47.

9. *Ibid.*, p. 352.

10. *Ibid.*, pp. 345-365, *passim.*

11. *Ibid.*, pp. 619-620.

12. *Passages from the French and Italian Note-Books*, Boston and N. Y., 1909, Fireside Edition, pp. 126-127.

13. Allingham and Radford, *op. cit.*, pp. 221-222.

14. William Bell Scott, *Autobiographical Notes*, N. Y., 1892, 2 vols., I: 239.

15. *Ibid.*, p. 240.

16. Janet Camp Troxell, *Three Rossettis—Unpublished Letters*, Cambridge, 1937, pp. 48-49.

17. Ralph L. Rusk, ed., *The Letters of Ralph Waldo Emerson*, N. Y., 1939, 6 vols., IV: 23 *n.*

18. *Ibid.*, IV: 506-507.

19. *Ibid.*, V: 110.

20. *Ibid.*, V: 110-111, notes.

21. W. J. Stillman, *Autobiography of a Journalist*, I: 240.

22. Edward Waldo Emerson and Waldo Emerson Forbes, eds., *Journals of Ralph Waldo Emerson, 1856-1863*, Boston and N. Y., 1913, IX: 159.

23. *Poems by Ralph Waldo Emerson*, Boston and N. Y., 1918 (Riverside Press ed.), p. 189.

24. Edward Waldo Emerson, *The Early Years of the Saturday Club 1855-1870*, Boston and N. Y., 1918, pp. 175-176.

25. William Gaunt, *The Pre-Raphaelite Tragedy*, London, 1942, p. 71.

26. Charles Rowley, *Fifty Years of Work without Wages*, London, n.d., p. 118.

27. William Michael Rossetti, *Some Reminiscences*, N. Y., 1906, 2 vols., II: 400.

28. Herbert H. Gilchrist, ed., *Anne Gilchrist, Her Life and Writings*, London, 1887, p. 177.

29. *Some Reminiscences*, II: 404. See also Clarence Gohdes and Paull Franklin Baum, eds., *Letters of William Michael Rossetti Concerning Whitman, Blake, and Shelley to Anne Gilchrist and*

Her Son, Herbert Gilchrist, Durham, N. C., 1934, p. 54 and *passim.*

30. Gohdes and Baum, *op. cit.,* p. 27.

31. Elizabeth Porter Gould, *Anne Gilchrist and Walt Whitman,* Philadelphia, 1900, p. 30.

32. Troxell, *op. cit.,* p. 188.

33. Gould, *op. cit.,* p. 45.

34. George Birkbeck Hill, ed., *Letters of Dante Gabriel Rossetti to William Allingham 1854-1870,* N. Y., 1898, p. 181.

35. Caine, *op. cit.,* p. 177.

36. W. M. Rossetti, *Some Reminiscences,* II: 492.

37. Allingham and Radford, *op. cit.,* pp. 159, 171.

38. Esther Wood, *Dante Gabriel Rossetti and the Pre-Raphaelite Movement,* London, 1894, vii.

39. Merle Curti, *The Growth of American Thought,* N. Y. and London, 1943, p. 630.
Professor Harry Hayden Clark has kindly suggested to me the importance in this connection of Vida D. Scudder, whose personal study under Ruskin directly shaped her later interests in Christian Socialism. As a professor of English at Wellesley for many years, she showed Ruskin's influence on her thought in such valuable works as *Social Ideals in English Letters* (N. Y., 1898), and *Socialism and Character* (N. Y., 1912).

40. Ralph Henry Gabriel, *The Course of American Democratic Thought,* N. Y., 1940, p. 308.

41. Alfred Kazin, *On Native Grounds,* N. Y., 1942, pp. 181-182.

42. *Ibid.,* p. 173.

43. Cf. Nikolaus Pevsner, *Pioneers of the Modern Movement from Morris to Walter Gropius,* London, 1936, pp. 99-121.

44. Charles R. Anderson, ed., *Centennial Edition of the Works of Sidney Lanier,* Baltimore, 1945; "Retrospects and Prospects," V: 298. Other stylists cited include Carlyle, Hugo, Richter, Hawthorne, and Poe. The final metaphor refers to "Prose" rather than to Ruskin himself.

45. *Ibid.,* "The Death of Byrhtnoth," IV: 292.

46. *Ibid.,* VI: 46-47.

47. *Ibid.,* V: 214.

48. *Ibid.,* VIII: 79.

49. *Ibid.,* I: xliii *n.*

50. Richard Webb and Edwin R. Coulson, *Sidney Lanier, Poet and Prosodist,* Athens, Ga., 1941, p. 26.

51. Cf. Edwin Mims, *Sidney Lanier*, Boston and N. Y., 1905, p. 160.

52. Christina Hopkinson Baker, ed., *Diary and Letters of Josephine Preston Peabody*, Boston and N. Y., 1925, p. 131.

53. Josephine Preston Peabody, *The Piper, A Play in Four Acts*, Boston and N. Y., 1911, pp. 142, 150.

54. Horace Gregory and Marya Zaturenska, *A History of American Poetry 1900-1940*, N. Y., 1946, pp. 40-41.

55. Baker, *op. cit.*, p. 22.

56. *Ibid.*, p. 15 (entry dated Sept. 1893).

57. *Ibid.*, pp. 304-308.

58. Sara Teasdale, *Strange Victory*, N. Y., 1933, p. 27.

59. Sara Teasdale, *Dark of the Moon*, N. Y., 1926, p. 20.

60. Sara Teasdale, *Helen of Troy and Other Poems*, N. Y., 1928, p. 85.

61. *Ibid.*, pp. 27-29.

62. Muriel Miller, *Bliss Carman: A Portrait*, Toronto, 1935.

63. Richard Hovey, *The Holy Graal and Other Fragments* (introduction and notes by Mrs. Richard Hovey), N. Y., 1907, p. 14.

64. *Ibid.*, p. 18.

65. *Ibid.*, p. 8, preface by Bliss Carman.

66. Gregory and Zaturenska, *op. cit.*, p. 127.

67. Edwin Arlington Robinson, *Collected Poems: The Children of the Night, Captain Craig*, N. Y., 1927, pp. 49-50.

68. W. J. Stillman, "Sketchings," *Crayon*, I: 27 (Jan. 10, 1855).

69. William Rose Benét and Norman Holmes Pearson, *The Oxford Anthology of American Literature*, N. Y., 1938, p. 1680.

70. Gregory and Zaturenska, *op. cit.*, p. 399.

71. *Ibid.*, p. 172.

72. Edmund G. Gardner, "Introduction," *Poems and Translations by Dante Gabriel Rossetti* (Everyman's ed.), London and N. Y., 1915, p. xiii.

73. Ford Madox Hueffer, *Rossetti: A Critical Essay on His Art*, Chicago and N. Y., n.d. (c. 1912).

74. Richard P. Blackmur, "Masks of Ezra Pound," *Hound & Horn*, 7: 178, 202 (Jan.-Mar., 1934).

75. Yvor Winters, "Book Reviews: T. Sturge Moore," *Hound & Horn*, 6: 538 *n.* (April-June, 1933).

76. Ezra Pound, *Poems 1918-21 including Three Portraits and Four Cantos*, N. Y., 1921, p. 57.

77. Babette Deutsch, *This Modern Poetry*, N. Y., 1935, p. 117.

78. Ezra Pound, *Sonnets and Ballate of Guido Cavalcanti*, London, 1912, p. 6.

APPENDIX III. TWO MINOR AMERICAN PRE-RAPHAELITE PAINTERS: JOHN W. AND J. HENRY HILL

1. C.H.M. [Charles Herbert Moore], "An Artist's Memorial," in J. Henry Hill, *John William Hill: An Artist's Memorial*, New York, 1888, pp. 3-10.
2. *Ibid.*
3. *Ibid.*
4. *Ibid.*
5. Reprinted in J. Henry Hill, *op. cit.*, pp. 11-12. Signed E.C.
6. *Ibid.*
7. "Obituary—John W. Hill," New York *Tribune*, Sept. 27, 1879.
8. *Ibid.*, pp. 14-15.
9. J. Henry Hill, "Introduction," *Sketches from Nature*, Nyack Turnpike, N. Y., 1867.
10. *Ibid.*

INDEX

INDEX

THE FOLLOWING terms are not included in the index because of their constant appearance throughout the text: Pre-Raphaelite, Pre-Raphaelites, Pre-Raphaelitism, P. R. B. and P. R. B.'s. The titles of the Rossetti MSS listed in Appendix II are excluded also.